MASTERING
RELATIONSHIP
CONFLICTS

MASTERING RELATIONSHIP CONFLICTS

Discoveries in Theory, Research, and Practice

BRIN F. S. GRENYER

American Psychological Association
Washington, DC

Published by
American Psychological Association
750 First Street, NE
Washington, DC 20002
www.apa.org

To order
APA Order Department
P.O. Box 92984
Washington, DC 20090-2984
Tel: (800) 374-2721; Direct: (202) 336-5510
Fax: (202) 336-5502; TDD/TTY: (202) 336-6123
Online: www.apa.org/books/
Email: order@apa.org

In the U.K., Europe, Africa, and the Middle East, copies may be ordered from
American Psychological Association
3 Henrietta Street
Covent Garden, London
WC2E 8LU England

Typeset in Goudy by Monotype Composition, Baltimore, MD

Printer: United Book Press, Inc., Baltimore, MD
Cover Designer: Naylor Design, Washington, DC
Technical/Production Editor: Emily I. Welsh

The opinions and statements published are the responsibility of the authors, and such opinions and statements do not necessarily represent the policies of the American Psychological Association.

Library of Congress Cataloging-in-Publication Data
Mastering relationship conflicts: discoveries in theory, research, and practice/ by Brin F. S. Grenyer.– 1st ed.
    p. cm.
Includes bibliographical references and index.
ISBN 1-55798-827-7
1. Psychotherapy. 2. Interpersonal conflict. 3. Metacognition. I. Title.

RC480.5 .G735 2001
616.89′14 – dc21

2001035751

British Library Cataloguing-in-Publication Data
A CIP record is available from the British Library.

Printed in the United States of America
First Edition

CONTENTS

FOREWORD

Only rarely does a major concept that has been around for many years—a century at least—get revived by a fine operational definition and then applied in studies that explain and support the concept and point to what more needs to be done. All of that is what happened here with Brin Grenyer's concept of mastery in psychotherapy.

This new work actually started almost a decade ago when Brin Grenyer from Australia visited me in Philadelphia to discuss his research ideas about studies of mastery. Like other clinicians and researchers, I had already written about the concept of mastery as a logical and necessary one. After we went over his plans, however, I saw they were likely to generate and vastly expand our understanding of mastery. I offered to help in any way I could and especially by offering him access to two data sets: the Penn Psychotherapy Study and the Penn Short-Term Major Depression and Chronic Depression Dynamic Psychotherapy Study.

The work he has done with these and other data sets makes a special contribution to our field—it makes research on and clinical implementation of mastery much more generative. The contribution has a strong appeal to those attracted by methods that have both a clinical side as well as an empirical research side. The discoveries reported here will appeal broadly to those who practice many forms of psychotherapy, because mastery has a common ingredient across psychotherapies—it helps in the development of self-understanding and self-control. It should appeal to many psychoanalysts, although a few might reject it because of the illogical reason of its association with empirical research (Schachter & Luborsky, 1998).

Many major findings have come from his work:

1. The patient's improvement in psychotherapy is associated with growth in mastery.

2. Patients go through developmental stages toward augmented mastery.

3. Different diagnostic groups show some specific changes.

4. Telling one's relationship narratives helps to develop mastery.

5. Grenyer's new Mastery Scale is a meaningful tool for evaluating improvement in psychotherapy.

Because the Mastery Scale is so central in Grenyer's method, it should be further explained here. As it should be, the method is applied to the heart of psychotherapy—the verbatim transcripts of psychotherapy sessions. Within the session the relationship episodes are scored on 23 categories, with the categories arranged in levels of 1 to 6 item sets ranging from *lack of impulse control* (Level 1) to *self-control* (Level 6). This description I have just given is enough to make it clear that the scoring is based on the text of the session, so that it has basic relevance to the clinician. The scoring system is reasonable and the mastery method has shown good evidence for reliability and for validity, which makes the method suitable for the researcher.

The way in which the research on mastery fits into personality theory and research has received a big boost in the past few years through its inclusion within "positive psychology." Our field of psychotherapy grew up with the concept of mastery as emerging from the resolution of conflict. However, positive psychology maintains that positive individual traits do not necessarily emerge from the resolution of conflict. The focus of positive psychology is on such qualities as hope, wisdom, creativity, honesty, and spirituality. This new development of positive psychology has mostly come about through the leadership and writings of Martin E. P. Seligman, as illustrated, for example, in a recent issue of the *American Psychologist*, which was mostly devoted to articles on this topic; the issue was introduced by Seligman and Csikszentmihalyi (2000). In contrast, Brin Grenyer's work is really a combination of both the old and the new concepts of mastery, that is, personality as a product of conflict as well as personality as a biopsychosocial development.

So we are all grateful to Brin Grenyer for helping us to see that we should reconceptualize the role of mastery both in development and in therapy. He starts his book with the theory of the role of mastery, presents his research on his Mastery Scale, shows us how to use his theory in clinical practice, and demonstrates how it can be used with specific populations, such as patients with depression and substance abuse problems. He concludes the book with cogent recommendations for research areas that are most likely to further advance knowledge of mastery.

Lester Luborsky
Professor of Psychology in Psychiatry
School of Medicine, University of Pennsylvania
Philadelphia

PREFACE

This book arose out of an attempt to capture the remarkable transformative effect of psychotherapy. These remarkable, exciting, and relatively common changes are witnessed firsthand by clinicians but to date have been shared with others only through narrative case descriptions that have been criticized for their subjectivity (Grünbaum, 1986; Wallerstein, 1993). Through psychotherapy, people are able to cultivate a deeper understanding of themselves and to develop control over their problems and their responses to others in their lives. Mastery is defined here as the development of self-control and self-understanding. Developing a reliable and valid way for measuring the development of a patient's mastery became a goal, and showing how this new method could help delineate these changes for different client problems and presentations became a central aim of this study.

My purpose is to present a complete and coherent set of new discoveries about an important process in psychotherapy: the patient's development of mastery over symptoms, conflicts, and problems. The book shows how the process of mastery works and demonstrates its significance for the client's progress in psychotherapy. It is through these discoveries that clinicians can target their interventions to enhance the development of mastery in their clients. It bridges the scientist–practitioner divide by providing a practitioner-focused guide on how to enhance clients' mastery and showing how these principles are directly supported by original research.

The book is intended to appeal to a broad range of professionals involved in psychotherapy practice and research. I believe the book is of benefit because it shows how mastery plays an essential role in the psychotherapy process. It provides a complete reference source for the theory, research, measurement, and clinical application of mastery. The theoretical basis of the concept of mastery draws on understandings from a range of theories, and the conclusions rest on a series of original quantitative studies, most of which are presented here for the first time.

I have attempted to bring the concepts to life through extensive case studies with transcripts of actual dialogues between clinicians and clients. The book describes the process of seeking mastery over conflicts from the client's perspective and explains the kinds of changes that patients must make to overcome these conflicts and achieve greater mastery. The clinician can see how key therapeutic techniques, such as supportive techniques focused on a positive therapeutic alliance and expressive techniques that challenge and confront, help to promote mastery in their clients. This approach provides a guide as to when certain interventions are appropriate and when they are not, depending on the patient's existing level of mastery. Psychotherapists will be able to relate to the presentation of the kinds of defensive and symptom-laden responses clients who exhibit low mastery display, and they will be able to see how clients overcome these conflicts and develop more mature ways of responding to their difficulties. As such, the book provides guidelines that help clinicians determine when clients are ready to terminate therapy.

Part II of the book begins with a comprehensive theoretical framework of mastery. The scientific paradigm is a biopsychosocial drive theory approach, which provides a suitable basis for new approaches, such as those from cognitive, behavioral, object relations, self psychology, and attachment theory. It can therefore be seen as an interpersonal theory with a foundation in scientific research. Throughout I have tried to provide a bridge between theoretical language and landmarks and the practical application.

Part III presents the Mastery Scale and the reliability and validity studies that support it. To facilitate its understanding and adoption by other researchers, I have included detailed instructions on how to score and analyze the scale. Research studies show the relationship between mastery and familiar outcome measures often used by psychotherapy researchers, such as the Beck Depression Inventory (Beck, Ward, Mendelson, Mock, & Erbaugh, 1961), the Symptom Checklist (SCL and SCL–90–R; Derogatis, Lipman, Covi, Rickels, & Uhlenhuth, 1970; Derogatis, Rickels, & Rock, 1976), the Health–Sickness Rating Scale (Luborsky, 1962, 1975), and the Global Assessment of Functioning Scale (Endicott, Spitzer, Fleiss, & Cohen, 1976). These are used to support the reliability and convergent and discriminant validity of the mastery method. The book also presents results that illuminate the relationships with other well-known process measures, including the therapeutic alliance (Penn Helping Alliance Scale; Luborsky, Crits-Christoph, Alexander, Margolis, & Cohen, 1983), experiencing (the Experiencing Scale; Klein, Mathieu-Coughlan, & Kiesler, 1986), and the core conflictual relationship theme method for understanding transference responses (Luborsky & Crits-Christoph, 1989).

Part IV shows how to apply the mastery theory and method in clinical practice. The relationship between therapist techniques and patient developments in mastery is documented through case studies. Micro-analyses of verbatim case study material allow the practicing clinician to get a unique perspective of client change as it actually occurs during the clinical hour. The concept of mastery acts as an organizing and guiding principle that provides a new perspective on clinical change through psychotherapy. An exploration is made of the relationship between mastery and early relationships with the patient's parents to help show the early origins of relationship conflicts and the importance of mastery of these early relationship difficulties. Focus is then given on differential paths to change based on diagnosis, with studies of patients with either depression, personality disorders, or substance abuse. For example, patients with substance abuse problems studied using the Mastery Scale revealed some important predictors of clinical improvement. Those who improved most developed not only self-control but also an interpersonal awareness of their problem by developing skills in assessing, challenging, and probing others' responses rather than blindly accepting them. It was found that the helplessness and hopelessness often found in drug users may have interpersonal roots in the way they respond to others. The findings presented here suggest that therapists need to focus not only on drug use behaviors but also on the interpersonal context of the person's problems and the way he or she relates to others. By studying the verbatim transcripts and applying the Mastery Scale, it is possible to reveal those changes in self-control and self-understanding that are most associated with improvement so that clinicians can target their interventions wisely onto those most helpful predictors of improvement.

The clinical focus of the book is the contemporary integrative view of psychotherapy and counseling. The book aims to promote an approach to clinical work that is informed and responsive to research findings irrespective of the specific form of therapy conducted by the clinician. Specifically, it represents an attempt to apply a new methodology to studying the psychotherapy process, using verbatim transcripts of psychotherapy as the evidential base. The book develops this original research within an articulated theoretical framework and uses the results to contribute toward an understanding of what makes psychotherapy effective and how this knowledge can help guide the clinician. This work represents the culmination of almost a decade of programmatic clinical study of psychotherapy. The enduring theme throughout has been the centrality of interpersonal relationships for past, present, and future mental health and personal enrichment.

ACKNOWLEDGMENTS

I am deeply grateful to the many people who made a contribution to this work. I thank the many patients who, by their trust and generosity in consenting to have their treatment recorded and used in research, have opened a window on patient change. All names and identifying data of patients and therapists reported in this volume have been altered to protect their privacy. I also thank the many therapists, both in Australia and North America, who have contributed to this psychotherapy research by allowing their work with patients to be examined.

This project benefited from the support of Lester Luborsky from the Center for Psychotherapy Research, University of Pennsylvania Medical School. He provided helpful advice, warm hospitality, and a critical review, and he generously allowed access to data from several psychotherapy research studies. Nigel Mackay (University of Wollongong) helped enormously to improve the clarity of the ideas presented here and provided expert advice on the theoretical aspects of the project. Nadia Solowij (National Drug and Alcohol Research Centre, University of New South Wales) was central to the success of this project; she reviewed many iterations of this volume and provided clarifying feedback at critical junctures. Stanley Messer (Rutgers University) and Bertram Cohler (University of Chicago) provided reviews of an earlier version, John Maze (University of Sydney) reviewed chapter 2, and Glen Gabbard (Menninger Clinic) reviewed an early version of chapter 8. Samantha Reis (University of Wollongong) generously provided time to review the whole book, which improved its readability.

The bulk of the time-consuming and exacting part of this research, scoring psychotherapy transcripts, was diligently and carefully undertaken by a number of very special people: Richard Rushton, Mary Carse, Annalisa Dezarnaulds, Nadia Solowij, Kealey Worthen, and Garreth Wild. Kealey Worthen and Garreth Wild also contributed a portion of the data analysis in chapter 8, and Nadia Solowij and Richard Peters contributed to the acquisition of the original data set of people with cannabis dependence. Assistance with various parts of the project was also provided by Louis Diguer, Suzanne Johnson, David Seligman, Kelly Schmidt, Susannah Burrell, Linda Barry, Vera Auerbach, and Ken Russell. Linda Viney (University of Wollongong) and Russell Meares (University of Sydney) were supportive during the developmental stage of the project, as were Robert Barry, Len Storlien, Rhonda Griffiths, and Frank Deane from the University of Wollongong.

I warmly thank the staff at the American Psychological Association, particularly Anne Woodworth, Emily Welsh, and Margaret Schlegel, who provided excellent editorial advice and guidance in transforming the early manuscript into a finished book, and I also thank Gary VandenBos and Julia Frank-McNeil for their vision and faith in the project.

It has been gratifying to see the mastery methods translated and used in research by colleagues in other countries; they have provided useful clarifying advice and feedback. Reiner Dahlbender provided generous hospitality in Ulm, Germany, during my visits and expressed ongoing enthusiasm for the mastery method, as did Gertud Reichenauer. Gherardo Amadei and Cinzia Bressi at the Istituto di Clinica Psichiatrica and Universit[grave]a degli Studi di Milano in Italy provided ongoing feedback about their mastery research. Paola Lucenti from Universit[grave]a Cattolica del Sacro Cuore of Milan, Italy was generous in her contributions to mastery research through a 9-month visiting fellowship at the University of Wollongong.

This book is dedicated to my wife Nadia and children Kees and Titus, who supported me the most during the journey of its discovery. I must acknowledge my family's ongoing support and love, especially my mother and father and Sue, Gwilym, David, Kate, Paul, Jaros, Luba, Natalka, Ed, Tayissa, and my godson Semmon. The tranquil waters of Jervis Bay and tropical palms of Austinmer Beach have provided calm and inspiration during the long hours of work on this project.

Several chapters contain revisions of previously published work, which are reproduced by permission. Part of chapter 7 includes a revised version of Grenyer, B. F. S., & Luborsky, L., "Positive versus Negative CCRT Patterns," in L. Luborsky and P. Crits-Christoph (Eds.), 1998, *Understanding Transference: The Core Conflictual Relationship Theme Method* (2nd ed., pp. 55–63), Washington, DC: American Psychological Association. Copyright 1998 by the American Psychological Association. Reprinted with permission. Chapter 4 includes a revised version of *Mastery Scale I: A Research and Scoring Manual*, by B. F. S. Grenyer, 1994, Wollongong: University of Wollongong. Copyright 1994 by B. F. S. Grenyer. Chapter 5 is a revised version of two previously published works: (a) "Dynamic Change in Psychotherapy: Mastery of Interpersonal Conflicts," by B. F. S. Grenyer & L. Luborsky, 1996, *Journal of Consulting and Clinical Psychology*, 64, 411–416. Copyright 1996 by the American Psychological Association. Reprinted with permission; and (b) Grenyer, B. F. S., & Luborsky, L., "The Measurement of Mastery of Relationship Conflicts," in L. Luborsky and P. Crits-Christoph (Eds.), 1998, *Understanding Transference: The Core Conflictual Relationship Theme Method* (2nd ed., pp. 261–271), Washington, DC: American Psychological Association. Copyright 1998 by the American Psychological Association. Reprinted with permission.

This research has been supported by a number of grants: the Australian Research Council (research scholarship 1991–1994; small grants 1995, 1996, 1998); the Commonwealth Department of Community Services and Health (Research into Drug Abuse Grant 1995–1997); and the Illawarra Institute for Mental Health (1998–2000).

I

INTRODUCTION

1

MASTERY AS A CENTRAL INGREDIENT IN PSYCHOTHERAPY

Central to this study is an understanding of the essential process of change that comes about through psychotherapy. How does psychotherapy lead to change? What change does it bring about? One psychological construct that appears to encompass the change process is mastery. J. D. Frank (1971) underscored the role of mastery when he suggested that "all successful therapies implicitly or explicitly change the patient's image of himself from a person who is overwhelmed by his symptoms and problems to one who can master them" (p. 357). Despite its evident importance, mastery as a concept is poorly defined and seldom researched. Yet it is implicitly and sometimes explicitly evoked as a central ingredient in nearly all therapy approaches (see Liberman, 1978) and has been regarded as conceptually related to other psychological constructs, such as locus of control (Rotter, 1966), self-control (D. H. Shapiro & Bates, 1990), attributional processes (Alloy, Abramson, Metalsky, & Hartlage, 1988; Seligman & Elder, 1985; Weiner, 1988), transference (Luborsky, 1977), morale and hope (J. Frank, 1968; J. D. Frank, 1974; Gottschalk, 1974), insight and self-understanding (Crits-Christoph, Barber, Miller, & Beebe, 1993), competence (White, 1959), ego strength (Barron, 1953; Jacobs, Muller, Eisman, Knitzer, & Spilken, 1968), and optimism (Seligman & Csikszentmihalyi, 2000).

Freud (1920/1955a) discussed how neurotic patients try to achieve therapeutic resolution through "mastering or binding" the various threads of their problem (p. 35). Freud (1937/1964a) observed at the end of one of his successful cases, "in these last months of his treatment he was able to reproduce all the memories and to discover all the connections which seemed necessary for understanding his early neurosis and mastering his present one" (p. 217). In their work in psychodynamic psychotherapy, Luborsky and colleagues offered an explanation for the changes in psychotherapy of the most and least improved patients in terms of mastery of conflicts, and they discussed how "patients in psychotherapy develop an increased sense of mastery expressed in part as greater tolerance for their thoughts and feelings" (Luborsky, Crits-Christoph, Mintz, & Auerbach, 1988, p. 160). Klerman, Weissman, Rounsaville, and Chevron (1984) focused on interpersonal forms of dynamic psychotherapy, and they maintained that the goals of treatment, from the patient's perspective, include "helping you to master current problems by changing how they seem, how you deal with them and developing new friendships and relationships" (Weissman, 1995, p. 10). In psychodynamic therapy, mastery is used to denote the hoped-for result of the process and outcome of psychotherapy.

Using a cognitive therapy approach, Beck (1976) discussed how the patient achieves a "sense of mastery" (p. 232) and how this mastery is acquired: "Psychological problems can be mastered by sharpening discriminations, correcting misconceptions, and learning more adaptive attitudes. Since introspection, insight, reality testing, and learning are basically cognitive processes, this approach to the neuroses has been labelled cognitive therapy" (p. 20). The goal of cognitive therapy is the mastery of problems. Beck maintained that lack of mastery leads people to seek psychotherapy: "Those who come to the professional helper, and inadvertently acquire the label of patient or client, are drawn from the residue who have failed to master their problems" (p. 215). He thus acknowledged that the central aim of therapy is to foster mastery.

Although there is considerable agreement among the different schools of psychotherapy concerning the centrality of enhanced patient mastery during therapeutic change, what actually constitutes mastery remains ambiguous. There are no major studies that focus on defining and researching the process of gaining mastery. This book represents such an attempt. It is proposed here that compared with individuals with a low level of mastery, those with a high level of mastery have a greater sense of adaptive control over their emotional reactions when faced with conflicts in interpersonal relationships and are better able to understand the origins and motives behind these conflicts. Individuals without mastery blindly react with great distress to a host of interpersonal situations without awareness of the sources of their conflicts and problems. I define *mastery* as the development of self-control and self-understanding in the context of interpersonal relationships (Grenyer, 1994). This volume (a) develops a comprehensive theory of mastery; (b) presents a new reliable and valid method for studying psychotherapy, the Mastery Scale; (c) shows how the mastery concept is relevant to articulating patient change; (d) provides guidance for the therapist in using the mastery concept in clinical practice; and (e) develops a series of empirical studies of psychotherapy and shows how mastery is essential to patient improvements. This study of mastery should help to advance the understanding of one of the central mechanisms of change in psychotherapy.

This chapter is intended as a broad outline of how the concerns of this study may be located within contemporary trends in psychotherapy research. It is not, nor is it intended to be, an exhaustive review of the field. More detailed discussions of specific studies of immediate relevance are reserved for later chapters.

CONTEMPORARY DEVELOPMENTS IN PSYCHOTHERAPY

Two questions in the science of psychotherapy research are fundamental: does it work? (i.e., is psychotherapy an effective treatment for mental disorders when analyzed using appropriate research methods?), and if so, how does it work? (i.e., what is the process by which it works?). These two fundamental questions underlie two major areas of study in psychotherapy: psychotherapy outcomes and psychotherapy processes.

The early years of scientific psychotherapy investigations were primarily concerned with developing a theoretical understanding of the process of the treatment, with intense focus on single case studies (e.g., Freud, 1905/1953, 1918/1955c). From the start attempts were made to collect together these single case studies to draw firmer conclusions concerning whether the outcomes of psychotherapy were positive (e.g., Fenichel, 1920–1930; E. Jones, 1926–1936). In a controversial study that was based on 24 early studies of psychotherapy from 1920 to 1951, Eysenck (1952) concluded that the findings "fail to support the hypothesis that psychotherapy facilitates recovery from neurotic disorder" (p. 323). Almost as soon as the article appeared, however, this conclusion repeatedly has been shown to be wrong (e.g., Luborsky, 1954, 1972; Malan, Bacal, Heath, & Balfour, 1968; Rosenzweig, 1954).

More recently, research methods for studying psychotherapy and evaluating its outcomes have grown in sophistication. The overwhelming conclusion from the past 25 years of research on psychotherapy is that it is highly effective (for excellent comparative and summary reviews, see e.g., Andrews & Harvey, 1981; Lambert & Bergin, 1994; Luborsky, Chandler, Auerbach, Cohen, & Bachrach, 1971; Smith & Glass, 1977; Smith, Glass,

& Miller, 1980). Howard (1993) has concluded that with more than 500 studies demonstrating efficacy, psychotherapy is the "best documented medical intervention in history" (p. 3). Recent reviews all share the view that psychotherapy is effective when compared to no treatment or placebo treatment.

MORE PSYCHOTHERAPY, GREATER IMPROVEMENTS

An additional source of evidence supporting psychotherapeutic efficacy was an influential analysis of the effect of dose to response in psychotherapy (Howard, Kopta, Krause, & Orlinsky, 1986), which showed that more psychotherapy leads to greater improvements. The authors found that

> 10% to 18% of patients could be expected to have shown some improvement before the first session of psychotherapy, . . . by eight sessions, 48% to 58% of patients would be expected to have measurably improved . . . about 75% of patients should have shown measurable improvement by the end of six months of once-weekly psychotherapy. (Howard et al., 1986, p. 162)

Not only does psychotherapy work, but the larger the dose the greater the gains, particularly over the first 6 months. Longer treatments show continuing gains, but at a diminishing rate—the steepest improvement occurs usually in the first 6 months of treatment (Howard et al., 1986).

EQUIVALENCE OF DIFFERENT PSYCHOTHERAPY TYPES

In comparative studies of psychotherapy, authors typically have concluded that there is no difference in overall effectiveness between therapies of different theoretical orientations (e.g., Anderson & Lambert, 1995; Crits-Christoph, 1992; Elkin et al., 1989; Luborsky, Singer, & Luborsky, 1975; Smith et al., 1980; Stiles, Shapiro, & Elliott, 1986). This is the case despite measurable differences in the delivery and technical aspects of the different treatments (e.g., DeRubeis, Hollon, Evans, & Bemis, 1982; Luborsky, Woody, McLellan, O'Brien, & Rosenzweig, 1982). Any differences that exist can, by and large, be attributed to bias arising from the allegiance of the researcher to one of the treatment modalities (Luborsky, Diguer, Seligman, et al., 1999).

Another attempt to differentiate treatments has arisen from the efforts to establish practice guidelines on the basis of empirically supported results (Nathan, 2000). The Division 12 (Clinical Psychology) American Psychological Association guidelines list behavioral treatments as being empirically established (Division 12 Task Force, 1996). However, this does not imply that behavioral treatments are superior to other therapies, but rather that they have been more thoroughly studied. When studies do compare different treatments under similar conditions, the results almost always suggest equivalence in results despite nonequivalence in therapeutic technique. This familiar conclusion was confirmed even when therapeutic outcomes were measured using a different method: consumer surveys (Seligman, 1995).

To repeat this important conclusion: Therapists who deliver different therapeutic modalities under similar conditions with similar sets of patients achieve mostly equivalent outcomes (Wampold et al., 1997). Having established the overall effectiveness of psychotherapy, researchers have increasingly turned their attention to investigating in more detail the processes of psychotherapy (Beutler & Crago, 1991; Orlinsky, Grawe, & Parks, 1994). Some authors claim that each therapy has specific effects, but studies have not been designed to provide optimal opportunities to detect them (e.g., Beutler, 1991). Similarly, meta-analyses obscure the real topic of interest in psychotherapy—not "do treatments work?" or "which treatments work?" but rather "how do treatments work?" (Howard, Krause, Saunders, & Kopta, 1997; Howard, Leuger, Maling, & Martinovich, 1993). A commonly held view is that general nonspecific characteristics shared among the therapies probably override any specific techniques unique to a modality and that these nonspecific factors depend crucially on the quality of the therapist–patient relationship. That is, as long as patients form a good relationship with their therapists and the therapy has a direction or goal, then this will to a large extent be sufficient to produce good results. Alternatively, it may be the case that mastery is the unifying construct that develops across all therapies and that all therapies foster mastery despite differences in approach.

EFFECTIVENESS OF DIFFERENT PSYCHOTHERAPISTS

Despite the overall consensus that different treatments are equally effective, individual therapists are not equally effective. Studies of therapists have repeatedly shown that some therapists achieve better outcomes than others (e.g., Blatt, Sanislow, Zuroff, & Pilkonis, 1996; Crits-Christoph & Mintz, 1991; Hiatt & Hargrave, 1995; Luborsky, McLellan, Woody, O'Brien, & Auerbach, 1985; Najavits & Weiss, 1994; Shapiro, Firth-Cozens, & Stiles, 1989; Strupp, 1960). Factors that appear to be associated with more effective therapists include fidelity to a treatment manual or model, personal preference or suitability for one treatment modality compared with another, quality of case notes and evidence of effective anticipation and planning for client difficulties, willingness to work harder with patients with more difficult and complex problems, and the ability to form a good working relationship with the patient.

INTERPERSONAL CLIENT–THERAPIST
FACTORS AND OUTCOME

Authors have suggested that a likely common or nonspecific factor responsible for the effectiveness of psychotherapy is the helping relationship between the therapist and the patient (e.g., Bordin, 1979; Rosenzweig, 1936). Rogers (1957) considered the therapeutic relationship as providing the "necessary and sufficient conditions" (p. 95) of change. The helping relationship is also variously known as the *therapeutic alliance*, the *working alliance*, and the *therapeutic bond*. Bordin (1979) described the relationship as follows: "I propose that the working alliance between the person who seeks change and the one who offers to be a change agent is one of the keys, if not the key, to the change process" (p. 252). In general, research has supported this view, and it is now accepted that the quality of the relationship between the therapist and patient is one of the most important variables affecting therapeutic effectiveness (e.g., Horvath & Symonds, 1991). After an extensive review of all empirical studies of the helping alliance, Orlinsky and colleagues (1994) concluded that "the strongest evidence linking process to outcome concerns the therapeutic bond or alliance, reflecting more than 1,000 process–outcome findings" (p. 360). Similar studies concur with this conclusion, including a recent meta-analysis of 79 studies (Martin, Garske, & Davis, 2000). Although the therapeutic alliance is known to predict outcome, the precise mechanisms that make this variable effective are not known. Why does a good relationship with a therapist lead to improvement in mental health? How does patient mastery develop through the relationship with the therapist?

There is considerable debate as to the distinctiveness of the therapeutic alliance and transference (Henry, Strupp, Schacht, & Gaston, 1994). In Freud's view (1912/1958a), the therapeutic alliance is the ego-syntonic part of the "transference" relationship with the therapist. Some authors have argued that the two terms are describing similar processes and stress that the main focus of therapy should be on interpreting the transference (e.g., Curtis, 1979). Others have maintained that the two aspects are distinct, a view that has some empirical support (Gaston, 1990). It is pertinent that one important empirically based measure of transference (the core conflictual relationship theme; see chapter 3) evolved by accident through a process of trying to understand in depth the therapeutic alliance. Using transcripts from psychotherapy, Luborsky (1977) developed a method to

> describe the patient's typical relationships and examine how the helping relationships fit into these. It was these experiences, in attempting to describe each person's patterns of relationships, that led me to what I came to recognize as a deep psychic structure: the core conflictual relationship theme. (p. 368)

This serves to illustrate the intimate connection between the therapeutic alliance and the more dynamic transferential representations of the patient's typical relationship patterns. It may be that the therapeutic alliance is a simple and observable measure of the therapist's and patient's ability to form a basic relationship that, through its vicissitudes, also touches the patient's (and therapist's) deeper core relational (hence transferential) patterns.

The term *transference* as used in this book refers to the regular characteristic personality style of the patient. Definitions differ. The narrow view holds that the object of transference is the therapist and that early images of childhood and other relationships are the subject of the transference. The broad view holds that the term refers to the overall patterns of relationships that patients have with all people in their life. This broader view more correctly describes the repetition compulsion (see chapter 2), but the term is used because it is the common parlance of psychotherapy researchers and clinicians.

PATIENT TRUST IN THE THERAPIST

The common clinical view is that the supportive aspect of the relationship between the patient and the therapist is the bedrock on which the more expressive, interpretive aspects rely. The distinction between the supportive versus expressive aspects of treatment is a useful one (Gabbard, 1990; Luborsky, 1984; Wallerstein, 1986). The stronger the supportive relationship, the deeper the exploration that can be afforded into more "expressive" maladaptive pathological beliefs and transferential patterns of relating. Most of the techniques in cognitive therapy fall within the expressive domain, such as challenging unhelpful thoughts and correcting misperceptions. Similarly, behavioral techniques such as exposure therapy are expressive in that they aim to challenge and confront fears or problem behaviors. To gain the cooperation of the patient in the treatment, the clinician must establish considerable trust and feelings of goodwill and support with the patient. The more fragile the relationship, the more attention the clinician must devote to fostering support at the expense of expressive activity (Gabbard, 1990; Grenyer, Luborsky, & Solowij, 1995). In a recent research trial, researchers investigated the relative efficacy of interpretive versus supportive versions of dynamic psychotherapy (Piper, Joyce, McCallum, & Azim, 1998; Piper, McCallum, Joyce, Azim, & Ogrodniczuk, 1999). Although there were few differences between the two forms of treatment, fewer patients dropped out from the supportive form, and the interpretive form led to greater improvements in the quality of object relations. These results offer support for the idea that alliance building in the supportive part of treatment helps to retain patients in therapy, and the interpretive part improves patient interpersonal functioning. Together, both contribute to the development of mastery (see chapter 6 for further discussion of the relationship between supportive–expressive techniques and mastery development).

Empirical support for this view comes from the work of the San Francisco Psychotherapy Research Group (Silberschatz, Curtis, Sampson, & Weiss, 1991; Weiss, 1990b; Weiss, Sampson, & Group, 1986). Through an intensive study of psychotherapy transcripts of Mrs. C, a patient in long-term psychoanalysis, several complementary studies have shown that patients need a trusting relationship with their therapists to feel safe enough to reveal and explore deeper thoughts, feelings, and behaviors. Patients develop this feeling of safety in part through the therapist's ability to "pass tests" (i.e., respond to them in a way that does not confirm their pathological beliefs or their core maladaptive relationship pattern). In other words, the helping relationship must go beyond simply being a nondifferentiated "good" relationship; it must also address patients' need to master their problems. The mastery of problems proceeds through the therapist's sensitivity to patients' deeper problems and conflicts.

Weiss and colleagues (1986) discussed how the findings from their group have implications for our understanding of the therapeutic alliance: "Ordinarily . . . a patient who consciously hates the analyst, who wishes to terminate, or who is manifestly bored and indifferent to his treatment is thought to have a poor therapeutic alliance with the analyst" (Weiss, 1986, p. 330). On the basis of research and theory concerning the testing of deep-seated transferential patterns, the patient may in fact be

> unconsciously working closely with the analyst . . . . Indeed, a patient's wish to stop treatment, his hatred of the analyst, or his boredom may indicate that he has made considerable progress in his treatment and is working with the analyst more directly than before. (p. 331).

Just as the therapist is concerned with maintaining a good therapeutic alliance, so also is the client. In fact, some authors have suggested that clients may sometimes keep parts of their presentation and history secret from the therapist in part to bolster their own image in the eyes of the therapist (Kelly, 2000).

Progress in psychotherapy probably occurs across a spectrum of relationship intensities, from the basic sense of concordance between the therapist and patient to the deeper levels of interpersonal exploration of the patient's central problems. What is crucial, however, is how patients come to achieve a sense of mastery of their interpersonal difficulties (Grenyer & Luborsky, 1996).

FOSTERING MASTERY

It can be argued that patients' self-control and self-understanding is augmented through interactions with their therapists. Fundamental to this development is a good, trusting, working relationship. A good therapeutic alliance provides the bedrock for therapists to help patients deal with more challenging and core difficulties. Depending on the orientation of the therapist, these techniques may seem on the surface to be dissimilar. For example, the cognitive therapist may focus on "challenging automatic thoughts," whereas the dynamic therapist may "analyze transference conflicts." However, despite their apparent diversity, they share the same goal: to help their clients to become aware of maladaptive aspects of their thinking and behavior and to help them change these patterns. In so doing, the overall goal of therapists of different persuasions is the same: to foster mastery. So, although considerable attention has focused on one nonspecific factor in psychotherapy, the therapeutic alliance, I maintain that another, fostering mastery, is at least as important in accounting for the similarity in outcomes between therapies of different theoretical orientations.

CONCLUSION

In summary, most schools of psychotherapy regard mastery as a central benefit of therapy. However, what constitutes mastery has been seldom studied. An underlying driving force behind this research is the finding that although psychotherapy has been shown in general to be efficacious, psychotherapies of different practical and theoretical orientations appear to lead to similar outcomes. This has led researchers to focus on common factors in psychotherapy, and the one that has drawn the most interest and most research support is the quality of the interpersonal relationship between the therapist and the patient.

A study of the therapeutic alliance has led researchers deeper into examining the interpersonal functioning of patients. What has so far received only scant research is how patients come to master these interpersonal problems, both at the level of the relationship with the therapist and more generally with others. This involves a focus on the patients themselves and how, through their work in therapy, they overcome their difficulties. Focusing on mastery, then, might help unlock the problem of how both supportive and expressive techniques lead to therapeutic change. It might also help to elaborate in more detail some of the mechanisms of the change process.

Studying mastery might help to uncover a central change process in psychotherapy. Such research is consistent with, and follows from, central research activity occurring across a large number of leading contemporary psychotherapy research groups. This is best characterized by the work of members of the Society for Psychotherapy Research; the Society for the Exploration of Psychotherapy Integration; groups within international societies for the advancement of cognitive and behavior therapies; the studies reported in Bergin and Garfield's (1994) *Handbook of Psychotherapy and Behaviour Change* (4th ed.); a review of international programmatic studies and research teams investigating psychotherapy (Beutler & Crago, 1991);

and work included in the 11 volumes of *Comprehensive Clinical Psychology* (Bellack & Hersen, 1998). Consistent with the work of these groups and individuals is the effort to develop better instruments to measure phenomena. Galileo is reputed to have said "measure what can be measured, and make measurable what cannot be measured." Consistent with this idea is the development of a new measure of mastery. A theory of mastery that helps delineate the different components of mastery to be used in the development of the mastery scale is presented in Part II of this book; a new measure of mastery is presented in Part III.

II

THEORY AND BASIS OF MASTERY

2

A THEORY OF MASTERY THROUGH PSYCHOTHERAPY

If fostering mastery is a central feature of most schools of psychotherapy and accounts for many of the broad gains patients make through different types of therapy, it is useful to consider how it might be conceptualized theoretically. A theory of mastery is also a necessary precursor to developing the Mastery Scale presented in Part III. A set of guiding principles that delineates what mastery involves and how this relates to personality change and therapeutic improvement is required. As noted in chapter 1, *mastery* is defined as the development of self-control and self-understanding. Here I show how this definition was reached. The chapter presents a thorough survey of several theories of therapeutic change. My goal here is to articulate and justify a comprehensive biopsychosocial theory of clinical change in psychotherapy and to show how mastery is at the core of this theory.

Readers who are less interested in clinical theory may bypass this chapter. Chapter 3 shows how researchers have tried to understand patient gains by developing new methods for studying therapeutic processes. Doing research on verbatim therapy transcripts opens a new window into the interior of psychotherapy, and how researchers have begun to develop reliable and valid methods to investigate this interior is reviewed to provide a context for the development of the Mastery Scale method. Chapter 2 is for those who wish to learn more about how mastery can be understood as a basic process within a comprehensive theory of personality and therapeutic change. This chapter begins by outlining some key principles on which the conceptualization of mastery is based.

A COMPREHENSIVE BIOPSYCHOSOCIAL THEORY OF PERSONALITY

A biopsychosocial theory encompasses not only psychological factors but also the social, interpersonal, and biological foundations (e.g., genetics, neurophysiology) of being human. The biopsychosocial theory developed here begins with biological motivators or drives, which profoundly influence psychological processes that in turn influence interpersonal and social relations. Mastery is a process that refers to the way biological, psychological, and social demands are reconciled for mental health. Patients in psychotherapy work with a therapist on their problems to reduce symptoms of distress and reconcile competing demands and desires. If they achieve some relief and satisfaction, then they may be said to have achieved some degree of mastery of their conflicts and problems. In so doing, they are able to gratify more of their basic desires, needs, and wishes than they (the self, or masterer) were able to previously.

This conception of mastery rests on the same premise of scientific explanation as the natural sciences: Psychological events and social phenomena (no matter how complex) can be explained ultimately by fundamental causes in biological motivators. This conception of mastery allows a scientific theory of psychotherapy process and change to be developed and, in turn, for mastery to be measured empirically from clinical psychotherapy data. Developments in science usually proceed by the hypothetico–deductive method (Popper, 1934/1959). In this chapter I develop a theory of mastery through a critique of various theories of clinical change. I then go on to consider in some depth the theoretical notions of working through conflicts, maladaptive behaviors, and interpersonal-transference–related social processes as commonly described in psychotherapy writings and how they may lead to the patient developing mastery of problems and conflicts. The chapter then concludes with a summary of how mastery is defined in the context of interpersonal and social relations.

Metatheory or metapsychology is the essential framework of assumptions made in developing a psychological theory. The basic proposition of science is that the explanation for an event depends on the discovery of its cause. For a psychological theory to be both useful and scientific, it should explain why behaviors occur, why we act the way we do, and how we are likely to act in the future. It must therefore be deterministic. In science, theories that invoke the concept of free will and human agency as causes of behavior are untenable. A scientific view of mastery must therefore be deterministic and subject to the same rules of the natural sciences, as are physics, biology, chemistry, medicine, and the neurosciences. Some schools of psychology and psychoanalysis embrace subjectivist, phenomenological, or hermeneutic bases, but they are not addressed here.

In psychology, there are a number of deterministic theories, the most prominent and well-articulated of which are the behavioral and the psychoanalytic theories. Behaviorism (and its cognitive offshoots) has been criticized because it has no theory of motives (Maze, 1983). Cognitive or information-processing theory is regarded in some circles as untenable because of perceived philosophical problems such as circularity, a self-contradictory slide into purposivism, and difficulties inherent within representationism (which include solipsism and relativism; Coyne & Gotlib, 1983, 1986; Dyck, 1991; Mackay, 1989, 1994; Maze, 1983, 1991). Psychoanalysis is also to some extent limited as a theory, because its archaic language is based on 19th-century understandings of human functioning.

Moreover, whereas recent psychoanalytic research has applied scientific methods rigorously, the early psychoanalytic writings have been criticized for using a case study approach, with intuitive and speculative interpretations of case material. Through the recent adoption of scientific methods (Crits-Christoph, 1992), this objection has been largely overcome (for fuller discussion of this issue, see the set of papers that accompany Grünbaum, 1986). The strength of the psychoanalytic theory of motivation derives from its kinship with the natural sciences, its propositions being related to the workings of basic biological processes. As argued by Maze (1983), Freud's unfinished early theory lays the groundwork for a scientific psychology. It is a coherent explanation for organismic behavior, just as central state materialism (Armstrong, 1968) is a coherent account of the ontology of the mind as brain states.

To argue all the points regarding the coherence of competing accounts of psychology and psychoanalysis is beyond the scope of the present book. What is important here is to lay the theoretical groundwork for the understanding of mastery. Here I outline how mastery can be understood within a biopsychosocial drive theory and how this theory can provide a sensible explanation of the interpersonal, narrative, attachment theory, and object relations developments prevalent today.

BIOPSYCHOSOCIAL DRIVE VERSUS EGO PSYCHOLOGY THEORY

Two prominent metapsychological systems in psychoanalysis are relevant to mastery. The first is biopsychosocial drive theory, which was first articulated by Freud (1915/1957a, 1915/1957c) mainly in the few years before and after 1915 and maintained in its most coherent form up to 1923 (with the publication of The Ego and the Id, 1923/1961). It was the theoretical basis for his most important clinical papers on technique (1912–1915, collected in vol. 12 of the *Standard Edition*). Although he modified his theory later in his life, the basic threads of his position remained the same throughout his career. The second system is the autonomous ego psychology school, a revision of the biopsychosocial drive theory, which has been developed over the past 50 years and continues to be a major influence in modern psychoanalytic thinking (Eagle, 1984).

A biopsychosocial drive theory is a suitable theoretical basis for understanding the process of mastery. The theory holds that psychological and social processes have a biological basis that "drive," or motivate, them. This theory of mastery contrasts with the theory in the later ego psychology accounts, which posits the existence of a drive that "seeks to master," and this mastery drive or mastery instinct is a faculty of the ego, independent of the primary drives. This view has a contemporary expression, for example, in Weiss's control–mastery thesis developed as part of the Mt. Zion Psychotherapy Research Group (Weiss, 1990a; Weiss et al., 1986). Eagle (1984) very carefully argued that Weiss's work rejects the Freudian biopsychosocial drive theory, and he traced the lineage of Weiss's ideas to ego psychology conceptions of psychoanalysis that define drives by their aim (such as the aim or instinct to master) rather than by their source (in basic biological processes):

> As is the case with all the other recent developments in and modifications of psychoanalytic theory I have considered, the Mt. Zion group both implicitly and explicitly rejects Freudian instinct and drive theory. The basic image of the person that emerges is not one who is primarily engaged in the direct and indirect pursuit of instinctual gratifications, but one who is seeking mastery of the conflicts, anxieties, and destructive beliefs that cause him suffering and limit his satisfactions, productiveness, and awareness. This emphasis on mastery links the work of the Mt. Zion group to the concepts of Hendrick (1943) and White (1960; 1963). Indeed, the formulations of the Mt. Zion group can be seen as an elaboration and application of Hendrick's and White's concepts to the therapeutic situation. One can also find links between the Mt. Zion formulations and both Fairbairn's emphasis on ego aims and certain of Rogers' (1959; 1961) concepts. However, Weiss and Sampson ignore all these links. Instead they try to show how their formulations are derived almost entirely from Freud's late writings, an attempt which appears more political than scholarly. (pp. 100–101)

It is useful here to expand on this ego psychology view of the "instinct to master" and trace the lineage that Eagle sketched from Hendrick through White to Weiss. Fairbairn and Rogers are also discussed. Weiss's control–mastery theory forms a recent credible psychoanalytical account of mastery as a concept of central importance. Because the present study also proposes mastery as a central psychoanalytic concept, it is necessary to carefully differentiate the present view of mastery from that of Weiss and his predecessors.

In the article "Work and the Pleasure Principle," Hendrick (1943b) argued that the pleasure of achieving something is a pleasure in itself and does not need to be traced to basic drives. Hendrick gave the following example:

> when a housewife takes pleasure in cleaning up she is normally not merely finding a substitute for a tabooed pleasure in dirt; nor is she merely preparing a clean genital substitute (her house) for exhibition to her guests that evening; nor simply protecting herself from the reproaches of her finger-snooping mother-substitute lady-friends . . . she is also performing work; and in those hours of house cleaning which yield pleasure . . . the pleasure is primarily again in the job well done, in efficient performance of a useful task. (p. 323)

On this basis, he argued that "the work principle be regarded as an expression of an instinct to master whose goal is control or alteration of environmental situations through the effective development of integrated intellectual and motor functions" (p. 327). This in a nutshell is Hendrick's view of mastery. The desire to master work (such as house-cleaning) is an ego function that does not need to be traced back to primary drives in the id.

In a later discussion of the "instinct to master," he stated that "this hypothesis was suggested to provide a dynamic explanation of the force impelling the development and exercise of ego functions" (Hendrick, 1943a, p. 561). Hendrick tried to counter the criticisms of his colleagues, including Thomas French, Karl Menninger, Robert Waelder, and Edward Bibring, who objected to his departure from the biopsychosocial drive theory (see Hendrick, 1943a), yet maintained the existence of an instinct to master as a faculty of the ego related to "efficiency of performance" (p. 565).

Some 20 years later, Robert White (1963) proposed the existence of "independent ego energies." The importance of this idea for ego psychologists is that it allows more lofty ideals, such as the intrinsic pleasure in work and in achieving mastery of something, to be given a place within psychoanalysis free from the necessity to trace them back to more base and basic biological drives. White's theory was very close to Hendrick's (1943a) mastery theory, but in place of the word *mastery* he uses the term *competence*. White began with the observation that children, and animals, through their play, appear to be doing more than just gratifying basic instincts. During play, children seem to be actively seeking mastery of their environment through their inquisitive explorations of things. He interpreted this as evidence that the biopsychosocial drive theory is not adequate for explaining the meaning of behavior. In an important passage, White (1960) stated,

A whole series of workers, including Harlow (1953), Butler (1958), Montgomery (1954), Berlyne (1950), and Meyers and Miller (1954), have pointed out that animals show persistent tendencies toward activity, exploration, and manipulation even when all known primary drives have been satiated. Clearly the original drive model, based on hunger and other internal deficits, stands in need of extensive revision. (p. 101)

These observations led him, like Hendrick, to suggest that the biopsychosocial drive theory needs revision through the addition of independent ego energies or drives.

Independent ego energies and their satisfactions are conceived to be just as basic as the instincts. They are not, however, related to particular somatic sources or to consummatory patterns of discharge. Conceivably they can be equated with the inherent energy of the nervous system. But their significance for development lies in their direct relation to the formation of psychic structure. Effectance is a prompting to explore the properties of the environment; it leads to an accumulating knowledge of what can and cannot be done with the environment; its biological significance lies in this very property of developing competence. Instinctual energies, of course, likewise produce action, effects, and knowledge of the environment, thus making a contribution to competence. Both their contribution is necessarily narrower than that of neutral energies which stand ever ready to promote exploration for its own sake. (1963, pp. 185–186)

White wanted ego energies to be seen as basic and did not want to tie them to a more basic biological or somatic source. He posited the existence of an instinct that drives humans to explore and develop competence in the environment, just as Hendrick proposed that there is an instinct that drives people to work. The two theories therefore share essentially the same ground with the same theoretical aims and directions. Hartmann (1938/1958; see also Hartmann, Kris, & Loewenstein, 1964; Rapaport, 1967) also proposed autonomous ego instincts as primary forces for adaptation. Similar views about the ego, with different terminology, are proposed by Kohut (1978), Feffer (1982), Gedo (1978), and Schafer (1976).

Weiss's control–mastery thesis is very similar to Hendrick's and White's theories, but he propounded his within an explicitly psychotherapy research milieu. Like his predecessors, and in contrast to the biopsychosocial drive theory, Weiss upheld the idea of the ego as having autonomous drives. He regarded these ego drives as having a similar aim: to develop control or mastery of the world. He called his thesis the "higher mental functioning hypothesis" (Weiss, 1990b) in contradistinction to the deterministic biopsychosocial drive theory of Freud, which he called the "automatic functioning hypothesis." Like White (1960), who began with a consideration of human and animal development, Weiss (1993) drew on infant and developmental psychologists in outlining his case. He referred in particular to the work of Stern:

Stern (1985, p. 238) has written that his direct observations of infants do not support the idea of one or two basic instincts. According to Stern, motivation needs to be reconceptualized as organized by interrelated systems that unfold developmentally. These are classified as "ego instincts," and they include attachment (to parents), exploration, certain perceptual preferences, cognitive novelty, and pleasure in mastery. (p. 26)

The idea that mastery of the world is one of the primary motives is similar to White's notion of competence. Weiss wanted to put the ego instincts including the mastery drive at the center of his psychology, not merely an addition, like a footnote, to the basic drive theory. He wanted to overhaul the theory: "The present theory assumes that the patient's central organizing motive is to adapt to his interpersonal world" (p. 206). *Adaptation*, *mastery*, and *competence* are all terms that have a similar lineage and arise from the wish of some theorists to get rid of the idea that humans are driven by basic biological processes and substitute the idea that they act out of desires to explore and master the world.

CRITIQUE OF THE EGO PSYCHOLOGY VIEW OF MASTERY

The ego psychology view has several problems, all of which center around the problem of trying to separate drives or energies from basic somatic sources. The following arguments point out these conceptual muddles and difficulties yet indicate at the same time how the biopsychosocial drive theory avoids these problems and is therefore the preferred theoretical base on which to build an understanding of mastery (in this context, see also Mackay, 1989, and Maze, 1987, 1993).

The first point is that there is nothing conceptually wrong with ego instincts. Freud conceived of these as modifiers of id impulses in the light of empirical experience (e.g., Freud, 1923/1961). The problem is that Hendrick, White, and Weiss (among others) posited them as independent and autonomous of basic biological sources. What remains unclear in these authors' accounts is why we want to achieve mastery. Why bother to work? Why try to achieve competence? To say merely, as these authors do, that we have a drive or instinct to achieve mastery and competence is a pseudo-explanation. These authors need a basic theory of motives specified in terms of basic sources (in definable processes) rather than by a theory of motivation specified in terms of the aim (to achieve mastery). This is discussed in detail. These authors must have implicitly assumed a basic biopsychosocial drive theory to explain why we do anything at all, including why patients try to improve or master their psychological conflicts. In critiquing Hartmann, Maze (1987) made the point that independent or autonomous motives or drives are untenable:

Hartmann himself (1964, pp.123, 152) inclines toward the Allport conception of the functional autonomy of motives (Allport, 1937)—the conception that although a mode of action may have been taken up originally in the service of a primary drive, in the course of time it can develop its own intrinsic motivation. That is, it can become, like virtue, its own reward, no longer being dependent on any primary drive gratification to maintain it. Apart from such difficulties as explaining why one action becomes functionally autonomous and another not—why a factory worker may perform the same action countless times and give it up the moment it is no longer necessary to earn a living—Allport's conception is rather like saying that the spinning of a record player turntable can become functionally autonomous of the electric motor which originally drove it, and of every other motor. Of course, in the case of human beings, the underlying notion is that they choose to continue certain occupations and cause themselves to do so—but such self-caused activities would be beyond the scope of scientific explanation. (pp. 192–193)

Freud's original deterministic view of psychology holds that ultimately all human behavior can be explained by a relatively small number of primary biological drives (Freud, 1915/1957a; Mackay, 1989). This theory of motivation is parsimonious in that all behavior can be linked to its source within biological processes, a position similar to the assumptions of biological psychiatry, the neurosciences, and molecular biology today. It also avoids problems with defining motivational principles by their aim, for example, in the instinct or tendency to "self-actualize" (see Maslow, 1970). Teleological theories of motivation have the problem of ambiguity as to the number of aims there are. For instance, is there an "instinct to master," an "instinct to get food," an "instinct to be competitive," an "instinct to learn"? It is never clear where such a list ends. For example, the question "why did she suck her thumb?" in a theory defined by aims or goals could be explained as "to satisfy her thumb-sucking instinct." Similarly, a cat stalking a bird might be said to have a hunting instinct, but this explains nothing and is circular: It just renames the observation in a form that implies we know more than we do.

Teleological descriptions are adequate in ordinary conversation but perform very badly in scientific discourse. That is why Freud (1895/1966) set out to develop a theory of psychology that was mechanistic, that rested on basic laws and explanatory principles just as molecular biology rests on DNA as a fundamental element. Freud rested his theory of psychology on basic biological processes (called, archaically, *instincts*), which are irreducible and which fuel behavior. Although Freud's ideas about the functioning of the nervous system (such as the hydraulic model) are now obsolete, that does not preclude the substitution of more modern knowledge of biological processes into the basic structure of Freud's metapsychology. Modern developments in biological psychiatry and neuroscience share this basic view of science and are therefore complementary to the basic biopsychosocial drive theory of psychoanalysis.

Is there good reason to postulate a mastery or competence instinct? Freud (1915/1957a) anticipated the problem of where to draw the line with the number of instincts:

> What instincts should we suppose there are, and how many? There is obviously a wide opportunity here for arbitrary choice. No objection can be made to anyone's employing the concept of an instinct of play or of destruction or of gregariousness, when the subject-matter demands it and the limitations of psychological analysis allow of it. Nevertheless, we should not neglect to ask ourselves whether instinctual motives like these, which are so highly specialized on the one hand, do not admit of further dissection in accordance with the sources of the instinct, so that only primal instincts—those which cannot be further dissected—can lay claim to importance. (p. 123)

Which of the drives are most basic and primary was never fully enunciated by Freud, and in this sense his theory is unfinished. It has been left to future scientists to continually update and incorporate modern knowledge about our biological system into the theory. What appears clear, however, is that the ego psychology view that mastery is a basic instinct cannot be defended because it has no obvious biological source. A question of primary importance is whether we need to add an extra level to Freud's basic drive theory, namely, independent ego drives, to account for the observations of Hendrick, White, and Weiss. In the case of Hendrick's housewife, it seems reasonable to argue that anyone who cleans his or her house is gratifying a self-preservation instinct by cleaning away dirt, dust, bacteria, mold, and invading rodents and insects and is thus helping to maintain sufficiently sanitary conditions to prevent infections and disease. Second, cleaning the house is also a way of contributing to the well-being and favor of the person's cohabitants, on whom the person may rely in a complementary fashion for love and erotic satisfaction. The pleasure of the work can be tied, without any conceptual difficulty, to the satisfaction of these needs. So a criticism of Hendrick's, White's, and Weiss's positions is that the additional ego drives are unnecessary and therefore do not satisfy Occam's razor (the principle that the fewest number of assumptions are to be made in the explanation of a thing).

Another problem with the idea of mastery or competence, as developed by these authors, is that there are no obvious criteria for judging that this goal has been met. What might be masterful competence for one person might be beginners' level for another. What one considers to be competent another might consider to be incompetent. The concept therefore relies on subjective accounts that preclude the objectivity required for science.

As mentioned by Eagle (1984) above, the idea that we have some inherent drive to master is similar to Carl Rogers's ideas applied to psychotherapy. In Rogers's view, a good therapeutic alliance between the therapist and patient is necessary and sufficient for change, because inherent within the patient is a drive to master problems or "self-actualize" (Rogers, 1957). Similarly for Weiss (1990b), after patients feel safe with the therapist (who has passed the "tests"), then they allow their problems to rise up from the unconscious and to be mastered:

> patients bring forward their pathogenic beliefs as well as other unconscious thoughts and feelings only when they decide they may do so safely. . . . It seems that the cognitive capacities of the unconscious mind have been under appreciated and that human beings can unconsciously carry out many intellectual tasks, including developing and executing plans for reaching certain goals. (p. 109)

The implication of this theory for psychotherapy is that patients exert a degree of control over their drives and can regulate their expression within therapy on the basis of whether they feel safe to do so. Such an idea, even if true, does not require the additional postulate of an independent mastering and controlling mechanism for the reasons outlined above. It should be stressed here that the empirical research on psychotherapy by the Mt. Zion group is not affected by these theoretical arguments; what is being brought to task is the adequacy of the theoretical basis for directing and explaining the empirical research. The point is that patients are more likely to be motivated to master their problems in psychotherapy because of symptoms such as depression and anxiety that have arisen because the patient is unable to successfully meet primary basic needs (such as for a close, loving, sexual relationship) rather than because of a mastery instinct.

A central feature of the biopsychosocial drive theory is that one drive can only be opposed by another drive. For example, if we assume that there is a need for self-preservation and a need for affiliation, we can understand the enormous conflict that some people experience in close loving relationships where there is also domestic violence. Two needs are in conflict and have to be reconciled in some way. Needs that are unfulfilled or threatened lead to anxiety and other symptoms (Freud, 1926/1959).

In summary, the view of mastery postulated by ego psychologists is inadequate because of problems with their conceptualization of the motivation of behavior. The biopsychosocial drive theory avoids these problems and is an adequate theoretical basis on which to build a theory of mastery. Only recently have prominent ego psychologists begun to recognize the limitations of their approach and to acknowledge that patient functioning is often "of a more primitive sort than had been adequately dealt with in the ego-psychological framework" (Schafer, 1999, p. 342).

WORKING THROUGH TOWARD MASTERY:
FREUD'S EARLY WRITINGS

The biopsychosocial drive theory is probably one of a number of theories that meet criteria for theoretical coherence and clarity. I chose the theory as a good example from which to build a theory of mastery. A good way to articulate and conceptualize psychotherapy is to construe it as a process of mastery. Freud's term for this process of change is *working through*, although as shown below, Freud also used the term *mastery* in a similar way to that developed here. Mastery is both the process and outcome of working through.

This discussion necessarily reflects the archaic "psychic energy transfer" language of Freud, because it presents an attempt to explicate Freud's writings on working through to develop the notion of mastery. Where possible, more contemporary vernacular is used to show how the basic Freudian ideas can be transferred into a modern psychotherapy research context. This is done to demonstrate how the biopsychosocial drive theory and processes in therapy are related and how mastery can be understood using both nomenclatures. Accordingly, the *masterer* (ego or self) and the *mastered* (conflicts or relationship patterns) are alternatively articulated in original terms as the ego drawing energy from the bound up impulses in the id (as in Freud's famous maxim "where id was, ego shall be"; 1933/1964, p. 80), and in modern language as the self or patient learning to understand and control problematic relationship patterns and overcoming traumas.

Only twice did Freud explicitly write about working through. The first exposition of working through, in 1914, falls into the period of his first theory of metapsychology, which was based on unconscious, preconscious, and conscious processes. This work was titled *Remembering, Repeating and Working-Through* (Freud, 1914/1958e) and constitutes a coherent conception for understanding mastery. Most weight in this discussion is given to this 1914 publication. From about 1920, Freud formulated a second metapsychology, which he presented in *The Ego and the Id* in 1923. His second discussion of working through, in 1926 (Freud, 1926/1959), falls into this latter period. To understand Freud's 1914 account of working through, it is important to first sketch out in more detail the basics of his metapsychology.

Freud's metapsychology is described as dynamic because it posits that the constituents of the psychical apparatus are based on motivational principles defined by their source in the biological drives. The first analyses of patients were those with "hysterical" symptoms, with the first methods primarily aimed at removing symptoms (Breuer & Freud, 1895/1955). From the outset, Freud believed in a determinist causal theory of mind. Thus, his method of cure was to trace the causes of the symptoms in mental life, identify the hidden logical links between "thoughts" and symptoms, and reveal them to the patient. These thoughts are more correctly termed *wishes* or *fantasies*, which imply a motivational basis.

It should be noted here that Freud's emphasis on motivation (including wishes and desires) is the chief departure point between dynamic psychology and cognitive–behavioral information-processing psychology. The latter posits the existence of irrational or pathological thoughts as the genesis of psychopathology, yet denies their motivational basis, relying instead on models of learning and the cognitive–structural development of thinking. The absence of a theory of motivation is a primary drawback of the cognitive–behavioral approach, which leads to a number of difficulties in explaining behavior. For example, the cognitive–behaviorist has difficulty explaining the persistence of maladaptive dysfunctional behaviors and thoughts often seen in patients; a learning theorist would predict that such behaviors should have been extinguished long ago because of the lack of reinforcement contingency. According to dynamic psychology, all behavior is motivated, and therefore the reasons for thoughts and behavior should not be ignored (whether they be dispositional or genetic). In the dynamic biopsychosocial view, maladaptive behaviors and thoughts can be sensibly understood often in terms of what function they have served in relation to fulfilling powerful desires or needs during the patient's development or continue to serve in relation to the patient's current situation, of which the patient is often unaware.

The psychotherapy technique derived from Freud's early metapsychology was based on resistance analysis. The principal task of psychotherapy was the systematic removal of the resistances that block the repressed material. Freud noticed that these unconscious or libidinal wishes manifest themselves in behavior, in the sense that they attach themselves or transfer themselves to others in the patient's life, including the therapist. The analysis of transference thus became an important technique because repressed wishes or memories are repeated in behavior and are thus observable. In fact, the libidinal wishes appeared to be increasingly transferred onto the therapist, thus creating a transference neurosis in place of the symptom neurosis (Freud, 1912/1958a). The focus of technique thus shifted to an analysis of transference wherein the key to the repressed unconscious wishes could be found and overcome within the present patient–therapist relationship. The analysis of transference has resulted in increasing attention being focused on all aspects of the interpersonal relationship (Winnicott, 1956), which now forms a cornerstone of many schools of psychotherapy.

Freud's (1914/1958e) work *Repeating, Remembering and Working Through* is a detailed exposition of the central technique of resistance analysis and is based on his theory of mind and motivation. The sole cause of the neuroses, according to Freud's very early conception, was real trauma. The method of analysis was thus the recollection of the memory of the trauma and its abreaction. Freud modified this theory and came increasingly to recognize that although trauma was important, it was also the conflicts between innate forces and fantasies that were most heavily repressed and active in the etiology of neuroses (Freud, 1917/1963). The central feature of analysis was the uncovering of underlying repressed mental conflicts between the unconscious and conscious processes. However, a patient in therapy expects to receive help, and therefore the analysis of the dynamics of the psychopathology occurs in a process involving the analysis of resistances. Rendering any change in the patient required more strenuous effort, and this is what Freud referred to as *working through*. Interpretation and the helping relationship are the tools of the therapist in the working-through process. Central to the process of working through are recollection and repetition, each of which is considered in turn.

Recollection involves the recovery of the "forgotten" material of childhood or of some earlier time in the patient's life. The process of forgetting is the falling away of links, the dissociation of memories from conscious life. In the recall of the earliest memories, what often emerges are *screen memories*, compromise formations between the forces of remembering and those of resistance to remembering. The forces of resistance cause a displacement to occur. The process of working through in recollection is the effort expended by the patient to find the meaning behind the screen memories, to trace the causal chain in forgetting back to the source of the repression. It is difficult to ascertain the clinical importance of the recovery of memories; some commentators claim that it is not a necessary part of treatment (e.g., Fonagy, 1999). There is some evidence that many primal memories are not encoded verbally but are in a nonverbal, primitive memory trace that is not accessible to conscious language (Clyman, 1991). The activation of this kind of memory trace is thought to be evident or knowable only by the transference—the way the patient acts toward the therapist and others. This primitive memory is unconscious and can be made conscious and "spoken about" only through interpreting its effects on the therapist. There is some neurophysiological evidence that the emotion associated with these memories is deep seated (subcortical) and relatively resistant to change (LeDoux, 1995). Indeed, memory itself is highly personal, subjective, and malleable (Loftus & Ketcham, 1991), so in discussing even early real memories, preconscious mental models of relationships may distort the memory to be consistent with the internal representations of object relationships. The importance of memory for psychotherapy is probably in what it reveals about the underlying transference pattern or repetition compulsion.

Repetition is the second aspect of importance to the working-through process. Repetition is a form of remembering that is displayed in action or behavior:

> the patient does not remember anything of what he has forgotten and repressed, but acts it out. He reproduces it not as a memory but as an action; he repeats it, without, of course, knowing that he is repeating it. What interests us most of all is naturally the relation of this compulsion to repeat to the transference and to resistance. We soon perceive that

the transference is itself only a piece of repetition, and that the repetition is a transference of the forgotten past not only on to the doctor but also on to all the other aspects of the current situation. (Freud, 1914/1958e, pp. 150–151)

Transference is thus a repetition, which in action replays the forgotten past. The transference pattern of relating to the therapist is only one instance of the patient's broader personality-like pattern of relating to others throughout his or her life. Freud (1912/1958a) stated,

each individual, through the combined operation of his innate disposition and the influences brought to bear on him during his early years, has acquired a specific method of his own in his conduct of his erotic life. . . . This produces what might be described as a stereotype plate (or several such), which is constantly repeated—constantly reprinted afresh—in the course of the person's life. (pp. 99–100)

One of the chief tasks of psychotherapy is to bring this repetitive pattern of relating to the awareness of the patient so that it can be understood and controlled. This is particularly the case in instances where a repetitive way of behaving (e.g., interpersonal withdrawal) prevents the fulfillment of wishes (e.g., to be close to others) emanating from the drives (e.g., to seek libidinal gratification).

THE PROCESS OF WORKING THROUGH TO MASTERY

Working through is a core mechanism of change in psychotherapy. Freud (1914/1958e) stated, "This working-through . . . is a part of the work which effects the greatest changes in the patient and which distinguishes analytic treatment from any kind of treatment by suggestion" (p. 155). Working through requires a "period of strenuous effort" (1926/1959, p. 159) and "may in practice turn out to be an arduous task for the subject of the analysis" (1914/1958e, p. 155). Repetition phenomena such as dreams, symptoms, obsessive rituals, acting-out behaviors, and transference reactions are all re-enactments of certain elements of unconscious conflict or trauma. Freud discussed in many passages how primary biological (or instinctual) energy becomes attached to libidinal wishes or objects and how this then leads to a fixation at a developmental stage or psychical inertia. When the wish becomes fixated, it is then compulsively repeated, until it is undone by the working-through process.

In traumas, the organism is flooded with excitations; therefore, "another problem arises . . . the problem of mastering the amounts of stimulus which have broken in and of binding them, in the psychical sense, so that they can be disposed of" (Freud, 1920/1955a, p. 30). When energy becomes fixated on an object, it is usually the result of a failure to master this stimulus. Freud thought that attempts at mastering stimuli are usually successful in everyday life. This everyday process of mastery can be seen in, for example, children's play:

> It is clear that in their play children repeat everything that has made a great impression on them in real life, and that in doing so they abreact the strength of the impression and, as one might put it, make themselves master of the situation. (1920/1955a, pp. 16–17)

Traumas arrest development until the problems are mastered. Freud regarded the repetition compulsion as an unsuccessful attempt at mastery, which usually requires addressing during psychotherapy. In traumatic dreams (which include flashbacks), Freud (1920/1955a) noted that "these dreams are endeavoring to master the stimulus" (p. 32). In children's play, for example,

> children repeat unpleasurable experiences for the additional reason that they can master a powerful impression far more thoroughly by being active than they could by merely experiencing it passively. Each fresh repetition seems to strengthen the mastery they are in search of. (p. 35)

Thus, the work of therapy is to overcome the compulsion to repeat, work through it, and master the conflict underlying its presentation.

MASTERY AS SELF-UNDERSTANDING AND SELF-CONTROL

If one assumes that the major outcome of the working-through process is mastery, what then is achieved in mastery? According to Freud's drive theory, mastery releases the energy that has been bound up or fixated in the id, where it fuels the repetition compulsion, so that it can be used effectively by the ego (such that "where id was, ego shall be"). These released energies are used in productive acts, which satisfy the demands of reality, the id (in the long run), and the super ego. Working through is thus concerned in part with overcoming old unhelpful patterns of attachment that are arresting mature development and also in overcoming traumas. Overcoming these problems or fixations releases energy that was previously bound up with these problems and appeared as symptoms (e.g., of anxiety); that energy then becomes available for more mature and constructive relationships and activities.

While using the language of his energy drive theory, Freud also wrote in terms intelligible to the psychotherapist in training, whom he regarded as the audience for his work on technique. In describing the benefits of the prospective therapist undergoing analysis with a senior therapist, Freud (1912/1958d) highlighted what might be considered to be the two fundamental aspects of mastery seen from the perspective of psychotherapy:

> everyone who wishes to carry out analyses on other people shall first himself undergo an analysis by someone with expert knowledge. . . .

Anyone who can appreciate the high value of the self-knowledge and increase in self-control thus acquired will, when it is over, continue the analytic examination of his personality in the form of self-analysis. (pp. 116–117)

Freud considered self-knowledge and self-control to be the benefits of psychotherapy and are held here to be the two fundamental aspects of mastery. It is worth considering how the processes of working through, as discussed above, may in fact lead to increases in self-understanding and self-control, and hence, mastery. This work is also relevant to the development of a measurement of mastery (described in chapter 4). Exhibit 5.1 (see chapter 5) shows in seven summary statements the changes that are made in psychotherapy as a result of working through. The seven statements and their relationship to the theory are developed in more detail below.

1. *Self-understanding is developed about the transference and other forms of the repetition compulsion in the person's life.* Through therapy, and especially during transference analysis, the therapist engages the patient in the job of noticing and bringing to awareness the mechanisms of his or her pathology as they are manifested within interpersonal relationships. Patients begin to notice that their ways of behaving and understanding are distorted by transference-related schemas and expectancies.

2. *Self-understanding is developed about previous events (e.g., trauma or fixation) and how these have been active in present relationships through the repetition compulsion.* Freud regarded the recollection of past events and tracing neurotic symptoms to their roots as one important task of therapy. The important point about recollection lies in what it reveals about the origins of transference patterns, because early memories may not be accessible to consciousness. He also showed how these past patterns of relating repeat themselves in the present. Patients begin to see that their distorted maladaptive understandings and behaviors are derived from earlier experiences in their lives.

3. *Relationships with others will improve given the self-understanding of the distorted and maladaptive transferential repetitive relationship patterns.* One task of therapists is to help link the transference relationship with common patterns of relating that are currently active in the patient's life. Patients begin to understand and behave toward others in a less distorted way and develop ways of meeting their needs that are more satisfactory.

4. *Self-understanding of relationships with others should improve given the greater degree of objectivity obtained following the process*

of working through. Working through links forces and ideas that have previously been separated. Through these increases in self-understanding, the person should be able to focus more clearly and objectively on relationships with others. Patients are able to reflect on others and begin to understand how the same distortions and transference schema they found in themselves are also active in other people. This understanding enables patients to begin separating others' reactions from their own, leading to a more objective appraisal of their relationships.

5. *Self-control is enhanced as greater energy becomes available for mature relationships.* Whereas previously patients are dominated by their conflicts, the working through of these frees these energies to be used elsewhere. Patients who had previously been dominated by their negative symptoms and anxieties are able to refocus afresh on new, more constructive activities and ways of interacting.

6. *Self-control increases as repetition or acting-out behaviors are lessened and new ways of responding in relationships emerge.* The libido becomes freed from its unconscious bonds or fixations and attaches to new objects. Patients in therapy may begin to have marked improvements in existing relationships through more flexible responding, with a consequent opening of new and promising relationships and interests.

7. *Self-control increases due to the enhancement of the ability to self-analyze conflict.* Improvement in self-knowledge and self-control further enhances self-analysis, which in turn operates as a protective factor against psychopathology. Being able to reflect on one's own behavior, rather than acting out, provides the opportunity for monitoring potential problems and conflicts and managing them more effectively.

The first four of these statements relate to self-knowledge and the final three to self-control. The reason for the emphasis on "self" knowledge and control derives from the recognition that there is a distinction between the *masterer* (the self that masters) and the *mastered* (the conflicts). According to ego psychology, the person is driven by an instinct to master, but in the view presented here, the person works to master conflicts through pressure from primary biological drives, which are either in conflict or are not being gratified.

Which of the two fundamental elements of mastery, self-knowledge and self-control, most predicts change in psychotherapy? Freud made it clear that self-control is primary, because it signals a successful transfer of ego-enhancing energy. In fact, he warned against attaching too much importance on self-understanding:

In the course of the treatment yet another helpful factor is aroused. This is the patient's intellectual interest and understanding. But this alone hardly comes into consideration in comparison with the other forces that are engaged in the struggle. . . . The patient, however, only makes use of the instruction in so far as he is induced to do so by the transference. (1913/1958c, pp. 143–144)

Transference, then, is the primary sphere in which analysis proceeds, and the internal conflictual relationship patterns must be not only understood, but more important, controlled and mastered.

In another passage, Freud (1913/1958c) cautioned against accepting intellectual evidence as a sole basis for assessing the progress of analysis:

in the earliest days of analytic technique we took an intellectualist view of the situation. We set a high value on the patient's knowledge . . . and in this we hardly made any distinction between our knowledge and his . . . we hastened to convey the information and the proofs of its correctness to the patient, in the certain expectation of thus bringing the neurosis and the treatment to a rapid end. It was a severe disappointment when the expected success was not forthcoming. (p. 141)

Strupp (1970), too, emphasized the importance of self-control: "One of the chief purposes of psychotherapy, if not the primary purpose, is to promote the acquisition of self-control" (p. 393).

Mastery is achieved through emotional effort—the effort required to re-experience the past and to understand the way interpersonal relations are distorted in the present. Freud (1920/1955a) maintained that the therapist must get the patient to

re-experience some portion of his forgotten life . . . which will enable him, in spite of everything, to recognize that what appears to be reality is in fact only a reflection of a forgotten past. If this can be successfully achieved, the patient's sense of conviction is won, together with the therapeutic success that is dependent on it. (p. 19)

Mastery as self-control is achieved when the patient no longer unknowingly reacts emotionally to conflicts in the present because of forgotten past traumas, but rather sees the present for what it is without undue distortion.

When mental conflict arises, Freud (1937/1964a) maintained, an essential talent is to have sufficient internal self-control resources to master it: "Under the influence of education, the ego grows accustomed to removing the scene of the fight from outside to within and to mastering the internal danger before it has become an external one" (p. 235). There must be adequate ego strength or resources to deal with external and internal conflicts, and the process of working through aims to endow the ego with these resources so that conflicts can be successfully mastered.

MASTERY AND ITS RELATIONSHIP TO NEW DEVELOPMENTS IN PSYCHOTHERAPY

The conception of mastery presented in the preceding section also provides a link between what some consider to be two separate camps of theory. In recent times theorists have begun to make a distinction between the so-called "drive/structural" model and the "object relational/interpersonal" dynamic model (Greenberg & Mitchell, 1983; Messer & Warren, 1995). Because drive theory begins with basic individual biological processes, it has been labeled an *intrapsychic theory* (or *one-person psychology*), in contradiction with object relations/interpersonal theory, which begins with the primacy of relationships and is so called *two-person psychology* (Aron, 1990). Mitchell (1988), for instance, defined the *relational model* by stating that "we are portrayed not as a conglomeration of physically based urges, but as being shaped by and inevitably embedded within a matrix of relationships with other people" (p. 3).

It might be tempting to use this kind of distinction to discredit the biopsychosocial drive theory and champion the relational approach as being the more modern and relevant. This would be particularly the case because patients do not generally talk about gratifying sexual or hunger needs, but rather about interpersonal relationships, work, and future aspirations. Some have argued that reducing the complexity of human behavior and emotion, in all its myriad variety (and sameness) to fundamental biological states is distasteful, and they champion more noble motives such as love and attachment. Some see the move away from the biopsychosocial drive theory as heralding a fundamental "paradigm shift" (Kuhn, 1970) sweeping across psychoanalysis (Greenberg & Mitchell, 1983). Many theorists have criticized drive theory for ignoring the interpersonal nature of psychology. For example, a text on the intersubjective approach to psychotherapy stated,

> We must emphasize, because we are often misunderstood on this point, that the intersubjective viewpoint does not eliminate psychoanalysis's traditional focus on the intrapsychic. Rather, it contextualizes the intrapsychic. The problem with classical theory was not its focus on the intrapsychic, but its inability to recognize that the intrapsychic world, as it forms and evolves within a nexus of living systems, is profoundly context-dependent. (Orange, Atwood, & Stolorow, 1997, pp. 67–68)

Adherents of the so-called interpersonal model include Sullivan (1953) and Fairbairn (1941/1952), a central figure in the object relations school; both proposed that a relationship with an object is a primary motive, rather than one derived from gratification of biological drives. However, if a primary motive is to seek objects, then the question becomes, For what purpose? For Fairbairn, the purpose is to gain love, but by itself this drive is of dubious utility within a deterministic science. Central to the problem is that a love drive can only be defined by its aim, so it is difficult to know when it is or is not achieved. How deep does love have to go before it is real or satisfied? Science cannot shed light on these matters. This is the same problem presented in the critique of ego psychology that postulates a mastery drive. Drives that are defined by their aim are nearly impossible to fully operationalize, and they become arbitrary theory-making additions that are neither necessary nor sufficient (Maze, 1983). In contrast, drives defined by their source do not have this shortcoming because it is clear when they are consummated. As long as one accepts the proposition that theory must ultimately rest on a fundamental biological basis, there is no difficulty in reconciling modern developments in psychotherapy within the one cohesive theory of mastery.

Object Relations Theory

It is not necessary to see object relations theory as an alternative to the biopsychosocial drive theory. There is a fundamental compatibility between biopsychosocial drive theory and object relations theory, and it is clear that object relations theory needs drive theory to be theoretically coherent (Maze, 1993). The overall approach cannot ignore either the intrapsychic or interpersonal, and it must be a "one- to two-person psychology." The interpersonal is thus understood in the context of the personal. Indeed, mastery is an object relations interpersonal concept, yet it rests on drive theory. It is well known that Melanie Klein, the founder of the object relations school, was able to explain such interpersonal object relations mental processes as projection, identification, depression, and transference through the drive–structural model. Klein never abandoned drive theory, although she relied at times on the less coherent and muddled conceptualizations evident in Freud's (1933/1964b) later writings (such as the death instinct). Some of the confusions in Klein's conceptualizations have been well documented by Mackay (1981).

In Klein's view, the mastery of conflictual transference patterns is central to clinical change. She saw transference not in the narrow terms of the patient's relationship with the therapist, but in broad terms as a ubiquitous personality template that influences all aspects of the patient's life. This led to the understanding that transference was a "total situation," meaning that it applied to all aspects of a patient's life and that mastery of it could only be achieved by working through:

> It is my experience that in unravelling the details of the transference it is essential to think in terms of total situations transferred from the past to the present, as well as of emotions, defenses and object relations. . . . My conception of transference as rooted in the earliest stages of development and in deep layers of the unconscious is much wider and entails a technique by which from the whole material presented the uncon-

scious elements of the transference are deduced. . . . It is only by linking again and again (and that means hard and patient work) later experiences with earlier ones and vice versa, it is only by exploring their interplay, that present and past can come together in the patient's mind. . . . When persecutory and depressive anxiety and guilt diminish, there is less urge to repeat fundamental experiences over and over again, and therefore early patterns and modes of feelings are maintained with less tenacity. (1952/1986, pp. 209–210)

Tracing wishes back to their original source in biological drives is probably not therapeutically useful; it is enough to use the language of love, wishes, self, play, attachment, and early development in working with patients. Winnicott (1965) shed light on this by specifying the conditions for "good-enough" satisfaction of needs through early care. Good-enough care for infants means that their needs and wants can be sufficiently satisfied for them to develop sufficient trust and confidence in the world, paving the way for their future mental health. It is only in theory that scientific consistency requires the postulation of primary drives. Maze (1993) made the point that in psychotherapy, tracing the original source of the need may not be important. In discussing a case of the psychoanalyst Betty Joseph, Maze pointed out,

> Joseph's strategy was to bring him to see what it was that he was doing in the "here and now"; that he was acting out these feelings with regard to her, not merely to an imago of his parent. Yet this is not to deny the instinctual basis of his behaviour, nor that it had begun as an instinctual reaction in early life, and one might argue that the recognition of such a basis is necessary to understand the irrationality of his behaviour. In some such terms one may be able to see the complementarity of object relations theory and a clarified instinctual-drive theory. (p. 469)

It may be enough to work on mastery of the transference pattern as it presents itself in the present life of the patient. Tracing its roots to early developments may not be clinically necessary, because early conflicts can be seen to be still operating in the present, and it is with these that the therapy concerns itself.

Self Psychology

Another development in psychotherapy, self psychology, focuses on the quality and development of inner objects called self-objects (Kohut, 1977, 1978). Self psychology developed particularly in response to the forms of psychopathology found in serious personality disorders (such as borderline and narcissistic personality disorders), where self-mutilation and body boundaries are often psychologically permeable (Kohut, 1971). Two self psychologists posit the drive to play as fundamental (Meares & Coombes, 1994), yet from a theoretical perspective this suffers from the same conceptual muddles as proposals for a drive towards mastery or a drive toward love as discussed above. Nevertheless, self psychology presents new discoveries about primitive personality states and linguistic symbolization, and by emphasizing problems in the early development of the self, it contributes much to our understanding of the role of therapy in helping patients develop mastery and the therapeutic role of empathy in treatment. Again, the fundamental discoveries and applications of self psychology are compatible with the biopsychosocial drive theory for the same reasons as the object relations theory.

Attachment Theory

Ego psychologists Hendrick, White, and Weiss (discussed above) were all impressed by infant developmental research, which suggests that young children appear to actively seek mastery of their environment. In a similar context, following research with young children separated from their parents, and studies by others (e.g., Harlow & Zimmermann, 1959), Bowlby (1988) proposed that the need for attachment is central to mental health. One of the great strengths of Bowlby's attachment theory is that it rests on fundamental biological drives, such as the need for survival (self-preservative instincts). Bowlby's contribution is to show that individuals respond to threat, particularly in infancy, by seeking proximity to objects that are protective. His work, and that of his followers, have discovered much about how different qualities or patterns of early relationships produce characteristic styles of relating that are predictive of future mental health or psychopathology (Simpson & Rholes, 1998). This work has provided data on the development of early models of relationships forming the transference template, which is so important for future interpersonal mastery. At times, attachment theorists talk as if the attachment need is a primary drive (e.g., Stern, 1985), but this notion is vulnerable to the same criticisms as the ideas of a drive toward mastery (cf. the ego psychologists), the primary need for love (interpersonal theory), and a primary drive for play (in the self psychology perspective), as discussed above.

Freud would no doubt agree that attachment is centrally important, but he would insist that this concept should be explained further, in that "all the emotional relations of sympathy, friendship, trust, and the like, which can be turned to good account in our lives, are genetically linked with sexuality and have developed from purely sexual desires" (1912/1958a, p. 105). Similarly with mastery or competence, infants' inquisitiveness can be seen ultimately as motivated by the need to satiate drives. An example of this would be discovering what is edible by putting all variety of objects in the mouth, which can be linked to the self-preservative instincts including the hunger drive. Mastery can thus be adequately explained within the biopsychosocial drive theory. Where to draw the line as to what is primary and what is secondary is still a matter of spirited debate. For our purposes here, it suffices that in biopsychosocial drive theory there are a small number of irreducible drives that are primary and linked directly to biological processes from which the multitude of needs can ultimately be linked (Freud, 1915/1957a).

MASTERY AND THE INTEGRATION OF PSYCHOTHERAPY

To the casual observer, the history of psychotherapy in the 20th century could be interpreted as being marked by a great number of violent splits, resulting today in a variety of schools of therapy. However, at the root of all schools is a remarkable sameness. Generally speaking, each builds on those that preceded it and expands into new areas of investigation, such as very early infant development or severe personality disorders, to further the field. One of the key lessons for Renaissance artists, as they sought inspiration from classical Greek sculpture and painting, was how our perceptual system is naturally primed to more readily see the differences between things than sameness. One of the difficult tasks for artists was to overcome their natural tendency to overemphasize individual features (the extreme of which is caricature) to distill classical subtlety and purity. Psychologists, too, are just as guilty of looking for differences among things, drawing distinctions, and forming into camps. As scientists, we should instead be impressed by the overall fundamental sameness among the various theoretical positions and their practical applications.

Even when comparing cognitive–behavioral therapy and brief dynamic therapy, it can be seen that these approaches are far more similar than they are different. Both refer to schemas and distortions in thinking, and both discuss how work with the psychotherapist can help correct these distortions, which in turn leads to a lessening in symptoms and improved relationships. Research appears to bear this out, with little or no measurable differences in effectiveness among different schools of therapy (Luborsky et al., 1975; Smith et al., 1980). The application of the mastery concept might point the way toward what is changing in patients, how they are benefiting from the therapeutic relationship and the changes that it may be effecting. This can be studied from within a deterministic scientific framework. The theory of mastery developed here was directly applied to the development of a Mastery Scale to measure levels of mastery within psychotherapy transcripts. Chapters 4 and 5 explain the scale in more detail and elaborate on the correspondence between the theory and the scale.

CONCLUSION

Mastery can be seen as the outcome of the working-through process. It can be understood as the development of self-control and self-understanding in the context of interpersonal and social relations, to better meet fundamental needs, wishes, and desires. The biopsychosocial theory developed here begins with biological motivators or drives, which profoundly influence psychological processes. These in turn are expressed within interpersonal and social relations. Individuals with mastery therefore have a greater sense of adaptive control over their emotional reactions when faced with conflicts in interpersonal relationships, are more able to understand the origins and motives behind these conflicts, and can find more adaptive ways of meeting their fundamental needs and wishes. Individuals without mastery react with distress to a wide domain of interpersonal situations without awareness of the sources of their conflicts and problems and are overcome by symptoms of anxiety or depression when their needs and wishes remain poorly fulfilled.

Mastery is a process and outcome which is best understood within a scientific paradigm exemplified by the biopsychosocial drive theory approach. This provides a suitable basis for new learning, such as that from object relations, cognitive, behavioral, self psychology, and attachment theory approaches and are informed by psychotherapy research data. It can therefore be seen as an interpersonal theory with a solid foundation in a deterministic approach to science. Developments in object relations, self psychology, and attachment theory help to explain how the transference template is formed through early developmental experience and predicts subsequent behavior. Furthermore, the mastery theory provides clues as to how psychotherapists should work through the various manifestations of the template in the patient's life to achieve mastery.

In the next chapter, a number of studies are reviewed that are congruent with the idea of psychotherapy as being the development of mastery. New and innovative scientific methods of studying psychotherapy through examining and scoring verbatim transcripts are reviewed. An examination of these studies provides the context from which the Mastery Scale is later presented.

3

MASTERY AND CURRENT TRENDS IN PSYCHOTHERAPY

In the past 15 years, new, innovative scientific methods for studying psychotherapy have been developed. My purpose in this chapter is twofold: (a) to present the current state-of-the-art methods that have been used, their strengths and limitations, and how they might be adapted to measure mastery, and (b) to review studies that are relevant to the mastery concept developed here. As previously discussed, *mastery* is the acquisition of self-understanding and self-control. An important part of the development of mastery involves the working through of the repetition compulsion (including transference). Relevant studies reviewed here are those dealing with narratives, empirical measures of transference, and changes in transference and self-understanding over the course of psychotherapy. It is proposed that clients remember and tell negative narratives during psychotherapy to try to master the conflicts contained in them. In this chapter I provide detailed coverage of attempts to operationalize the pattern of conflictual narratives, including the core conflictual relationship theme (CCRT; Luborsky, 1977) method. I review studies of self-understanding as another line of research relevant to the study of mastery, and I conclude with a discussion of the implications of current research.

Excluded from the current review are traditional psychotherapy outcome studies that look only at changes in symptoms and that have a more remote relevance to the processes of mastery. Although virtually all studies of dynamic psychotherapy directly or indirectly investigate aspects of the change process developed by Freud, (1914/1958e), it is well beyond the bounds of this chapter to review all these studies (for more comprehensive reviews, see, e.g., Henry et al., 1994; Lambert & Bergin, 1994; Luborsky, Barber, & Crits-Christoph, 1990; Luborsky et al., 1988; Luborsky & Spence, 1978; Miller, Luborsky, Barber, & Docherty, 1993; Orlinsky et al., 1994; Strupp, 1992). What follows, then, is a discussion of only the most pertinent studies, selected from a deep pool of research.

RESEARCH ON NARRATIVES TOLD DURING PSYCHOTHERAPY

People usually come to psychotherapy because their psychological symptoms have become too severe for them to handle on their own. Patients typically illustrate to their therapist the kinds of problems and symptoms they are experiencing, and the history of the illness, by telling narratives. The study of narratives is now one key area of psychotherapy research relevant to mastery, along with the therapeutic alliance and the transference introduced in chapter 1.

Methodologically, this research depends on advances in the audio recording of psychotherapy sessions (Mahl, Dollard, & Redlich, 1954; Rogers, 1942), which provide more reliable information on the process of psychotherapy than therapists' case notes. Videotapes and audiotapes of therapy are the equivalent of the astronomer's telescope—they provide a more detailed and sharper picture of psychotherapy for study. Recorded sessions are usually transcribed verbatim, and qualitative and quantitative studies are made on the transcripts (Kächele, Thomä, Ruberg, & Grünzig, 1988). This method to some extent answers the concerns of critics of psychoanalytic scientific method who have in the past objected to the evidential basis of subjective case reports (for discussions of psychoanalytic research and the scientific method, see Wallerstein, 1993, and Grünbaum, 1986). Because transference and the therapeutic alliance are interpersonal phenomena, the key data of relevance in this context are the instances where patients discuss their interpersonal relationships in psychotherapy. These discussions are usually told as narratives, and through technological developments in the recording and transcribing of psychotherapy sessions, these narratives can be examined in detail.

Freud (1913/1958c) advised prospective therapists that "what the material is with which one starts treatment is on the whole a matter of indifference" and that the patient should be instructed to "say whatever goes through your mind" (pp. 134–135). The opening communications by the patient are usually along the lines of describing the history of the difficulties, the symptoms of distress, and the manifestations of these symptoms in daily life. A common feature to be found in such accounts are narratives of interactions with others. Luborsky, Barber, and Diguer (1992) have found through the intense study of verbatim transcripts of psychotherapy that narratives of interpersonal interactions are ubiquitous throughout the course of the psychotherapy encounter. These narratives, frequently about negative interactions, illustrate the problems brought to therapy:

> Negative interactions are more memorable and so are more ready to be told than positive ones because they deal with conflicts in relationships that are harder to master. The remembering and telling probably is in the service of trying to master the conflictual relationships. (p. 284)

Patients attempt to master their problems and conflicts within the psychotherapy hour, and one way of doing this is through telling narratives of conflictual relationships. Recent psychological research is increasingly being focused on the significance of narratives in psychotherapy, and more broadly in psychology generally, because these narratives contain rich information on people's attempts to make sense of adversity and to maintain coherence in their lives (Cohler, 1991; G. S. Howard, 1991; Russell & Van Den Broek, 1992; Toukmanian & Rennie, 1992; Viney & Bousfield, 1990).

Early in his career, Freud (1895/1955b) noticed the connection between the stories patients tell and their problems:

> It still strikes me as strange that the case histories I write should read like short stories and that, as one might say, they lack the serious stamp of science . . . . Case histories of this kind are intended to be judged like psychiatric ones; they have, however, one advantage over the latter, namely an intimate connection between the story of the patient's suffering and the symptoms of his illness. . . . (p. 231)

As Freud's statement implies, stories told to the therapist often have an "intimate connection" to "symptoms of his illness"; thus, it is reasonable to conclude that these conflictual interpersonal narratives probably contain within them the core of the neurosis. The study of narratives is now an emerging and important area of psychotherapy research, and it has applications to several psychotherapy schools and more broadly to psychology in general. The study of narratives provides a window into patients' mastery, their therapeutic alliance with the therapist, and their characteristic transference pattern.

RESEARCH ON THE TRANSFERENCE PATTERN: THE CCRT METHOD

Psychotherapy researchers have been focusing their attention on this transference "template" or pattern. Freud's translator (James Strachey) originally used the term *stereotype plate* to refer to it (Freud, 1912/1958a, p. 100). This has been renamed *transference template* after the German psychoanalyst

Helmut Thomä suggested to Lester Luborsky that it was a better translation from the original German (L. Luborsky, personal communication, April 23, 1995). This is important for the concept of mastery because it is in part through an analysis of transference-related patterns that mastery may be developed. Despite the importance of transference as a clinical concept in psychoanalysis, little attempt was made to investigate it in quantitative terms until the early 1950s, and only in the past 15 years have research advances allowed the development of objective measures.

Chance (1952) operationalized *transference* as the similarity of descriptions of the significant parent and of the psychotherapist given by the patient. Various researchers have developed Q-sort questionnaires of self-descriptions, which are used to compare descriptions of therapists (e.g., as nurturing or critical individuals or as a role model), with descriptions of father or parent figures. Crisp (1966), for example, found that attitudes toward the therapist during therapy changed with, or prior to, symptom changes. This follows from a psychoanalytically derived view that symptoms arise from, and are shown in, relationship conflicts. Luborsky et al. (1988) concurred, reasoning that a lessening of symptoms proceeds with changes in the pervasiveness of transference-related core conflictual relationship themes. Other early measures of transference included systematic clinical formulation and rating methods, whereby judges made independent ratings of transference. Such studies suffer from the disadvantage that there is little agreement among clinicians on the way formulations are made, and consequently the studies often have low statistical reliability.

At least 12 new methods have been developed to assess such repetitive patterns in psychotherapy. Some of the methods were designed to measure transference reactions, and some stem from the perspective of psychodynamic diagnosis and formulation. Although they appear different, they measure the same kinds of phenomena, namely, the structure and features of the transference template.

Definitions of *transference* differ (see chapter 1). Some define it strictly in terms of the patient's relationship with the therapist; others take a broader view of it and define it as the overall pattern of a person's relationships with others, including the therapist. Either way, narratives told about interpersonal conflicts with others outside the consulting room are evidence of transference (or repetition compulsion; see chapter 2) as equal in importance to transference enacted with the therapist. Empirical research has found significant correlations between the quality and amount of transference interpretations by the therapist and clinical outcome, which supports the crucial role of focusing on the present transference relationships, both inside and outside the therapy room, in therapeutic change (Crits-Christoph, Cooper, & Luborsky, 1988; Silberschatz, Curtis, & Nathans, 1989).

These new approaches to researching transference phenomena use content coding methods consisting of transcripts or tapes recorded from in vivo psychotherapy sessions. Available measures include the following: CCRT (Luborsky, 1977), configurational analysis (M. J. Horowitz, 1979), frame method (Teller & Dahl, 1981), script method (Carlson, 1981), patient's experience of relationship with therapist (Gill & Hoffman, 1982), consensual response formulation (L. Horowitz, Weckler, & Doren, 1983), dynamic focus (Schacht, Binder, & Strupp, 1984), plan diagnosis (Weiss et al., 1986), and idiographic conflict formulation method (Perry, Augusto, & Cooper, 1989). Many of the methods have been investigated only once. The CCRT is a popular method, and it is the one to which most others have been compared (see Luborsky, Popp, Barber, & Shapiro, 1994, for comparative studies of the transference measures). It is also perhaps the quickest, simplest, and most reliable to use, and research supports its reliability and validity (Luborsky, 1977; Luborsky & Barber, 1994; Luborsky & Crits-Christoph, 1990, 1998).

The CCRT measures the person's needs or wishes and how successful he or she is at gratifying them within the context of relationships with others. It thus draws heavily on Freud's (1915/1957a) basic theory of drives (expressed as wishes, needs, and wants) and their gratification or frustration (through successful or unsuccessful interactions with the person's social environment). This is an important link between Freud's metapsychology of instinctual drives and its application within a modern psychotherapy research tool.

Luborsky's CCRT technique (Luborsky, 1977; Luborsky & Crits-Christoph, 1990) involves the extraction from therapy transcripts of patient narratives that detail relationship interactions, such as those with close relatives, friends, or the therapist. Relationship narratives are often identified by an index such as "I remember when . . ." or "Like, for example, when . . . ." Narratives of relationships often illustrate a problem or emphasize an observation, and they contain within them the transference template—the regular characteristic conflictual personality style of the patient.

Morgan and Murray (1935) analyzed fantasies from Thematic Apperception Test responses into a tripartite structure of

> (1) a driving force (or fusion of forces in the subject), (2) an object (or group of objects) toward which or away from which the force is directed, and (3) the outcome of their interaction expressed in terms of subjective feeling—satisfaction or dissatisfaction. (p. 293)

Luborsky's CCRT method also has three elements: (a) the wishes of the speaker, which correspond in psychoanalytic theory to instinctual needs or drives (e.g., to obtain love and nurturing); (b) the reactions of others to the patient, such as hostility or aggression; and (c) the response of the self (e.g., withdrawing and becoming depressed). The three elements of the CCRT therefore code the dynamics of the relationship interaction and document patients' basic attempts to get their needs or drives satisfied. They narrate the expression of a wish, how this was received and responded to by another person, and then how this response affected them.

What does the CCRT show regarding the narratives of patients? Studies (Luborsky & Crits-Christoph, 1998; Luborsky, Crits-Christoph, Friedman, Mark, & Schaffler, 1991) have supported its validity as an objective personality measure of the transference template. The CCRT captures the conflict between the instinctual needs (expressed as wishes) and the meeting of these wishes (in the response from others and the self). Psychotherapy patients' narratives show marked conflicts, which generally involve wishes being met with negative responses from others and the self. The CCRT shows a unique and pervasive pattern for each patient, supporting the notion of a template that "repeats," deriving specifically from each patient's unique upbringing and inheritance. CCRTs of early memories of parental figures are similar to current relationship episodes with other people: a result consistent with the view that the transference template originates in early experiences. The CCRTs of narratives of interactions told in dream recall are highly consistent with the CCRT of interactions in the waking state, adding weight to the pervasiveness of the transference template and its unconscious derivatives (Luborsky & Crits-Christoph, 1990).

The CCRT is a relatively new tool, and more than 100 studies currently in progress are using it, extending it, and assessing its validity (e.g., Luborsky, Diguer, Kächele, et al., 1999). The question of importance here is this: How can we measure the degree to which patients have developed mastery of their problematic transference patterns? Empirical research reported in chapter 7 contributes to this quest.

DYNAMIC CHANGES IN PSYCHOTHERAPY

French (1958) developed a reintegrative model of recurrent cycles in psychoanalysis, whereby conflicts are repeatedly activated and attempts are made to master them. French discussed how problems in the external world have an internal resonance, just as narratives also contain a blend of reality and fantasy. He wrote that

> primary problems in adjustment to external reality and . . . secondary problems concerned with mastery of internal pressures . . . gives us another criterion by which we can recognize a patient's successive neurotic cycles. Each cycle begins with a primary problem and continues then with problems of internal mastery until the activated pressures are discharged. (pp. 115–116)

This working-through cycle is akin to Freud's (1914/1958e) comment that analysts must bring the "pathological character-traits" and other daily compulsive recurring phenomena "piece by piece, within the field and range of operation of the treatment" (pp. 151–152).

Pfeffer (1963) conducted a research study using French's (1958) model, which involved follow-up interviews with successfully analyzed patients. Although the therapist who was conducting the interviews had not treated the patients, he noticed two striking phenomena: Patients approached the interviews as if they were in analysis, and the symptoms and transference conflicts dealt with in the original analysis briefly recur. These conflicts do not last long: "The quick subsidence of symptoms appear to support the idea that conflicts underlying symptoms are not actually shattered or obliterated by analysis but rather are only better mastered with new and more adequate solutions" (p. 234). In other words, the conflicts are not fully resolved or cured; instead, they are mastered.

In concert with these findings, the patient's image of the therapist following analysis is not of a "neutrally experienced helpful physician who has given assistance," as would be predicted by those who maintain that the transference is shattered at the end of successful analysis (as reviewed a little later in this chapter). Rather, Pfeffer found that the transference remains alive and well but that it is simply better mastered by the patient.

This mastery arises out of finding solutions to the repeated conflict:

> In analysis repetition is not eliminated, but rather the content or substance of what is repeatable is changed. That is to say, the neurotic repeats the conflicts of the infantile past, whereas the satisfactorily analysed patient in new situations that require mastery is capable, in addition, of repeating the solutions of these same conflicts as achieved in the analysis. (Pfeffer, 1963, p. 241)

Because Pfeffer was studying patients in long-term analysis, it is not surprising that the transference repetitions became recognizably organized around infantile conflicts. Thus, a remarkable feature of mastery is the rapid regression and progression from and to infantile conflicts in the service of the adaptive ego functions.

On the basis of this study, it would seem reasonable to hypothesize that the narratives of successful patients should show similar CCRT conflicts in early and late stages of therapy. However, what should change is the mastery of the conflict, as demonstrated by a greater recognition of reality, greater monitoring and ease of emotional reactions, self-questioning of reactions, and insight into the past–present transference links. As Pfeffer (1963) noted, the neurotic conflict is repeated "as well as the repetition of the adaptation facilitating resolution of these same conflicts" (p. 242).

Schlesinger and Robbins (1975) used the same research design as Pfeffer (1963) and found that a "repetition" in "miniature" of the analytic process was evident in the follow-up interviews of successfully analyzed patients, even when they are interviewed by a therapist they did not know. Schlesinger and Robbins argued against the "analytic myth" that the outcome of an ideal analysis is the obliteration of the transference neurosis, and they put forward evidence that the conflicts remain, with the difference that the patient develops mastery over them. They studied a single patient who demonstrated repetitious patterns of conflict and attempts at mastery that the conflict patterns successively instigated. As the case moved toward termination, the cycles of transference conflict intensified. Toward the end of analysis, a full cycle was evident within a single session. In the six follow-up interviews 2 years and 9 months after termination, all the relationship themes from the analysis were still evident:

> The case study demonstrates a persistence of the recurrent pattern of conflicts. It is our hypothesis that such recurrent patterns of conflict remain relatively immutable as a childhood acquisition. They are a unique outcome of the maturational and developmental influences shaping an individual's early experience and are intrinsic to the organization of the infantile neurosis. (p. 776)

However, rather than signaling the failure of analysis, the authors noticed a change in the mastery of the transference template: "The effect of the analysis is not any obliteration of conflict, but changes in the potential for tolerance and mastery of frustration, anxiety, and depression through the development of a self-analytic function" (Schlesinger & Robbins, 1975, p. 776). The authors considered that this self-analytic function included the ability of patients to observe their internal reactions, to question them, and to see the links and connections of their reactions with the past; the ability of patients to control regressive emotions and to understand them when they occur; and finally the ability of patients to acknowledge libidinal wishes that were initially repressed. In summary, the patient's "ego resources were enhanced for self-analytic work in the mastery of her conflicts" (p. 778).

Crits-Christoph and Luborsky (1998a) explored the changes brought about by the use of the CCRT in dynamic psychotherapy. They reasoned that the repetitive maladaptive relationship conflicts, which typify the transference template, should become less pervasive over the course of therapy. That is to say, the CCRT pattern (of wishes, responses from others, and responses from self) should become more positive, with a wider range of relationship patterns indicating greater flexibility in emotional responding to conflicts. They hypothesized also that a decreased pervasiveness of conflictual relationship patterns should parallel the reduction in symptoms, because the two are causally related in psychodynamic theory. The individual ratings of two judges' CCRTs were transformed into standardized categories and then combined with 95% agreement to form a single CCRT formulation. The five units included in this study were the wish, positive and negative responses from other, and positive and negative responses from self. *Pervasiveness* was defined as the sum of relationship narratives with identical CCRT patterns divided by the total number of relationship narratives.

Thus, this study simply assessed change in the CCRT pattern over therapy, with the hypothesis that the pattern should disperse (i.e., become less pervasive) over the course of successful psychotherapy. Thirty-three nonpsychotic patients from the Penn Psychotherapy Project were included; they had weekly or twice weekly psychodynamic treatment sessions for periods ranging from 21 to 149 weeks (median = 43). Early sessions (typically Sessions 3 through 5) and late sessions (around the 90% mark, to avoid termination issues) were transcribed, and two judges coded the CCRT components. Symptomatic improvement was assessed by a modified self-report Hopkins Symptom Checklist–85 (Derogatis, Lipman, Covi, Rickels, & Uhlenhuth, 1970) and the clinician-assessed Health–Sickness Rating Scale (Luborsky, Diguer, Luborsky, McLellan, et al., 1993).

The results supported the hypothesis that over the course of dynamic psychotherapy, the pervasiveness of negative CCRT components significantly decreases. Not surprisingly, the wishes, which correspond to instinctual needs, did not alter in pervasiveness (66.3% early in therapy versus 62.9% late in therapy), which indicates that these are relatively stable within the personality. Significant decreases were found in the pervasiveness of negative responses from others (40.7% to 28.5%) and negative responses of the self (41.7% to 22.8%). Significant increases were found for positive responses from others (8.6% to 18.7%) and positive responses of the self (13.4% to 19.1%). By and large, these results were related to symptom reduction on the two measures. A striking finding was that despite the decrease in pervasiveness of the CCRT components, much of the CCRT patterns were still evident. The dynamic changes were small, with considerable transference patterns evident despite symptom improvement. This is consistent with the findings of Pfeffer (1963) and Schlesinger and Robbins (1975) reviewed above, who also found that the transference template remains relatively intact throughout the course of psychotherapy. Further original research on the positive and negative dimension of the CCRT and its relationship to mastery is presented in chapter 7.

Although the measure of pervasiveness used by Crits-Christoph and Luborsky (1998a) is highly relevant to dynamic theory, it does not appear to go far enough in capturing the development of mastery, which Schlesinger and others found to be the significant outcome of dynamic therapy. Despite the small but significant changes in the transference patterns evident in the above studies, overall it would seem reasonable to conclude that transference phenomena are alive and well in the most successfully analyzed patients and that this does not indicate the failure of therapy. What was not empirically verified on a large sample, however, was the hypothesized development of mastery. Three studies that attempted precisely such verification on a large sample are the focus of chapters 5 and 8.

STUDIES OF SELF-UNDERSTANDING

Self-understanding is an important aspect of mastery. Crits-Christoph and Luborsky (1998b) investigated changes in self-understanding of transference patterns on a slightly expanded sample (43 patients) from the Penn Psychotherapy Project. Only two early sessions (generally Sessions 3 through 5) were scored. Originally they hoped to compare these two early sessions with two later sessions, but they abandoned this approach because it was difficult to derive meaningful and comparable scores for the later sessions (P. Crits-Christoph, personal communication, June 25, 1993). This problem is discussed in detail below.

Five-point rating scales (ranging from *none* to *very much*) were constructed for self-understanding. These were used to rate patients' self-understanding or insight as evidenced in the CCRT in general (i.e., their awareness of their transference pattern) and toward specific people the patient discussed in therapy (the therapist, parents, and two main other people). Each rating was originally divided into the three CCRT components (wish, response from other, response of self), giving three separate scores per rating, but these were averaged to give a single score of self-understanding. Thus, four ratings per patient were made on self-understanding (general, therapist, parents, others). Each session was read as a whole and then rated by two judges on the self-understanding scales.

The results suggested that this method of scoring was good; the intraclass correlation for pooled judges was .85. The level of self-understanding in general for these early sessions was generally low (scores around 2.16; on this 5-point scale, average self-understanding = 2.5) and did not differ in any clear way between the two sessions. The data were then further analyzed to assess levels of patient symptoms (measured by Health–Sickness Rating Scale for the two sessions) and improvement in self-understanding between the two sessions. Results suggested that there were no changes between sessions but that overall level of self-understanding was related to outcome in some analyses.

The authors of this study relied on finding a convergence between patient self-statements and CCRT components, but they had difficulty in coding later sessions. This measure of insight was tied to specific material associated with particular people (i.e., therapist, parents, two prominent others), and after 50 or so weeks of therapy it would hardly be surprising that the content of the material and the specific persons referred to in the narratives would change. For example, the patient and therapist may have discussed the transference so often in the early stages of therapy that it is seldom mentioned after 50 sessions. Unless the patient is specifically asked or probed for statements related to insight, then the insight, even if present, may not come up as self-statements that can be coded. This problem cannot be overcome easily, and it may threaten any attempts to make content comparisons of self-statements between early and late sessions. The authors suggested that one solution is to study a single content theme throughout a brief therapy.

Another approach to this was developed by Blacker (1975), who traced a single memory over multiple instances and occurrences in therapy using process notes. Blacker found that over the course of the therapy the patient shifted from being a passive observer to being an active and insightful commentator, a change attributed to a strengthening of the ego. It might just as well be said that the patient's mastery increased.

Another approach, which uses the method of tracing a theme throughout psychotherapy, comes from the University of Sheffield Psychotherapy Research Program (Field, Barkham, Shapiro, & Stiles, 1994). This study relies on what is known as the *assimilation model*, which posits that change in psychotherapy is based on a manifestly cognitive information-processing model. This model proposes that patients need to clarify, understand, synthesize, and accommodate problematic experiences into cognitive schemas (Stiles et al., 1990; Stiles, Meshot, Anderson, & Sloan, 1992; Stiles et al., 1991). The Assimilation of Problematic Experiences Scale (Stiles et al., 1990) measures eight levels of assimilation: (a) warded off, (b) unwanted thoughts, (c) vague awareness, (d) problem statement and clarification, (e) understanding and insight, (f) application and working through, (g) problem solution, and (h) mastery. Fully assimilated experiences are said to be mastered, a process the authors described as when the "client successfully uses solutions in new situations; this generalizing is largely automatic, not salient. Affect is positive when the topic is raised, but otherwise neutral (i.e., this is no longer something to get excited about)" (Stiles et al., 1992, p. 83). This view of mastery involves the extent to which a previously problematic experience can be talked about with ease. It does not address the issue of changes in transference patterns or self-control (even though these may be present); it mainly measures the patient's ability to solve a problem with self-understanding.

Field and colleagues (1994) studied a transcribed single case of psychodynamic–interpersonal psychotherapy that lasted eight sessions. The theme selected for study was based on the patient's self-reported problems. Two hundred and forty-five passages from four sessions (Sessions 1, 3, 5, 7), in which the patient discussed her relationship with her mother or some parental theme, were extracted for analysis. These were then reduced to 65 passages on the basis of whether judges could recognize the mother theme within them. The 65 passages were then evaluated to determine how meaningful they were in relation to the patient's core problem; 24 passages met the criteria and were used in the subsequent analysis. These 24 passages were then randomly presented to judges to be rated on the assimilation scale. Results indicated that, at least for this theme, there were increases in assimilation congruent with predictions arising from the model.

The problem with methods that try to trace single themes throughout psychotherapy is the enormous loss of data that typically occurs toward the end of therapy. In other words, the problems that a patient brings to therapy often change as the treatment proceeds. Even for patients in short-term (8 sessions) therapy, judges could recognize and score all the required features in only 24 out of 245 passages. This raises questions about how valid and generalizable the results are in terms of the overall process of change. Indeed, with patients who had had long-term therapy (more than 50 sessions), Crits-Christoph and Luborsky (1998b) had to abandon trying to match similar themes. These difficulties will probably always negatively affect attempts to trace literal content themes through therapy. Perhaps a better approach is to look at changes in the process of how problems are discussed irrespective of specific content. As an example, assessing changes in the CCRT pattern is preferable to looking for relationship episodes experienced by one patient throughout the course of therapy.

Another method of studying self-understanding that has been investigated at Vanderbilt University involves the use of a questionnaire (Connolly, Hollon, & Shelton, 1993). Patients are asked about the extent to which they see their current problems as being related to the past. It thus specifically targets how much patients understand the links to the origins of their problems, but it does not assess awareness of the transference pattern in the present. One limitation of using a questionnaire is that it does not accurately convey the correspondence between patients' responses and how they conduct and understand themselves in real interactions. One virtue of transcript methods is that genuine interactions and narratives are unobtrusively recorded in real time.

O'Connor, Edelstein, Berry, and Weiss (1994) assessed insight over the course of therapy and found a U-shaped curve: Patients began with high levels of insight, progressively lost this insight as therapy proceeded (a result of the patient "testing" the therapist, the authors suggested), then regained it at the end of therapy. However, this finding may be an artifact of the study design: Early and late interviews from this project specifically probed for insight statements, whereas middle sessions did not (G. Silberschatz, personal communication, June 11, 1993).

Rating scales have also been used to judge the importance of insight within therapy (for a further discussion of insight, see Crits-Christoph et al., 1993). For example, one study of 43 patients used clinical ratings of insight and found that gains in insight after 2 years predicted longer dynamic changes after 4 years. Unfortunately, however, the subjective nature of the rating task led to considerable disagreement among the judges (Høglend, Engelstad, Sorbye, Heyerdahl, & Amlo, 1994).

Another way of articulating the concept of self-understanding is to use the notion of *emotional insight*, the integration of affect and cognition (Gelso, Hill, Mohr, Rochlen, & Zack, 1999, p. 264; Gelso, Kivlighan, Wine,

Jones, & Friedman, 1997). This is probably also linked to the more generalist and popular notion of *emotional intelligence* (Ciarrochi, Chan, & Caputi, 2000). For example, Gelso and colleagues (1999) regarded insight as comprising two components—intellectual insight, which they found to be relatively high throughout treatment, and emotional insight, which connects intellect and affect and which starts off relatively low and improves with successful therapy. They maintained that emotional insight is crucial for resolving transference distortions. The practical implication is that therapists should be attending to the emotional processing and experiencing of their patients, particularly when patients are dealing with narratives that are laden with activated transference-related conflicts.

Although they regarded emotional insight as part of self-understanding, Gelso and colleagues' notion of it comes closest to my formulation of self-control as an essential component of mastery. This idea is hardly new: Strachey (1934) made such a distinction. Perhaps what is now recognized is that intellectual insight may not be sufficient for change, but rather that emotional insight, or self-understanding, particularly toward the transference template, is more predictive of mastery and subsequent change.

OUTCOME OF TRANSFERENCE CONFLICTS: RESOLUTION OR MASTERY?

Because a fundamental principle of psychoanalytic technique is analysis of the transference, it follows that the ideal outcome of therapy would involve some change in the pervasive negative transference patterns. There are two major theories of outcome of dynamic psychotherapy. One holds that transference reactions, particularly those that are negative and conflictual, are resolved in successful psychotherapy (Davanloo, 1980; Ekstein, 1956). For example, an account by practitioners working under Davanloo's methods stated that "this constant experiencing and linking of conflicts is believed to rapidly resolve neurotic symptoms and interpersonal patterns" (p. 84), such that at termination "review shows no residual problems" (Laikin, Winston, & McCullough, 1991, p. 95).

The second and more widely held view is that conflicts and transference reactions continue even after successful psychotherapy. In *Analysis Terminable and Interminable*, Freud (1937/1964a) questioned the extent to which conflicts could be resolved. He noted that it was only "the optimists' expectations . . . that there really is a possibility of disposing of an instinctual conflict (or, more correctly, a conflict between the ego and an instinct) definitively and for all time" (p. 223). Given the dialectical oppositions inherent in psychoanalytic metapsychology, it would be inconsistent to argue that instinctual forces can be eliminated. Moreover, on a clinical level, radical changes in personality are seen only in patients with severe psychotic, dissociative disorders or as a result of severe head injury or trauma, not as the result of successful psychotherapy. Mastery of emotional transference conflicts appears to be a more likely outcome of psychotherapy than does the possibility that psychological tendencies or problems can be cured, in the sense of being entirely resolved and eradicated.

What tends to change in successful psychotherapy is the patient's ability to "identify cues to recognition of the central relationship problems . . . since the relationship problems typically reappear in many seemingly different contexts" (Luborsky, 1984, p. 124). This involves "structural changes" in personality (Luborsky et al., 1988, p. 158), that is, alterations in the mastery of transference conflicts. Psychotherapy patients seem to internalize the image of their therapist and the kinds of interpretative techniques that the therapist uses to understand psychological conflict (Meissner, 1981). In summary, they develop through the internalization of therapeutic gains the ability to analyze themselves. In an empirical study discussed above, Pfeffer (1963) suggested that "the intrapsychic image of the treating analyst is used to cathect, comprehend, and comfortably adapt" (p. 240). This internalization is thus the basis for the development of the ability to analyze oneself and to maintain mastery over emotional transference conflicts.

CONCLUSION

The research reviewed suggests that mastery appears to involve (a) changes in the potential for tolerance of frustration, anxiety, and depression; (b) the ability to control regressive emotions and understand them when they occur; (c) the ability to acknowledge libidinal wishes that were initially repressed; (d) greater recognition of reality and self-questioning of reactions; (e) greater monitoring and ease of emotional reactions; (f) insight into the links and connections of their current reactions with the characteristic ways of behaving in the past; (g) being able to provide adaptive solutions to long-standing transferential conflicts; (h) the ability to identify cues that activate and maintain the central maladaptive relationship patterns; and (i) improvements in the ability to link intellectual knowledge with emotional experience.

No studies have specifically targeted the study of mastery as self-control and self-understanding. The study of narratives from verbatim transcripts appears to provide a window into mastery-relevant processes. Studying underlying processes through content analysis appears to be a more effective research strategy than tracing literal themes or making Likert-scale clinical ratings. Although changes in pervasiveness of the transference (CCRT) pattern have been researched, no study has looked at the mastery of the pattern. Studying this phenomenon is hampered by the lack of a research instrument to investigate mastery. Transference patterns appear to change only slightly over the course of therapy. What appears to change in therapy is the mastery (self-control and self-understanding) of these transference patterns, although this has only been indirectly studied.

There appear to be compelling reasons for developing a new measure of mastery. The development of new methods of studying psychotherapy processes, using content analysis of verbatim narratives told by patients in psychotherapy, appears to offer a new way of studying mastery processes. Chapter 1 has shown how the study of mastery contributes directly to the current state-of-the-art methods and themes of psychotherapy research. Chapter 2 has developed a way of conceptualizing mastery as self-control and self-understanding within a biopsychosocial theory, and this chapter has presented the evidence to date that is most relevant to understanding and researching mastery processes. The next chapter puts this together and presents a new research tool: the Mastery Scale.

III

MEASURING MASTERY

4

THE MASTERY SCALE METHOD

The Mastery Scale, Version I, is a comprehensive psychotherapy process research tool (Grenyer, 1994b). It is based on the biopsychosocial model of psychotherapy presented in chapter 2, but it may be readily applied to many clinical research investigations from different orientations. This chapter describes a method for operationalizing the concept of mastery and provides comprehensive guidelines for scoring the Mastery Scale.

There are three major phases in scoring. Phase 1 is to collect and prepare samples for analysis. This involves obtaining narratives of interactions, transcribing them verbatim, dividing the text into grammatical clauses, and identifying the clauses that can be scored in terms of mastery. Phase 2 involves applying the scale to the samples (i.e., allocating mastery scores to the identified clauses). Phase 3 involves the compilation of sample scores obtained from the method. Two types of researchers are recommended to score the Mastery Scale. The first type of researchers (*clausers*) complete Phase 1. The second type of researchers (*judges*) complete Phase 2. Phase 3 is usually done by the principal investigator.

This chapter describes the steps, in each of these three phases, required to use the Mastery Scale for the purpose of research. The intention is to provide an accurate, valid, and replicable measurement tool that can be used in different research contexts. The use of the Mastery Scale in clinical work is described in chapter 6.

PHASE 1: COLLECTING AND PREPARING SAMPLES FOR ANALYSIS

When using the Mastery Scale, the clinician must have speech samples to examine. Verbatim transcripts of psychotherapy sessions are recommended; under certain research contexts, it may be possible to score records of interviews, responses to stimulus materials (e.g., the Thematic Apperception Test; Morgan & Murray, 1935), or perhaps even written archival material such as diary entries, although to date this has not been attempted. Although it may be possible to score some features of the scale directly from audiotape or videotape, it is not recommended that the scale be coded from these materials alone until further studies are done to validate this procedure. A combination of transcript and tape would probably improve the validity of the ratings, but this has not been experimentally established; other content analysis scales using audio material compared to written transcripts alone have not been found to provide significantly more accurate results (Gottschalk, Winget, & Gleser, 1969).

Instructions for Collecting Verbal Samples

Data can be collected in many ways. Below are three methods that have proven very useful. All rely on making audio recordings of speech for later transcription and analysis.

Before the samples are recorded, the researcher records the following information on the audiotape: (a) date of recording, (b) time of day, (c) identification code of the interviewee, and (d) name of interviewer or therapist making the recording. A clear and clean recording is vital to ensure that the transcription is as faithful to the spoken speech as possible. Select a quiet and private echo-free room to conduct the therapy or interviews (Mahl et al., 1954). Endeavor to minimize all extraneous noise, disruptions, and interruptions. Sensible precautions include diverting telephone calls and putting a warning sign outside the door. Ensure that the recorder and microphone are functioning and are placed close enough to the research participant to maximize the ratio of the speech signal to ambient noise. Do not use tape recorders that are voice activated, because pauses and silences may be important pieces of information in understanding and coding the material.

It is important that the participant and interviewer are comfortable with the presence of the recording machine. Experience has shown that if the interviewer or therapist is comfortable with the recording device and can model the absence of concern about it (to put the recording device "out of mind," so to speak), then the interview usually proceeds smoothly. The interviewer should maintain appropriate eye contact with the participant to convey interest in what the participant has to say. The interviewer should avoid looking at the recording machine or fussing over it and should monitor the comfort of the participant, promptly answering any concerns and dispelling fears (e.g., about confidentiality) early in the interview, preferably before the data are collected. The essential qualities of the interviewer include those recommended in all therapeutic contexts, such as the ability to establish rapport, use listening skills, and empathize with the interviewee's concerns.

The basic principles of collecting data are those developed by Freud (1913/1958c) in his free association method. Freud wrote that "the patient must be left to do the talking and must be free to choose at what point he shall begin" (p. 134). In other words, the patient should be extended a general invitation to speak about his or her experience without undue shaping of this by the experimenter. The three methods discussed below all share this feature. The interviewer should avoid giving any more specific instructions as to content than those given below.

Method 1. Naturalistic Psychotherapy Sessions

Before the beginning of a contract between therapist and patient to engage in psychotherapy, informed consent should be obtained from the patient (and if relevant, the therapist) for the therapy to be audio or video recorded. The consent usually involves signing a consent form that has been approved by an ethics committee. The conditions of such consent commonly include the clause that the patient can withdraw consent for the audiotaping without prejudicing treatment in any way.

At the completion of the psychotherapy, verbatim transcripts of the sessions of interest are made. These form the database for scoring the Mastery Scale. In psychotherapy, the therapist provides an invitation to speak, but in general he or she does not direct or prescribe the content of the session (although this may not always be the case). The data are naturalistic in the sense that the patient leads the discussion and furnishes the content of the material as his or her personal needs dictate.

Method 2. Relationship Anecdotes Paradigm Interview Method

Luborsky (1998b) developed the relationship anecdotes paradigm (RAP) interview method, and interested readers are advised to consult this source for detailed information. The interviewer instructions generally are as follows:

> Please tell me some incidents or events, each involving yourself in relation to another person. Each one should be a specific incident. Some should be current and some old incidents. For each one tell (1) when it

occurred, (2) the other person it was with, (3) some of what the other person said or did and what you said or did, and (4) what happened at the end. The other person might be anyone—your father, mother, brothers and sisters or other relatives, friends or people you work with. It just has to be about a specific event that was personally important or a problem to you in some way. Tell at least 10 of these incidents. Spend about 3 but no more than 5 minutes in telling each one. I will let you know when you come near the end of 5 minutes. This is a way to tell about your relationships. Make yourself comfortable and enter into this RAP session as you would with someone who you want to get to know you. (Luborsky, 1998b, p. 110)

To derive good narratives, it is crucial for the investigator to use follow-up prompts where necessary, and especially after the first narrative is told, to be sure the patient gives specific concrete events and not only generalized accounts. For narratives that are too short, the patient must be asked to describe the events further. It is important to do this from the first narrative to ensure that the patient understands the amount of detail to provide so that the data can be analyzed usefully. The investigator should reduce the anxiety about finding narratives by suggestions such as "just tell me any incident, event or interaction with anyone that occurs to you now." The person who is struggling to remember exact details should be encouraged to "say what you remember now about it." Similarly, the person who cannot remember narratives that are "important" should be invited to recall "events or incidents as you think of them."

The RAP interview is tape recorded and lasts between 30 and 50 minutes. Relationship anecdotes can come from any period in the person's life; it is in fact preferable to have a variety of narratives. The narratives may be derived with specific research questions in mind. For example, (a) in marital therapy, derive narratives about each other; (b) in object relations studies, derive four narratives for each of the main people in the person's early life; (c) in psychiatric studies, use narratives told in the context of a clinical evaluation; (d) in addiction studies, narratives about relationships with other drug using acquaintances could be compared to nonusing acquaintances (see Luborsky, 1998b, p. 114, for more details on various methods).

The most important factor in deriving good narratives is that the patient has a good rapport with the investigator. References to the confidentiality of the interview and the positive value of the patient's contribution to understanding relationships can help to engender trust and cooperation.

Method 3. Five-Minute Speech Samples

Five-minute speech samples have been used for more than 20 years and have proved to be very useful in clinical research contexts. Gottschalk et al. (1969) explained in detail how such samples may be used. The instructions are given following the establishment of rapport with the patient, and responses are audio recorded. The original instructions of Gottschalk et al. are as follows:

> This is a study of speaking and conversational habits. Upon a signal from me I would like you to speak for 5 minutes about any interesting or dramatic personal life experience you have had. Once you have started I will be here listening to you but I would prefer not to reply to any questions you may feel like asking me until the 5-minute period is over. Do you have any questions you would like to ask me before we start? Well then, you may begin.

Viney (1983) developed alternative instructions for use in clinical and health psychology research contexts :

> I'd like you to talk to me for a few minutes about your life at the moment—the good things and the bad—what it is like for you. Once you have started I shall be here listening to you; but I'd rather not reply to any questions you may have until a 5-minute period is over. Do you have any questions you would like to ask now, before we start? (p. 545)

This method has been used to score samples on the Mastery Scale (see chapter 8). Depending on the research question, the interviewer may want to use the following instructions, which focus on the patient's perceptions of a relative or significant other (Gift, Cole, & Wynne, 1986):

> When I ask you to begin I'd like you to speak for 5 minutes, telling me what kind of a person (relative's first name) is and how you get along together. After you've begun to speak, I'd prefer not to answer any questions until the 5 minutes are over. Do you have any questions you'd like to ask before we begin? (p. 88)

Keep in mind that samples as short as those derived from the 5-minute method may not result in as valid a measure of complex constructs such as mastery compared with those obtained from narratives from multiple psychotherapy sessions or a long RAP interview.

Instructions for Transcribing Verbal Samples

The transcription of psychotherapy sessions is a time-consuming process; 1 hour of therapy can take 5 to 8 hours or more to accurately transcribe. There are generally three standards in transcription. Level 1 is a very quick transcription that renders the main spoken speech (which involves the transcriber only listening to the sample once or twice); Level 2 is more detailed, with full punctuation, nonverbal sounds, difficult to hear passages, stutters, and repetitions (which usually involves the transcriber listening to the sample two or three times); and Level 3 involves extremely detailed rendering of all nonspeech sounds (e.g., tongue clicks, breaths in and out) and uses special rules to render how each word is enunciated (e.g., with glides, emphasis, vowel markings), and this can involve listening to the speech sample four or more times. Very detailed rules are available for transcribing verbal material (Sacks, Schegloff, & Jefferson, 1974). There are also recommendations for transcribing psychotherapy samples (Mergenthaler & Stinson, 1992).

For the purpose of scoring the Mastery Scale, a Level 2 transcription standard is recommended. Very detailed transcriptions, as in Level 3 transcripts, have the disadvantage that judges may get lost in the detail of the transcription and miss the main communication message. Level 1 transcripts are probably suitable but not ideal; they may provide little information on how the words were spoken. However, all transcriptions are more or less accurate renditions of what is said, and a "perfect" transcription is unachievable with the present state of technology and the limits of verbal language in capturing voiced speech. Bordin and colleagues (1954) discussed these and other sources of error in such types of psychotherapy process research.

The following rules are useful in preparing transcripts:

1. *P:* refers to patient speech, *T:* to therapist speech.

2. All partial words, stutters, and repetitions are included.

3. Nonverbal vocalizations such as *ah* and *um* are included.

4. All words transcribed are rendered in dictionary-standard form, not in dialect (e.g., *yaknow* is rendered you know).

5. Unheard words are rendered as *xxx* (e.g., two unheard words are presented as *xxx xxx*).

6. Short sentences with proper punctuation are usually imposed on the speech sample to create comprehensible written dialogue.

7. A short pause is a comma, pauses up to 5 seconds are written as dashes (e.g., — — —), and silences longer than 5 seconds are documented in brackets (e.g., [pause: 1m.35 sec]).

8. Particular qualities of speech are included in brackets and followed by colons where appropriate (e.g., [softly: whispers: loudly: teary voice: quickly: shakily:]).

9. Nonspeech sounds are recorded in brackets (e.g., [cries, coughs, laughs, blows nose, sniffs]).

10. Very brief interjections and noises from the other speaker are inserted in square brackets within the main speaker's dialogue rather than on a separate line (e.g., [T: uh-huh] or [P: OK]).

11. An independent listener checks the entire transcript with the recorded tape for accuracy

12. The transcripts are triple spaced, with a wide margin on the right-hand side.

Instructions for Preparing Psychotherapy Transcripts for Scoring

The following methods are used when the data for scoring mastery are transcripts of psychotherapy. When the materials are derived through other means (e.g., 5-minute speech samples), the following can easily be modified as necessary. The research steps below should be followed, preferably by specific clausers who are not involved in Phase 2.

1. Remove or obscure sensitive information in the transcripts (if it has not already been done), such as information that may identify the patient (e.g., names, ages, places, nationality), the number of the session, the date of the session, and so on. This information may bias the judges (e.g., information that the session occurred late in therapy as opposed to early).

2. Identify and extract all narratives or relationship episodes (REs) from the transcripts. *Relationship episodes* are defined as "a part of a session that occurs as a relatively discrete episode of explicit narration about relationships with others or with the self" (Luborsky, 1998a, p. 16). These discrete episodes are identifiable because the narratives tend to have a stereotypic structure: (a) a beginning introduction; for example, "I will give you an example, yesterday I saw Kelly and she . . ."; or "I am depressed. The phone rang last night. It was Kylie and . . ."; (b) a middle, where the main details of the interaction are described, often with recollection of what each person said; and (c) an end, where the story as it happened is finished before the patient moves back into a more general discussion or a change of topic. A single horizontal line is drawn at the start of the narrative (at the beginning of the introductory comments or story), and another is drawn at the end (when the explicit telling is finished). Sometimes a story is interrupted by a digression, and then the rest of the story is finished afterward. In this instance, the start and end of the first part of the story are marked, with a note at the end (e.g., "continues on page x") and on the continuation page the beginning of the story resumption is marked, and so is the end. The digression is thus "cut out" and is not scored. Generally, judges only read the RE—they are not provided the context of the rest of the session, although in some studies context may be important and should be provided.

    The characters (apart from the narrator) in the RE are noted in the margin (e.g., father and mother). Sometimes the other person may be the therapist (either a recollection of an episode that happened earlier or an enactment at the time between therapist and patient, such as an argument about the cost of the therapy sessions). Occasionally the person may narrate an episode about himself or herself only, which is more than self-description and can be scored. It may be useful to note whether the narrative occurred early in the person's life or is a recent event.

Narratives are judged for completeness on a 5-point scale. Only those that are 2.5 or greater in completeness are used and scored. A 2.5 narrative or above has three identifiable components: (a) a wish by the speaker, either explicitly stated or clearly inferable (e.g., I wanted to get help from Pete); (b) a reaction of the other person to that wish (e.g., Pete told me to go away and stop bothering him); and (c) a reaction of the self (speaker) to the interaction (e.g., I felt rejected and hurt). This is the basic structure of the core conflictual relationship theme method from which it is derived (Luborsky, 1998a; see chapter 3). A narrative such as "Pete came over to my house and we played records all afternoon before I got very tired again" is not scored because it is not clear what Pete's reactions are in this example. An inferable wish is where what was motivating the person can be deduced. For example, in the narrative "we went to the movies together and then came back to my apartment for a drink," the wish might be inferred as "to be close" to the other.

3. Divide the narratives into clauses. Transcripts are of spoken words, and they must be divided into grammatical units (clauses) for content-analysis techniques. This is made by using slash marks (/) to indicate the division of the clauses. In the examples that follow, double slashes (//) are sometimes used when each clause is a separate example. A valid and reliable method for this has been developed by Auld and White (1956). The only exception to the rules of Auld and White used here are that nonrestrictive dependent clauses and independent clauses are also divided. This alteration makes this method of clausing consistent with the rules adopted by Gottschalk et al. (1969), and the reader is referred to that work for many scored examples. For a more general discussion of independent and dependent clauses, see Strunk and White (2000).

Decisions as to where to divide verbal samples are not always clearcut, and differences of opinion can arise that cannot be resolved by experts because the rules of grammar allow for different interpretations of the same problem. It is preferable to have one clauser undertake the clausing for all transcripts used in the study to keep this source of error constant.

1. Only independent and nonrestrictive dependent clauses are divided. A clause contains a subject and a predicate, and it may or may not contain other complements and modifiers. Clauses are either independent or dependent. Main independent clauses are normally separated by periods, commas, and conjunctions such as *and, or,* and *but.* Dependent (subordinate) clauses are either restrictive (they modify the meaning of the main clause) or nonrestrictive (they add additional information to the main clause). Restrictive subordinate clauses only qualify the main clause, they are not preceded by a comma, and they are not divided. They are usually introduced by words such as *that, what, when, where, who, how,* and *if.* For example,

/It was hot when I was in Rome/;Rome is where I found love/.

Nonrestrictive dependent clauses are divided (because they add additional independent information), they are usually preceded by a comma, and they are usually introduced by words such as *because, since, when, which, who, that, although, even though, so,* and *so what.* For example,

/I went to Rome,/which was hot/;I had a Roman holiday,/where I found love/.

2. In elliptical sentences, the subject or predicate may be missing, but the context makes the whole meaning clear. In these cases, the phrase is also divided. For example, if the therapist says "Are you cold?" and the client replies "Yes," the "yes" is treated as a separate clause because it can be understood to be saying "/yes I am cold/."

3. False starts are not divided (e.g., "/yeah I was going—I was going to Rome/.").

4. Filler phrases such as "you know" added to clauses are not divided (e.g., "/I am going to Rome, you know/").

5. Clauses that are interrupted by other clauses, as if in parentheses, are divided separately (e.g., "/I am going —/Lise asked me to marry her,/going to Rome,/where I'll get married/").

6. Contrary to Auld and White (1956), silences are not considered separate units.

7. Therapist statements are not claused or scored, unless that is part of the research design.

Instructions for Identifying Which Clauses Can Be Scored for Mastery

Following clausing, the clauser then identifies (by underlining or some other marking convention) all scorable clauses; this is done before the judges assign their content codes. This involves deciding which clauses are indicative of mastery. Only clauses that can be meaningfully scored on the Mastery Scale are identified. Clauses that are ambiguous in respect to mastery or require a high degree of abstraction or context to derive mastery scores should not be identified. The number of scorable clauses per passage can vary widely. For example, one passage may only have a few scorable clauses, whereas in another almost all clauses may be scorable. Statements in patient narratives that are quoted verbatim from others are generally not identified or scored (e.g., /He said "I don't know why you are acting this way today"/). However, the statement "/He seemed to be very confused about my behavior/" would be identified as scorable on the Mastery Scale because it is from the patient's phenomenological perspective.

The benefit of having a clauser identify the scorable clauses is that all judges make ratings on the same clauses, making calculations of interjudge agreement easy. Second, the task for the content-coding judges involves considerably less labor, an important consideration as the cost of coding is high and the extra task in addition to scoring can rapidly lead to fatigue. The clauser who identifies the scorable clauses should be very experienced and highly trained with the scale.

PHASE 2: APPLYING THE SCALE TO THE SAMPLES

The items that compose the Mastery Scale are listed in Exhibit 4.1. Mastery Scale judges should be given the following instructions:

Psychotherapy provides a forum for patients to work on their difficulties with the assistance of a therapist. The material brought to therapy by patients typically contains narratives of conflictual interpersonal relationships, which they wish to master. These narratives have been extracted from psychotherapy transcripts. You are to rate these narratives on a research content-analysis scale.

1. Rate each narrative separately before proceeding to rate the next narrative. Rate the narratives in the order in which they are presented to you. Read the narrative first to get a feel for the relationship interaction.

2. The scale requires you to make specific judgments about individual sentences (clauses). You are not rating the process as a whole.

EXHIBIT 4.1
The Mastery Scale I

Level 1—Lack of Impulse Control
  1A Expressions of Being Emotionally Overwhelmed
  1B References to Immediacy of Impulses
  1C References to Blocking Defenses
  1D References to Ego Boundary Disorders

Level 2—Introjection and Projection of Negative Affects
  2E Expressions of Suffering From Internal Negative States
  2F Expressions Indicative of Negative Projection Onto Others
  2G Expressions Indicative of Negative Projection From Others
  2H References to Interpersonal Withdrawal
  2I Expressions of Helplessness

Level 3—Difficulties in Understanding and Control
  3J Expressions of Cognitive Confusion
  3K Expressions of Cognitive Ambivalence
  3L References to Positive Struggle With Difficulties

Level 4—Interpersonal Awareness
  4M References to Questioning the Reactions of Others
  4N References to Considering the Other's Point of View
  4O References to Questioning the Reaction of the Self
  4P Expressions of Interpersonal Self-Assertion

Level 5—Self-Understanding
  5Q Expressions of Insight Into Repeating Personality Patterns of Self
  5R Making Dynamic Links Between Past and Present Relationships
  5S References to Interpersonal Union
  5T Expressions of Insight Into Interpersonal Relations

Level 6—Self-Control
  6U Expressions of Emotional Self-Control Over Conflicts
  6V Expressions of New Changes in Emotional Responding
  6W References to Self-Analysis

3. There can only be one score per clause.

4. You will only be coding references to the self and the patient's perceptions of others in relation to their interpersonal experience.

5. Score only the clauses identified as scoreable by the clauser. Record the scores above the underlined units or on a score sheet provided.

6. Occasionally you will find that individual aspects of the clause suggest different scores. You are rating the clause as a whole so the choice of the rating must reflect the whole clause, not one part of it. If in doubt, score the major theme that best reflects the mastery of the patient. If you cannot decide between two alternative codes, choose the higher code.

7. You are coding manifest or "surface" content; you do not need to make sophisticated inferences about the clause. You are coding content, not mood. Mood is relevant only if it is revealed explicitly in the content. You should generally take what the patient says at face value.

8. Reported fantasies and dreams and references to animals and to inanimate objects are coded for content in exactly the same way as other material.

9. Occasionally you will need to consider the context in making a score. As a general rule, you should make a conservative inference firmly on the basis of contextual evidence that occurs close to the clause, rather than making abstract inferences on the basis of remote evidence.

10. Remember that psychotherapy does not change a person into a genius or a god. You should consider scores in the 5 or 6 range to represent good, not outstanding, functioning. If the narrative is generally indicative of psychological health and well-being according to the criteria stated, then you should consider using these scores where appropriate.

11. Sometimes there will be confusion as to whether you are scoring the performance of the person in therapy or their performance in the narrated interaction. The truth about what really happened in the relationship interaction is unknown to you (and the therapist), so the only evidence you have for the mastery score is the verbal narrative of the interaction as told in therapy. The way the narrative is told may be just as important as the features of the interaction described.

12. You are judging the patient's present mastery as evidenced in the way he or she discusses material with the therapist. It does not matter at what time the interaction described actually happened (e.g., it may be when they were 5 years old). References to old ways of relating should be scored because they typically can relate to functioning in the present and can be differentiated from late narratives in the research design if needed.

For example, consider the statements "I used to get so angry when he did that/but now I don't." The first clause is scored 2F (expressions indicative of negative projection onto others), even though the statement is in the past tense. The second clause is scored 6V (expressions of new changes in emotional responding), because the old pattern of anger has been modified. The person is talking in the present about new changes in their emotional reactions. Note that talking in the past tense does not necessarily mean that the person is discussing an old way of relating. The statement "I got angry" is still scored because the assumption of this method is that patients are reporting problems in the attempt to assimilate them more fully (Vaillant, 1993). We take what they say seriously and at face value, because what is in their speech (no matter how distorted) is a window into their inner functioning and can thus be interpreted for mastery. The assumption of this scale is that statements concerning mastery are not all of equal importance: Those at Level 6 indicate very high mastery, and those at Level 1 indicate very low mastery.

Level 1: Lack of Impulse Control

1A. Expressions of Being Emotionally Overwhelmed

1A includes being globally emotionally overwhelmed and distressed. The state described is extreme, it dominates the person's state of mind, and it includes egressive features.

Example Clauses:

/I exploded//Everything all started//It is extremely painful//Nothing is easy//I felt very bad//I hate myself//I felt really sick//Everything is black//My sickness controls everything//It is all too much/.

Clinical Examples:

/He ought to open up his eyes (2F)/and look where his mother lives/if he wants to be ashamed of what he's, you know, his parents./Look at, oh, oh. I saw so many colors, (1A)/that room just went around. (1A)/And when he walked away/Jack said to me "Who the hell is he to ask a question like that?! It's none of his business!!"/He said "Why didn't you open your mouth?" / I said "Jack, I just couldn't. I just couldn't" (2H) / All the way home I was burning and burning and burning, (1A) / and my stomach's killing me. (1A)/.

* * *

/I didn't feel like being with people, (2H)/I was really depressed. (2E)/And all of a sudden I burst out crying and crying and (1A)/I just felt really horrible [pause] (1A)/and that scared me. (1A)/.

* * *

/I met a boy that I fell in love with, you know,/and he said "I don't care."/He didn't care./He didn't care./About me or anything,/and so, I mean, I was, this really upset me. (2E)/I was in shock, (1A)/and, uh, that's when I really wanted to commit suicide (1A)/and that's when I was very,/uh, uh, oh, what was it? (1C)/I was very emotional about it. (2E)/.

1B. References to Immediacy of Impulses

1B includes extreme loss of control in mind and actions, an overwhelming urgency to gratify needs, and an overwhelming urgency to escape.

Example Clauses:

> *Being out of control in mind and actions:* /I was heavily intoxicated and reckless//I want to destroy with a sledgehammer//I have lost all control//I couldn't stop laughing//I want to smash everything//I couldn't stop myself thinking about it/.
>
> *Overwhelming urgency to gratify needs:* /I put pressure, pressure on him//I pleaded to him//I begged her to let me do it//I would do anything at all to get it//I want it badly//All I want is this/.
>
> *Overwhelming urgency to escape:* /I want to get out of here//All I want to do is escape//As soon as possible I want to go//I felt really trapped/.

Clinical Examples:

> /I just. I felt bad. (1A)/You know, I just felt like you know, I felt like a little kid./You know, like I wanted my own way (1B)/and I couldn't have it/and it really made me mad. (1B)/I just wanted to stamp my feet (1B)/and just cry (1A)/and say "I have to go home, (1B)/you have to let me" (1B)/.

* * *

> /I was getting very hyper, you know? (1B)/And I asked the cook "Is such-and-such a thing cooked to order?"/He said "What gets you all hyped up?"/I said "You do."/And so I just turned around and ran and ran. (1B)/And I was waiting for an incident./I was./I was really feeling hyper. (1B)/I wasn't in a mood to argue./I, I had to be active. (1B)/I just had to do something./Physically, I just had to do something. (1B)/.

* * *

> /Now, my children upset me,/still, uh, something terrible (1A)/because, uh, I don't have this control, you know, that I speak of. (1B)/I just go to pieces / and feel driven to hit them, (1B)/and I lose all control of myself (1B)/and I go into the bedroom and scream. (1A)/.

1C. References to Blocking Defenses

1C includes blockages in thinking and feeling; repression of affects; and denial, forgetting, numbness, and avoidance.

Example Clauses:

> *Denial:* /I'm OK/and I don't want to change anything//I act normal//It doesn't bother me//It doesn't worry me at all/.
>
> *Forgetting:* /Oh, what was I saying?//Something just slipped my mind//I don't remember what happened//I forgot everything about what happened/.
>
> *Numbness:* /I can't think//I can't concentrate on anything//I feel blank about this//I feel at a loss//I feel nothing//There is a void inside me//I feel very sleepy//I was asleep through it all/.

Avoidance: /I just ignored it all//I pretend that it didn't happen//I don't think about anything in particular//I can't get down to it//I just didn't do it/.

Clinical Examples:

> *Therapist:* Had you come close to having sexual relations with the prior one or is there something about . . .
>
> *Patient:* /Yes, I mean I can't remember. (1C)/Yes and no. (1C)/I mean like I make out with them and everything/but um—no, I think that that was like you know the first you know the first time./I was I was sort of drunk. (1B)/I can't—I can remember what happened (1C)/.

* * *

> *Therapist:* Now you started saying something and then you stopped.
>
> *Patient:* [softly] I did? (1C)
>
> *Therapist:* Of course.
>
> *Patient:* Don't say of course. (2G)/I'm trying to remember. (3L)/That's what I'm sitting here trying to do./I—I don't know what I was going to say (1C)/.
>
> *Therapist:* I see.
>
> *Patient:* Now you think I'm awful. (2G)
>
> *Therapist:* Why do you say that? . . .
>
> *Patient:* Because it seems like,/I was thinking about what I was saying/and I, something else ran through my mind/And it confused me (3J)/because I was more or less thinking of two things,/and then I couldn't remember what I was thinking about originally. (1C)/And I was talking./I don't even remember what I was talking about. (1C)/Reminded me of when I was a child; (5R)/something went through my mind (3K)/.

* * *

> *Patient:* /Well I don't—I don't remember. (1C)/
>
> *Therapist:* Why not?
>
> *Patient:* /Because I'm not./If I don't remember—/I'd like to remember what he said,/so I can comment on it./I don't remember what he said. (1C)/
>
> *Therapist:* It may be deliberate that you're trying to block them out.
>
> *Patient:* /It's not undeliberate that I'm trying to block it out. (1C)/.

1D. References to Ego Boundary Disorders

1D includes serious disorders of ego functioning—fragmentations, ego boundary ruptures, and regression of the ego. Also included are dependency, submission, and masochistic passivity–aggression; identity instability; and omnipotent narcissism.

Example Clauses:

> *Dependency, submission, and masochistic passivity-aggression:* /I fall under his spell when I'm with him//I want my mummy and go home//I need someone to tell me what to do//I really had a love crush on him//I am subservient to you//I felt possessed by him//I told him to hit me//If you told me to believe it I would//I need someone to tell me what to do//I am leaving all the decisions up to you/.

> *Identity instability:* /I don't have an identity//I don't feel that I'm me//It feels like it happened to someone else, not me//I feel like a conglomeration of bits and pieces//It just seemed to invade my body/and then it suddenly left//I feel like a different person each time I arrive/.

> *Omnipotent narcissism:* /I just watch and observe others//I deserve special treatment//I live in my own world//I know you think about me all day//People should be calling me to offer me help//They will let me go to the front of the queue//I want it for me/.

> *Ego boundary ruptures:* /He spoke to me in my dream/and commanded me to act this way//She can read my mind//The lecturer is always looking at me/and giving me secret love messages//It is like they are an extension of me/.

Clinical Examples:

> I'm—I'm just—All I can do is watch. (1D)/And as soon as I—as soon as I go out with them,/I'm into their life (1D)/and I'm—and I'm—and I don't know what to do. (3J)/I mean I want to just sit back and observe them (1D)/. . ./But I mean when I do that I just—I just dissolve. (1D)/I'm not me. (1D)/I'm not—I'm not a person. (1D)/I'm nothing. (1D)/I'm just—I'm just [hesit.] this sh- this mirror reflecting their—the way they are. (1D)/And I have no way of—of getting into their life (2I)/.

* * *

> /I'm a very I'm a loner more than like it's it's more of a of an isolation (2H)/uh an isolation instead of an independence (2H)/and like when I depend on somebody,/I lose my independence almost, (1D)/I lose my identity getting so close to somebody. (1D)/You know I sort of merge with them. (1D)/I mean like they have to make—It's like I just well, I really it's really—it's strange,/it's uh uh I'm not aware of them as another person— (1D)/I'm aware of them as somebody who makes me do something (1D)/.

* * *

> /I don't feel that I'm me. (1D)/I feel that I'm just a conglomeration of a lot of [pause] bits and pieces (1D)/and [pause] everything else from a lot

of people, you know./I don't think I ever thought anything out on my own (1D)/.

* * *

/Sometimes when people look at you/they look as though they're looking at a point in the middle of your brain (1D)/rather than at your eyes/or your face,/or they're looking through you, (1D)/an—that's almost./I'm making it into something physical/unless you just like, reach through or something,/as though I was laid open (1D)/.

Level 2: Introjection and Projection of Negative Affects

2E. Expressions of Suffering From Internal Negative States

2E includes references to the self suffering—anxieties, melancholia, mania, guilt, shame, and jealousies.

Example Clauses:

/I felt panicked//I suffered a lot with depression//I've been feeling hyperactive/I feel so jealous and envious//I am ashamed at myself//I am useless and unworthy//I should have done a lot of things better//I'm frustrated about it//I started shaking//I got mad at myself//I am very upset about it//I really hate myself//I feel so guilty//I'm scared/and nervous/.

Clinical Examples:

/Last week I was —I was so upset— (2E)/and I didn't sleep for nights and nights and (1A)/I was feeling guilty for this, that and the other, (2E)/and (pause) I mean I—I know I did something wrong, (2E)/.

* * *

I'm also saying/that I don't know whether or not this is is, a manipulative thing (4O)/that I really didn't know, (3J)/that I was that upset (2E)/and confused (3J)/and distraught (2E)/that I was not even trusting when I was sitting down/and really trying to write an honest letter./.

* * *

And yet when I got home I, you know, I just, I don't say any,/I say less than I normally say/and I just feel dead (1A)/and I feel like a sad sack, (2E)/you can't even think of, you know, something to say. (1C)/.

* * *

/At one point I got very uptight with my mother (2E)/when she just asked me a question about a cross word puzzle/and it just struck me that her tone of voice seemed harsh (2G)/and I just sort of like got very anxious at that point. (2E)/And, and, I, I just pressed the pencil against the radiator and broke it (2E)/and went upstairs and started pacing up and down (2E)/because I thought like, well, here's an event that just transpired/that [pause] that it would be hard for me to explain to anybody what I was so upset about (3J)/[short laugh—pause] and I don't know what to do about it. (3J)/Like, I, I, I just feel lost. (2I)/.

/I don't know why I told her that./I was terribly hurt (2E)/or upset about that [pause] that thing last Autumn (2E)/when he was taking me out [pause]/and to me when he wanted to take me out it seemed, it see—/it seemed like he didn't care (2G)/[pause] and I was [pause] really wanted to hurt him. (2F)/.

2F. Expressions Indicative of Negative Projection Onto Others

2F includes negative internal states directed toward others—anger and blame, cynicism and repressed rage, resentments and defiance, vengeful and sadistic feelings, and domination and manipulation of others. Patients' negative emotions are intended to upset the others' feelings.

Example Clauses:

/I exploded at him//I got madder and madder at him//I blamed him for all my problems//I am not going to budge an inch//I was cranky at her//I just stormed out of the room//I was angry/because he never listens//I screamed at him//It's all his fault! /.

Clinical Examples:

I started hating my mother. (2F)/Not like—not like my mother, not like hating her because she's my mother, or anything,/or disliking her, you know./I mean, like, if she weren't my mother, she'd be fine, you know, like./But she just—, I'm just turning into—I'm just turning into the type of person she is. (5R)/It's utterly unable to relate to people, like, that, (2H)/and that's what screwed me up. (2F)/And I don't want to have kids if I'm going to mess them up like that./And I hate her for that. (2F)/.

* * *

/We talked about stuff,/and I said to my sister "come on"/and we went in my room./She said "I'm not interested."/I said "Jesus, you never are!" (2F)/so the hell with her! (2F)/.

* * *

/Well this is what makes me mad, (2F)/and that's—and—I'm just as angry at you for imposing this feeling on me (2F)/as I am for my husband doing it. (2F)/Why is it that I am the one who's supposed to always be something, (2F)/to do something./Why is it that I'm the one that always has to take the action? (2F)/.

2G. Expressions Indicative of Negative Projection From Others

The other is perceived to be punishing and rejecting self. 2G also includes paranoiac ideation about others' motives, no compassion or understanding of the other's point of view, and feeling laden down and the victim of the other. Others may be unaware of the distress, because the malevolent affects are a projection of the negative internal states of the patient.

Example Clauses:

/I get the feeling a lot of people think I'm dumb//They are not interested in me//They are playing a game against me//He is trying to get something out of me//She punishes me//I felt she didn't care about me//You are making this hard for me//I imagine she will be disappointed in me again//I felt she was hostile toward me//He uses me for his own ends/.

Clinical Examples:

/I just sit there./I mean why, you know, so I don't say anything/and then, you know, people just don't bother talking to you, (2G)/because you're not playing their stupid little game, (2F)/and then they think you're stupid. (2G)/.

* * *

/The one date I did have was the first night,/and um, it was a blind date,/of which I have had—this was—that was the second one in my life./I don't believe in having blind dates./I'd rather see them first./And she was a really nice girl,/but it bothered [laugh] for some reason I thought she didn't like me. (2G)/Just because she didn't—she just didn't talk a lot./And I found out later she didn't talk to anybody./She just didn't know—she was shy. (4N)/ But I had this thing in my mind/that she didn't like me. (2G)/I don't know. (3J))/I'll just keep away from her. (2H)/.

* * *

Patient: /You're going to be impossible, aren't you? [pause] (2G)

Therapist: Why do you say that?

Patient: / because you're very disturbed with me. (2G)/You are./You're very annoyed with me [pause] (2G)/I can tell./I can./

Therapist: Why am I annoyed with you?

Patient: /I don't know. (3J)/Just with me./You have been for a while. [pause] (2G)/Did you know that?/I did. [pause]/

Therapist: You seem to be able to identify my feelings better than yours today.

Patient: /Yours are obvious./Mine are all mixed up. (3J)/.

* * *

/If they really love me/why aren't they over here, you know, (4M)/so we could bang / and I get impatient (1B)/and I get mad [pause] (2E)/and I got like that—that last night./I felt like he wasn't paying enough attention (2G)/and oh "you're just like everybody else—/one thing—you, you know, you really don't care about me, you know ah, (2G)/all you want to do is sleep with me you know." (2G)/Well, I didn't say those things to him,/I was scared that what I was thinking was really true, (2G)/that you know, he really didn't care about me, (2G)/yeah, I don't believe that, (4O)/I don't think that that's the case. (4O)/I think it might be the case if I continue the way that I've been doing./I might push it into being the case. (5Q)/.

2H. References to Interpersonal Withdrawal

2H includes avoiding, withdrawing, and isolating the self from others. Also involved are interpersonal difficulties, timidity in approaching others, and moving away from others.

Example clauses:

/I don't initiate friendships//I don't want to get involved with people//I didn't talk to him//I deliberately didn't go and see him//I don't want to relate to others//I didn't tell him everything I wanted to//I didn't sit with them//I can't relate to them/.

Clinical Examples:

/I don't want to get involved with somebody (2H)/because I know I'm— I'm going to end it,/and so I just go around I don't bother with people. (2H)/I don't want to get involved with people. (2H)/I'm afraid to get involved with people. (2H)/I just want them to stay out of my life (2H)/.

* * *

/Well for instance, he wanted to uh [pause] he wanted to go down to the beach/and and I just—and I cancelled out on it (2H)/and [pause] and uh, a few other times he has—he has uh, changed his plans to fit mine/and then I have uh, you know, I cancelled out. (2H)/.

* * *

/and he says "If anything, they think about—they think of you as being ah one who doesn't involve yourself too much at work"/Which is true. (5Q)/Like, you know, since I've been, um sort of anxious around people (2E)/like I've been—I have not been the most sociable person in the world by any means. (2H)/.

2I. Expressions of Helplessness

2I, giving up, involves assertion problems, apathy, amotivation, and external locus of control. Also included are having no perceived choice and lacking self-value.

Example Clauses:

/There was nothing I could do//I don't care //I just sat there//I can't help it//I don't care about anything//I just shut up and didn't say anything//I am going to give up//These pills will cure me//I'm not good enough at it//I just couldn't make him go away//I want to give up//I couldn't find out what was wrong with me//I can't get on with anything/.

Clinical Examples:

/And I thought, well, you know, I'd come home [pause]/and you know, show her I did have something to offer after all [pause] (3L)/but I didn't feel that I, you know, I didn't feel any different [pause]./I didn't do anything. (2I)/I just—you know, I walked around./I watched the golf./I went to the parties/and I drank and I slept and I ate/. . ./I don't f- I don't feel worthwhile. (2I)/I don't—I don't feel I've anything to offer. (2I)/.

* * *

/I feel, you know, I just don't have any balls. (2I)/I can't stand up to anybody. (2I)/I can't say "no I don't want to distribute the god damn leaflets, go call somebody else" you know, (2I)/and I can't say, uh "I don't want you in the house" (2I)/or "I do want you in the house." (2I)/.

* * *

/ I'm not effective, you know, with the children, that's definite. (2I)/So that, that in itself you know is is a problem for me./As far as discipline goes, it, but—I just, just give in. (2I)/It isn't working out/and there is nothing I can do about it. (2I)/.

Level 3: Difficulties in Understanding and Control

3J. *Expressions of Cognitive Confusion*

3J includes the inability to predict or understand, things being left unresolved, and feeling uncertain, confused.

Example Clauses:

/I don't know//I don't know why//My dreams are very confused and mixed up//I don't know why he changed the way he did//I guess things haven't really been sorted out at all//I wasn't sure what to do/.

Clinical Examples:

/I guess I don't really know what my problems are, (3J)/or I do,/and then I—one day I think it's this thing,/and then another day I think it's another thing. (3K)/But—as far as she goes,/she can say exactly what her problems are. (4M)/Like my whole thing's just a- is all hazy. (3J)/.

* * *

/Oh, I feel, you know, I love him, sure./You can't begin to be through all I've gone through all your life without, without love there./I don't know. (3J)/I'm not sure if there's love there. (3J)/I don't know. (3J)/It's happening though./.

* * *

/You know, I can see a card in one way/and start to send it to somebody like oops, you know/they might see it in 10 different ways,/so I end up having a great collection of cards/that I don't send to anybody./I can't figure things out (3J)/and [sighs] not figure them out. (3J)/That's why I'm sorry. (3J)/I apologize for that./.

3K. *Expressions of Cognitive Ambivalence*

3K includes struggling to understand, partial awareness and hypothesizing, and difficulties communicating or putting things into words.

Example Clauses:

/Well it was sort of like this//It is hard to explain how it was//I don't know whether to feel one way or the other//I seem to be making sense of it/but I am unsure//It might be beginning to come together in my mind now//Sometimes I think that/but other times I don't//I sort of said that//I suppose that it was like this//I don't seem to be able to say it very well/.

Clinical Examples:

Patient: I was talking to another girl about it (5S)/and uh, we were just talking about it,/I don't know, (3J)/the subject just came up/and she said she met a girl who was a homosexual, you know,/and all this and uh, I sort of felt homosexual. (3K)/. . ./

Therapist: And here it points to express some of your own feelings.

Patient: /Well, I just felt that, uh, oh what it is it, (3K)/that before it may have been latent/and the feelings of homosexuality,/but they seem to be coming to the surface. (3K)/And, uh, I didn't feel physically attra- why, she is an attractive woman. (3K)/Ah, I didn't want to touch her. (1C)/Ah, I don't know, (3J)/I just of, homosexuality in itself/that, uh, perhaps I, that this maybe is a better life for me. (3K)/.

* * *

/Am I going to take those pills again? (3K)/I was wondering if I'm strong enough not to take them. [pause] (3K)/It takes willpower, you know./I haven't thrown them out./They're still in the house. [pause]/It's just like when I stopped smoking./Just one more./Maybe tomorrow, I'll take another one, (3K)/but not today./.

* * *

Therapist: So there were a few things you could have said clearer?

Patient: /Well, uh, maybe. (3K)/I said maybe, well maybe I said what he took down. (3K)/But, uh, at that time was only the second time/that I've spoken in a session like that./And, uh, I'm being, I mean he was, sort of I'm not sure. (3K)/I don't know, maybe I shouldn't have felt like, ah, he was against me (3K)/but um I felt like he wasn't really for me./

3L. References to Positive Struggle With Difficulties

3L includes expressions of struggling with difficulties and seeking change and control, in addition to references to effort, hope, and engagement in struggles to get better and improve.

Example Clauses:

/I am trying to get myself better and under control//I had to face it instead of ignoring it//I have to put up with it//I want to get over this//I can't pretend that it never happened//I am always trying to be the best I can//I know I had to do it//Talking and thinking about these things is very painful and hard//If I really want to do it I can/.

Clinical Examples:

/I like him a lot [sighs]/and I don't want to make any mistakes [laughs] (3L)/I don't want to start the same patterns over again. (3L)/.

/I wouldn't, you know, have, I wouldn't be constantly, uh, feeling anxiety./I would probably be a little calmer/but that would be the only thing/because it would mean I would probably be still—/I would still be working just as hard on my problems. (3L)/.

* * *

/If the clothes need washing,/he'll just go ahead and wash them./'Cause he's trying to understand me, he said./And I try to get these things done (3L)/because I know that he'll be happy when he comes home. (4N)/.

* * *

I'd want to see her,/but I, I couldn't just stand and wait./I'd have to fortify myself with reasons for being in that place (3L)/"while I was going over to get a Coke,"/and then I changed my mind and/"I came out to get some fresh air"/and I changed my mind again and/"I was going back to get the Coke"/and I looked at the displays in a display case,/and everything just, to justify the fact that I was in any given spot when she should happen to, if she should happen to appear. (3L)/.

* * *

/I just met her. [pause]/But, you see, the whole thing is,/I want to try to, try to, [pause] get, get to know her if if possible, you know, (3L)/if it will work out./.

Level 4: Interpersonal Awareness

4M. *References to Questioning the Reactions of Others*

4M includes probing, assessing, and challenging others' reactions rather than blindly accepting them.

Example Clauses:

/I asked him why he thought this//I don't agree with the way she is approaching it//She criticized me/and I asked her what it was that was bothering her//I asked him to tell me what he thought instead of just shutting up//I told him to stop because he was disturbing the children//She shouldn't be cranky with me//Do you know what I am saying?

Clinical Examples:

/Well when I asked you about it,/you—it didn't seem to me that you were being very straightforward, (4M)/you were like sort of, you had the answer/then you were thinking up a justification for it./That was my impression of what you were doing, (4M)/which led me to, at least partially led me to think the way I was thinking./.

* * *

/And he does the same things about my sister's boyfriend/because they've gone together now for 5 years/and he doesn't understand why they aren't married. (4N)/He has this fairy tale idea of romance,/but I mean, he just, he loused up his own life/so I don't know why he thinks he should, you know, try to give us advice. (4M)/.

* * *

/Another thing she said was "why did you ever go into therapy in the first place?" [laughs]/And after telling me I was schizoid,/I mean I-I mean I would think that the- that's a silly question. (4M)/Like, a person who's schizoid is bound to have problems. (4M)/.

* * *

/ He picked out just that one thing to, uh, you know, pinpoint./But then I said "well you have to look at the, uh, situation a little more openly than that." (4M)/I mean, you can't, uh, put it down to one thing. (4M)/You know, you can't say, "because he cries (4M)/that he's going to, uh, he's going to become, he's going to be feminine."/.

4N. References to Considering the Other's Point of View

4/N includes clear consideration of alternative perspectives, compassion and understanding toward another person, consideration of how the other may be viewing the self, and listing qualities of the other.

Example Clauses:

/He is sensitive about things like that//I can see from her point of view//Maybe he did this because of x//It could be that he reacted because of x//I wasn't sure if he would understand//I can understand how she feels//I know he doesn't mean it/because he is just a boy//I know he suffered//I can see she was jealous/.

Clinical Examples:

/I think they, you know, sort of, you know, put their hopes in me in a way, you know. (4N)/They want, they want me to succeed. (4N)/You know, they want me to, to ah do well, all things that they, well, especially well, (4N)/my father probably is, you know, he would feel more proud of me and all (4N)/if I succeed or anything if I did well./.

* * *

/He'll be worried sick (4N)/that he won't just, won't come out of his surgery./It'll be, uh, very upsetting. (2E)/And after all he is 70, uh, 71./And his health isn't in the best condition./I guess he, I'm hoping someday he'll try and get better./It's just the way he takes things. (4N)/He's just afraid. (4N)/.

* * *

/So, I had had about half a beer by that time,/and like I was kind of annoyed, (2E)/but I know the mood he was in, (4N)/and I knew he was—he wanted to get angry at somebody. (4N)/.

* * *

/One day my father came,/and he said "I have failed to inspire you—you don't practice your religion."/For him, it's like saying that he's a shit. (4N)/He doesn't see it as a condemnation of me. (4N)/He says it's a condemnation of himself. (4N)/He says "I have failed to inspire you."

4O. References to Questioning the Reaction of the Self

4O involves awareness of role of the self—one's own contribution to conflict or situation.

Example Clauses:

/ I wonder whether I do something to create conflict//I asked myself why I felt this about her//It was my fault really//What can I say?//I am seeing this in more of a negative way than it really is//I can see now that I caused this/and made her feel bad//I realized there are things that need to be dealt with here//I questioned my reaction in this situation//I think maybe I was the problem/.

Clinical Examples:

/Is it comfort I'm looking for? (4O)/Or someone to say "poor me"? (4O)/I don- I really don- I'd like to know that,/I don't know it. (3J)/.

* * *

/I wondered if he wanted to talk about it / and yell about it. (4N)/After that I, I didn't think about it,/but I came home [pause]/I suppose I should have said something. (4O)/.

* * *

/And [pause] well, anyway, that is one of the things I do (5Q)/and I suppose one of the things I have to stop doing (4O)/because [pause] I—it's uh, it's just, you know, too great of a burden to carry around, (4O)/having to be right all the time/or having to be, uh, taken seriously all the time./.

4P. Expressions of Interpersonal Self-Assertion

4P includes standing up for self with confidence, acting independently and stating views with ease, the free expression of ideas previously difficult to discuss, and prosocial attempt to get needs and wishes met displaying emotional modulation.

Example Clauses:

/I told him to stop interrupting me before I had finished speaking//I stood up against the bully//I asked him to stop calling me at home/because I needed some privacy//I said I found her behavior offensive when she acted that way//I am not going to be pushed around//I stated clearly what my fears were in this instance//She knows now that I do not agree with the proposal/.

Clinical Examples:

/He'd already mentioned to me about my hair./He said it was getting pretty long/and I said to him like "whoa, just let me do my own thing. (4P)/I don't bother you—you don't me. (4P)/It's going to get a lot longer" (4P)/and he said just "okay"/.

*   *   *

/He was always yelling at me that he would never be happy and every-thing like that./So, I got out of that (4P)/because I didn't want to be his whole life— (4P)/like I didn't want to be responsible for his sanity— (4P)/you know so responsible because he couldn't stand on his own two feet, you know? (4P)/.

*   *   *

/I said to him "Listen, Doctor, I don't know what you're saying to me. (4M)/Are you telling me she's competent or incompetent?"/He was fumbling and ignoring me./So then I declared that he was unable to make decisions himself [laughs] and (4P)/I made my own decision that the woman was not competent for the position. (4P)/.

*   *   *

/I looked up to him,/but on the other hand, um, [pause]/he has not in any way tried to force me/or tried to, uh, interest me in any way./And I will not permit it if he ever tries. (4P)/And I have enough stamina if, you know, myself to [pause] brush it off (4P)/rather than being scared to death/like I was before. (5Q)/So I don't want to push, being pushed around anymore (4P)/.

Level 5: Self-Understanding

5Q. Expressions of Insight Into Repeating Personality Patterns of Self

5Q involves making a self-observation about one's own personality—insight into transference pattern. Also included is awareness of maladaptive interpersonal patterns of relating to others.

Example Clauses:

/I always see a part of myself in others/and I realize I was fighting with a part of myself//I am the type of person that reacts this way//I realize I have a problem being confident with people/unless I know them really well//When I was young I was insecure,/and even now I have difficul-ties//I know/I am always worrying about these issues//I know it is hard for me to respond like that//I am the sort of person who likes to behave in this way//When he asked me that question/I saw what he was getting at—/that I am like that//I know I have a tendency to react that way in many situations/.

Clinical Examples:

/I say men are evil./Consequently, I act as if I—the situations/I have to agree to situations where I can prove it. (5Q)/And, you know, this is, this is what I think happens, (5Q)/I don't know what. (3J)/And I don't go out and say that now I am going to lace./But this seems to be what's happening. (5Q)/You know, and I don't do it intentionally. (5Q)/.

*   *   *

/It seems that one experience,/a kind of recurring thing that has happened throughout my life (5Q)/is that like I'll know somebody for a while./Then

I'll start picking out flaws (5Q)/and then sort of concentrate—start, well concentrating on their flaws (5Q)/or ah looking at those rather than the whole thing. (5Q)/And I kind of have done that with Ed. (5Q)/.

* * *

/I know what you are doing./I know why I'm doing—I know what you're doing. (5Q)/I understand exactly what is going on. (5Q)/I understand./I'm asking for reassurance. (5Q)/I'm asking for you to tell me something (5Q)/and you just won't do it./.

5R. *Making Dynamic Links Between Past and Present Relationships*

5R includes observations about similarities and differences in the patterns of relating between present situations and past relationships.

Example Clauses:

/I saw him like he was my father//I can see now that this is related to my upbringing//I treat my boss in the same way as I treat my father//He controlled me like my mother did//I used to see him in a different way than/I do now//I thought of my mother in that situation,/because she used to do the same thing//I can see now that the past and the present are different//I'm turning into the sort of person my mother is//I see you in the same way as my favorite teacher//I know my reaction toward my children is because of my own upbringing/.

Clinical Examples:

/I was standing in line to—going to the cafeteria/and this guy came out, very [deep breath] suave/and well not suave,/but—a—very proud of himself,/and—and a—can't think of a word [pause] (3K)/arrogant and with a smile on his face/and a toothpick/this is the point/a toothpick,/and—a—for no reason I just felt like hitting him all of a sudden, you know, (2F)/and I didn't,/of course I didn't do anything,/but I just felt like hitting him. (2F)/And I couldn't understand why, (3J)/but the first thing that came to me was,/I don't know whether this has any bearing on it,/but my father used to chew on a toothpick a lot, a lot you know (5R)/.

* * *

Patient: /So now I'm listening to him/

Therapist: And what do you think about that?

Patient: /It's not good./He's just being like my mother again. (2F)/Like I—I just./

Therapist: So who are you going to listen to?

Patient: /I should listen to myself, (4O)/but he's just like another mother image to me (5R)/

Therapist: Well, you're letting him be.

Patient: /Yeah, lots of times I'll even come out and tell him,/"who do you think you are (2F), my mother?" [pause]/Like I transferred all my dependence and my, you know, ah, from from my mother on to him. (5R)/Like I listen to what he tells me to do now. (5Q)/.

Patient: / I was dreaming the fact that she was, uh, so gentle and all that, (5S) / so warm, (pause) (5S) / so I guess maybe I don't hate her as much as I thought I did. (4O) /

Therapist: When you think of a gentle and warm person, what comes to mind?

Patient: [pause] / As soon as you said that, I sort of had a block. [pause] (1C) / And two faces went through my mind, / my girlfriend and my mother. [pause] / Um [pause] I wonder if in some way, [pause] um, in some strange way, / I—I equate my girlfriend with my mother. (5R)/.

* * *

/Most people don't think of me as a scared person./I'm afraid of myself. (2E)/[pause] Because it's, I don't know it's you know, it's a sort of a mixture/—a father–lover sort of thing (5R)/because it's, it, it is a romantic guilt. (5Q)/But it's also, it's also this thinking that [pause] it's also this hangover from when I was real young. (5R)/And when I really try to, uh, you know, I try to explain—/and I try, I wind up on a train,/I hid in the luggage car behind something/and trying to, and they got me, came and got me/and brought me back./And it's those moments when I thought that, you know, see my father/if he was really great he would have let me./But still I have to keep him great./And I do the same to you. (5R)/.

* * *

/Peter was eating chicken, and/somehow he struck me the wrong way,/and I got sick, (2E)/I got really, you know, so I could feel I was all hot in my face,/and I was, I—I really got ill, (2E)/and the only thing I could see, you know, I-I could see him—/I could only see him as my stepfather. (5R)/.

5S. *References to Interpersonal Union*

5S involves interpersonal support, closeness, and communication. Included are approaching others, intimacy between people including physical, offering and giving help to others or seeking and receiving help from others, and benefaction to the self from positive patterns of interpersonal relating.

Example Clauses:

/I know that/I can talk to her if/I need to//called her up on the telephone//Our conversation is full of jokes and laughter//I went to the doctors for assistance in these problems//I was trying to be there for her and help her//We slept together last night//She has helped me a lot to get over this//Coming to psychotherapy is a big help//Talking to someone is a relief//We get on really well//He really made me feel good about it//I felt respected by him/.

Clinical Examples: /I went with a friend who is very close to me. (5S)/And in many ways it was a beautiful weekend,/because, and, it's the first time in a long time I've shared a lot of experiences with people. (5S)/Just as an example,/if we were driving/and we see a nice sunset/or something like that,/we'll stop./And we did that./And there are very few people I really can do that with./It was very, I felt very, ah, fulfilled by things like that. (6U)/That went on the whole weekend/and we got on together extremely well. (5S)/.

* * *

/They did an awful lot for me. [pause] (5S)/Like when they bathed me,/and they washed me,/changed the dressing on my leg and neck./[pause] and, uh, [pause] so maybe, I don't know [pause] (3J)/I just felt that they did enough for me. (5S)/It's funny, I can't forget that./.

* * *

/I was there today/and he had—it was really amazing./He had all this— he was cooking lunch for me [laughs] on this hot plate. (5S)/He was making steak and string beans and potatoes [laughs] and everything. [laughs]/Well, there was not enough time to have lunch/and to try to compose music,/I mean to help write songs, (5S)/to have sex and, (5S)/you know do the whole thing in an hour/but, you know, we got certain things accomplished. [laughs]. (5S)/Yesterday I thought, well that it was going to develop into a full-blown affair. (5S)/I don't know, the scene had such—it had such romantic potential. (5S)/.

* * *

/I said we were going down there as friends, (5S)/and uh, at first when I got down there, it was very, very much beautiful./and, uh, and we got into our room/and we made love and things like that. (5S)/.

5T. Expressions of Insight Into Interpersonal Relations

5T includes insight into other people and the dynamics of their relationships with the self.

Example Clauses:

/I see now that my parents had trouble with this//She is the type of person that will react in this way//I think at first we were both hung up with problems//We differ in our views of this situation//I know I have the same problem as he does//He is as stubborn as I am//We rub each other the wrong way//I know it is true about him//I recognize he won't change on this issue//I notice the way they react to one another//I know how he feels about these things/.

Clinical Examples:

/She is something like me. (5T)/ She's afraid too. (4N)/It's like I—I know exactly how uncomfortable she is when we're looking at each other. (4N)/I don't like to look at people when I talk/and neither does she.

(5T)/.../And I also know how defensive she is with people (5T)/and she does the same thing I do. (5T)/Maybe not the same degree or maybe not in the same ways, (5T)/but the same sort of thing. (5T)/.

* * *

I talked to him very calmly (6U)/and told him that the house was more important than anything else/and that I just didn't feel anything else could go on until the house was done, if then./And so he made all sorts of promises and everything, he wouldn't take any more [laughs] 3-day vacations, etc., etc./I also said to him/that since the two of us tended to behave irresponsibly on our own (5T)/that I didn't feel that we needed to encourage each other to behave irresponsibly. (5T)/.

* * *

/What I am saying is that, uh, I am, uh, mild-mannered, (5Q)/and he is very—he's strong, you know,/he's, he's strong-willed,/so he's you know, at one end of the pole,/and I'm at the other end,/but we're not really meeting. (5T)/.

Level 6: Self-Control

6U. Expressions of Emotional Self-Control Over Conflicts

6U involves adequate freedom from mental conflict. Included are self-control, positivity, self-esteem, modulation of feelings, adaptive solutions, responding rather than reacting, constructive emotional distancing from conflict (not avoidance), and internal locus of control.

Example Clauses:

/Everything is alright//I will stand back/and see how it goes//I feel I'm a capable person//I've just got to let this sort itself out//I realize these things can't be changed overnight//I negotiated a peace between us that will stick//I left my anger in that situation/and got on with other things to build a better relationship//When things go wrong I have enough patience//I feel good enough to go home//I feel loved and respected//I felt okay about this//I didn't take it to heart//I realize it is up to me to get it done//I said that it was sensible to do it in this situation/.

Clinical Examples:

/I like the freedom to choose to come and go, (6U)/when I want to,/as I want to,/the way I feel like it, (6U)/rather than having this thing forced on me./Like he comes up at 10 o'clock with "come over and and cook me dinner"/And I'll just say "no" (4O)/.

* * *

/I can be very enthusiastic of him / and I can get really excited about things, (5Q)/you know, I can also be very critical (5Q)/but I'm also more, like not so much up and down, (6V)/but my, as I used to be with many different opinions,/I just seem to have a lot of enthusiasm in one direction or the other. (6U)/And I just feel very emotional actually and that too, (5R)/what I want from him,/which I feel better. (6U)/I feel more stabilized with him. (6U)/.

* * *

/I was serving as his blasting target, you might say./But I kn- I e- I knew what he was doing (5T)/and I kind of like [hesit.] said, you know, took it with a grain of salt. (6U)/And we continued to talk/and have a couple more beers,/and yh-w-we generally had a good night. (6U)/By the end of the night he was in a good mood (4N)/and I felt good that I had gotten him into a good mood (6U)/by the time he left the place./.

* * *

I've dated a lot of different fellows. (5S)/Now I'm just dating one and, (5S)/uh I guess it's, uh, sort of, um, making myself feel that I am attractive (6U)/and someone is interested/and it's sort of an ego builder sort of thing. (6U)/I really had a good time. (6U)/[pause] I met this fellow slightly last week and , uh/I flirted last night (5S)/and he took my phone number./It's fun. (6U)/It's sort of reassuring, you know [pause] (6U)/It's good to feel like a woman. (6U)/It's good to feel very feminine. (6U)/.

6V. *Expressions of New Changes in Emotional Responding*

6V involves changes in emotional reactions that are nontrivial; adaptability and flexibility in responses, and overcoming maladaptive repetitive patterns of reacting to problems and relationships.

Example Clauses:

/My feelings in this situation are different now than before//This is a new feeling for me//It is like I have opened my eyes for the first time//It doesn't seem so bad now as it did in the past//I felt better about myself this time//My feelings have changed and/I don't feel as bad//Yesterday my reaction was different//It is getting easier now to do it//It doesn't worry me as much//I look back and see what/I was like compared with now/(6V).

Clinical Examples:

/You know, I really find myself really disagreeing with my sister-in-law/where I think that for years I sort of accepted her as the oracle (5Q)/even though she was having terribly serious problems with herself./And I was sitting down there on a Sunday/and finally you know for the first time— (6V)/you know this has happened twice now— (6V)/I didn't find myself boring out my problems (6V)/or you know, throwing my behavior out for her to make judgements of/or to please her/or to show her how I'd improved/or you know trying to—that wasn't important to do that any more. (6V)/.

* * *

/I—it was just that I was feeling/that I was seeing everybody differently (6V)/and I was pleased about it. (6U)/And I have been pleased about it./I'm not so desperately trying to impress them (6V)/or even trying to make them see me favorably— (6V)/or whatever it was I was trying to do in the past. (5Q)/.

* * *

Like we were talking last night (5S)/and she was telling me about a number of personal things/and I was telling her about some personal things about me. (5S)/And it was good (6U)/because I wasn't telling her everything/because I've decided that's something I shouldn't do to somebody I don't know very well (6V)/—tell them everything./.

* * *

/Sunday I was out in the field flying kites./And you know, doing crazy things that I've never done before (6V)/because I was, before I was always concerned about how will I look if I run with this kite (5Q)/if I make it fly or something?!/Because it would be, you know, it wouldn't be uh behaving according to protocol or something,/and uh [pause] it feels like a sort of freedom. (6U)/.

* * *

/Well I wanted to go out Sunday/and I called a few people to see who was busy/and I said "Hi, how are you doing, so let's go."/Usually I wait for others to call./It's the first time I called and said "Let's go." (6V)/.

6W. References to Self-Analysis

6W includes references to introspection, self-monitoring, internal dialogue with the self, and carrying out psychotherapy of the self.

Example Clauses:

/I have thought all this through over the last week//This is my lay analysis of the situation//I have really sat down and thought about myself as a person//I talk to myself a lot now and find that this helps me//I thought about it carefully before I decided//I was thinking about it and a lot came out/.

Clinical Examples:

/I have really learned since I have been coming to see you I think, (6V)/more than—well I think I questioned things before anyway, (6W)/but now, I feel that I do so a lot more/and it's—it's very helpful to me you know,/I feel a lot more, um, I don't know, just, it makes my mind work more you know, (6W)/I don't just stagnat- stagnate you know / because I—I really think about things, (6W)/.

* * *

/He went away./He went to Varenna for two weeks./And for 2 weeks he was not around / and I was sitting down thinking everything out. (6W)/.

* * *

/I felt, I guess I felt that I should have acted more, ah, positively with this kid, (4O)/more aggressively than I did,/and you know this all came out when I was thinking about it. (6W)/I was trying to avoid/—but I was going to,/I didn't avoid thinking about it. (6W)/I said "Well, I'll think about it anyway instead of holding it back." (6W)/I just kept on, I just thought about it: (6W)/And ah, it was better—I thought it was better that I did. (6U)/.

PHASE 3: COMPILATION OF SAMPLE SCORES

There are many approaches to scoring content analysis scales, and each carries different assumptions about the underlying constructs embedded in the transcripts. Common to almost all approaches is the assignation of a single content category per scorable clause. After you assign categories to the clauses that are scorable within an extract, the problem is then how to accrete the scores. Most methods derive a mean or corrected score—in other words, the raw sum of scores is divided by a correction factor, which standardizes each scoring occasion (i.e., each psychotherapy transcript extract). Not all methods do this, however. Three options for scoring the Mastery Scale are presented in the sections that follow. The first method is the most commonly used; the others have specific applications to certain research questions. Mastery scores can then be combined and contrasted in various research designs within and between participants. As in all scientific research, the use of the Mastery Scale in different contexts depends on the quality of the raw data collected, the adequacy of the design, and the veracity of the methods of statistical evaluation used and conclusions drawn from them.

The basic scoring method devised for the Mastery Scale is to correct the raw summed score by the number of scoring opportunities. Mastery is probably to some degree traitlike and should be relatively independent of the number of words spoken. It is irrelevant to this particular approach if a patient talks for 5 or 10 minutes on a topic and gives no indication whether he or she has high, low, or moderate mastery. What is important is the level of mastery conveyed in those passages that do contain information on mastery. Therefore, one can sum the mastery scores and divide by the number of scored clauses. This method isolates for scoring only those clauses that contain information on mastery. The word count is irrelevant in this context. The final score is a value between 0 and 6.

Mastery Score = Sum of mastery scores/Number of scored clauses

Alternative Method 1

An alternative method, devised by Gleser in collaboration with Gottschalk et al. (1969), is to take the number of words spoken by the patient as an important moderator of the raw summed score. Individual categories (i.e., 1–23 mastery categories) are used in a separate analysis.

However, if the samples are short, with few scorable clauses, it is advisable to take each level as a category (i.e., 1–6 categories) because of the large amount of missing data likely if all 23 items were subjected to individual analysis. The Gottschalk–Gleser 5-minute speech sample scales are designed to measure transitory psychological states, and therefore the most important variable is the quantity of the state within a known number of words. To get a valid measure (i.e., enough chances of detecting the signal among the noise), a minimum of 70 words is required per sample. For technical reasons, in this method 0.5 is added to every score, but more importantly the entire result is subject to a square root transformation to correct for skewness. The aim is to reduce the correlation between the number of words spoken and the mastery score to zero.

After doing a word count and clausing and scoring the transcript, the next step is to ascertain the Correction Factor (C.F.), that is, 100 divided by the total number of words in the verbal sample (C.F. = 100/no. of words). This is a standard procedure for dealing with variations in the length of verbal samples (Gottschalk et al., 1969). For example, a verbal sample of 120 words would have a C.F. of 0.83. So compilation of final scores is relatively uncomplicated, and the number of references in each category is tabulated on score sheets. The raw score is obtained by multiplying the number of references (frequency) by the construct's number code (weight 1–6). The score is then defined in each case as Raw Score (frequency × weight) × C.F. Some verbal samples contain no scorable references on one or more category, and they would all receive a zero score on that category even though they differ in word length, with the longer verbal samples providing greater opportunity for such references. Therefore, half the C.F. is added to each score: (Raw Score × C.F.) + ½ C.F. To reduce distribution skew, the square root of this ratio is used as the final corrected score (Gottschalk et al., 1969).

In certain research contexts, it may be appropriate to use this as an alternative scoring method, although it is only recommended as an adjunct to the basic method. Examples of research where it may be considered important are studies where there is a time limit on the speech sample, and the researcher is interested in the degree to which the speaker can demonstrate self-understanding and self-control within the confines of the allotted time. Further psychometric investigation of this method is recommended, particularly because the square root transformation was devised to be used on an anxiety scale. Some studies in which this method was used successfully are detailed in chapter 8.

Alternative Method 2

The simplest method is to sum the scores and take the final score as the data point. This process is used in the "counting signs" method of scoring the helping alliance (Luborsky, Crits-Christoph, Alexander, Margolis,

& Cohen, 1983). The assumption behind this procedure is that a transcript is much like a questionnaire—all that is required is to add up the scores. Unlike questionnaires, however, which have a set number of questions, in psychotherapy transcripts there is the potential for great variability in the number of questions or instances that indicate the helping alliance. In this method, a uniform period of time is allotted in which the measure is rated (usually the first 20 minutes of the therapy). That there is variability in how much each patient talks within 20 minutes (some talk very fast, others very slowly) is not considered important. The significance of the number of words spoken is that the greater the number of words, the more chance there is of finding scorable helping alliance content. The helping alliance scale treats this variable as random error. Although not entirely a psychometrically sound method of scoring, it is simple, has obvious appeal, and appears to differentiate good from poor helping alliances. Although not used to date in scoring mastery, its potential could be investigated in future studies.

Alternative Method 3

Another scoring method is to do individual analyses of mastery scores. For example, all scores from 1A–3L may be assigned a score of 1 and all scores from 4M to 6W a score of 2, and then they are corrected for the total number of scores. These proportions could then be used in nonparametric analyses where the variable of interest may be high versus low mastery. Alternatively, all 23 items may be treated separately within an analysis (e.g., as if they were separate questionnaires). The disadvantage of this method is that, unless the sample is very long (or multiple samples are combined), there are many empty cells, because not all 23 codes are typically present in a sample. Another alternative is to investigate 3 levels (Level 1 + 2 vs. Level 3 + 4 vs. Level 5 + 6) as the variable of interest in a nonparametric analysis. One other method, used in cluster analysis (see chapter 5), is to treat the presence of a category as 1 (irrespective of the number of times it may appear in a sample) and all absences of a category as 0. In this way, it is possible to profile the clusters of categories that commonly occur together. The relative frequencies of Mastery Scale categories can also be computed. Profiles of categories within and across participants can be graphically represented and interpreted.

FREQUENTLY ASKED QUESTIONS IN SCORING THE MASTERY SCALE

Question: When should I consider the context surrounding a clause and when not?

Answer: In general, you should score each clause as a separate unit without considering the context. However, in scoring the higher levels of mastery (5 and 6), you may need to consider the surrounding clauses in order to judge whether the statements indicate high mastery. For example, to score the clause

/I was doing it again/

requires the surrounding context

/I could see what I was reacting to; (5Q)/I was doing it again. (5Q)/And now I understand this pattern of mine (5Q)/

to make sense of the clause and to score it. In general, scores at the lower end of the Mastery Scale require less context to score.

Question: How do I know if scores fall in Levels 1–3 or 4–6?

Answer: The equator of the Mastery Scale is between Levels 3 and 4. It is here that the patient shifts from predominantly focusing on the self to focusing on the self in relation to others. Self-absorption, focusing on inwardly felt pain, distress, confusion, ambivalence, and anger, marks the early levels of mastery. Thinking about the self in relation to others and their interpersonal world marks the later levels of mastery.

Question: How should I decide whether to score a statement as 1A, 2E, 4O, or 5E?

Answer: In deciding between scoring alternatives, the first question is to consider the way a statement is told. Is it self-focused and affect laden, or is it interpersonally focused and reflective? This helps organize the statement into either Levels 1–3 or 4–6. In deciding between 1A and 2E, the severity of the distress should be considered. 1A statements imply that the person is dominated by the feeling or thought; 2E statements indicate distress but not global distress. For example,

/I feel really bad about what I said (2E)/

is less extreme in nature than

/I can't stand life any more! (1A)/.

Statements at 4O and 5Q are both self-reflections generally within an interpersonal context. The difference between them is that statements at 5Q summarize a major trend in how a person characteristically behaves, thinks, or feels in many situations, whereas 4O is more self-questioning and less certain and usually concerns an analysis of only one event or situation. For example,

/I often feel myself withdraw when a woman approaches me (5Q)/

is more of a global observation than

/I can see now how I get timid with her (4O)/.

Question: What is the difference between 1A and 1B?

Answer: 1A is for global distress. It is marked by global, overgeneral-ized catastrophic thinking. Here patients describe their state as if there is no other; this is all they can think or feel at the present time. In contrast, 1B relates to the intensity and immediacy of felt affect. The key issue here is time, in that the feelings or thoughts are immediately pressing on the person with great urgency. For example,

/I collapsed into a heap and wailed and cried (1A)/

expresses a state in which there was no other, whereas

/I smashed my fist through the window (1B)/

refers to a more immediate and extreme loss of control that was probably more transient.

Question: What is the difference among 1C, 3J, and 3K?

Answer: The difference between these three codes is in the quality of the expression. Scores at 1C have a more global quality and are highly defensive and passive. There is a sense that the language is used as a wall to block thinking and feeling or to reject or dissemble any thinking or feeling, as in the example

/It means nothing (1C)/.

Scores at 3J and 3K indicate that the person is more engaged with the sub-ject and material and is actively wondering about it. There are two essential qualities of 3K: (a) ambivalence, as in the example

/perhaps but maybe not (3K)/

where two possibilities are entertained; and (b) emerging awareness with uncertainty, as in the example

/It could have been like that (3K)/.

In contrast, 3J is a simple expression of confusion without any emerging idea or ambivalence, as in

/ I don't know why it was like that (3J)/

or

/I don't know why (3J)/.

Question: What is the difference between 2F and 2G?

Answer: With both 2F and 2G a person's distress is seen as related to another person. The difference between the scores is how the person responds. Put simply, in 2F the person dumps on the other, and in 2G the other dumps on them. In 2F the person directs his or her emotional state outwards toward the other with anger and vengeance; for example,

/I'm going to make him pay for what he did to me (2F)/.

In 2G the person feels it is the other person who is punishing or neglecting them; for example,

/They are making me pay for this (2G)/.

Question: What is the difference between 2H and 2I?

Answer: The essential difference between these two scores is that 2H reflects an interpersonal emphasis (social avoidance), whereas 2I has a personal emphasis (the self is helpless and hopeless).

Question: What is the difference between 3L and 6U?

Answer: The essential difference between these two scores is that with 3L there is a sense that the person has not reached a goal, that he or she is struggling and striving toward it. With 3L there is the sense that effort is being expended; for example,

/I tried really hard to face it this time (3L)/.

In contrast, with 6U the change has occurred, a goal has been met, and the person is more calm with a situation rather than struggling with it; for example,

/I feel good about facing it (6U)/.

Question: What is the difference between 4O and 6W?

Answer: The difference between them is in emphasis. 4O emphasizes questioning and self-responsibility, whereas 6W emphasizes cogitation and engaging in analysis. With 4O individuals have an emerging awareness of themselves in a particular situation. Usually they question their reaction with a degree of uncertainty; for example,

/I wonder if it was the best way for me to react to her (4O)/.

In contrast, with 6W the emphasis is not on the wondering or emerging sense of self, but on the process of thinking clearly through a situation; for example,

/I thought it all through last night (6W)/.

Question: Should we combine two judges' scores into an average, or should we discuss each others' ratings and derive a single consensus score?

Answer: For scientific purposes, it is best for each judge to score the Mastery Scale independently. The scores are then compared for the purposes of assessing interrater reliability and for deriving an averaged score. In some cases, it is desirable to have a single consensus rating for each passage. In this case, judges should score the transcripts independently and then come together and discuss their discrepancies to arrive at a single consensus scoring.

Question: What should I do when I disagree with another judge about a score?

Answer: Discrepancies between judges are a normal part of scoring and usually arise from differences in emphasis between judges when assessing a clause. For example, in the clause

/I don't know whether she was thinking the same thing/,

one judge could put weight on the "I don't know" and score the clause 3J, whereas another could put weight on the "whether she was thinking the same thing" and score 4N. In general, the more significant part of the clause (usually indicating higher mastery) should be accepted, which in this case is 4N.

Question: Is it acceptable to have highly discrepant scores in one passage?

Answer: It is normal for passages to have combinations of high and low mastery scores. The overall mastery is determined by the total averaged score. It is common for people to display a variety of levels of mastery within their description and discussion of events. There may be extremes within a person, for example, having shafts of high insight in someone who is more generally distressed and avoidant, or vice versa: a person with generally high mastery can also lapse into confusion and display poor impulse control.

CONCLUSION

The Mastery Scale is a comprehensive research tool for analyzing transcribed speech samples for indices of mastery. The scale is generally applied to transcripts from psychotherapy that document narratives of relationship interactions, but it may also be applied to shorter speech samples collected outside of psychotherapy. The method involves dividing transcribed speech into clauses, and then assigning scores to those clauses that are indicative of mastery. The Mastery Scale is made up of 6 levels (lack of impulse control, introjection and projection of negative affects, difficulties in understanding and control, interpersonal awareness, self-understanding, self-control) representing the spectrum of functioning, with 23 individual content categories. The scores derived can be analyzed in a number of ways, including deriving a mean mastery score, individual scores or proportions per level of mastery, or finer grained analyses of the 23 categories. In the next chapter, I investigate the scale's reliability and validity when applied to verbatim transcripts of psychotherapy patients.

5

RELIABILITY AND VALIDITY OF THE MASTERY SCALE

In this chapter, I present an original study using the Mastery Scale. My purpose is to assess whether the Mastery Scale (a) can be reliably applied with good interrater and test–retest reliability by judges working independently and (b) demonstrates good internal consistency. In other words, is the scale technically sound, and can it be reliably applied? I also address the following hypothesis: Patients rated as showing greater gains in mastery have larger gains on measures of general psychological health–sickness and reductions in symptoms than those patients showing fewer gains in mastery. The hypothesis is concerned with whether the scale is valid in measuring the kinds of changes predicted by the biopsychosocial theory of clinical change (chapter 2), a process described as one of mastering the conflicts, with the outcome being a high level of mastery. Patients who show gains in mastery should also improve on objective ratings of psychological health–sickness. The assessment of the validity of the Mastery Scale is also a test of this theory of clinical change.

Luborsky, Diguer, Luborsky, Singer, and colleagues (1993) noted in relation to the dodo bird finding that all psychotherapies have equivalent outcomes (discussed in chapter 1) but that the measures of outcome typically used are not designed to measure specific types of psychodynamic changes:

The outcome measures may not be representative of the treatment's intended outcomes. The most typical example is dynamic psychotherapy: the therapy emphasized the development of insight, yet its outcomes are typically measured by global ratings of improvement—which may neglect changes in insight. The usual outcome measures also do not make an adequate distinction between short-term and long-lasting improvement, nor do they make a distinction between the parallel related changes referred to as nonstructural and structural change. A structural change is one that makes a long-lasting change in a central component of the transference. (p. 510)

The Mastery Scale has been designed to overcome these shortcomings. It measures both changes in insight and self-control in relation to basic interpersonal transference-related patterns contained within narratives of relationship interactions. Exhibit 5.1 illustrates the concordance between these dynamic concepts and the related Mastery Scale items.

Because of the number of widely used and accepted outcome measures (McCullough, 1993), I decided to compare the ratings of change in mastery from early in therapy and late in therapy with changes in health and sickness, as measured by the Health–Sickness Rating Scale (HSRS; Luborsky,

EXHIBIT 5.1
Seven Processes of Psychotherapy as a Result of Working Through to
Achieve Mastery (Self-Understanding and Self-Control), With Corresponding
Mastery Scale Categories

A. Increase in self-understanding

1. Self-understanding about transference and other repetition compulsion
   Mastery Scale item: 5Q Expressions of Insight Into Repeating Personality Patterns of Self

2. Self-understanding about previous relationship events and their influence on the present
   Mastery Scale item: 5R Making Dynamic Links Between Past and Present Relationships

3. Relationship improvements following self-understanding of maladaptive relationship patterns
   Mastery Scale item: 5S References to Interpersonal Union

4. Self-understanding of relationships following working through
   Mastery Scale item: 5T Expressions of Insight Into Interpersonal Relations

B. Increase in self-control

5. Self-control is enhanced as greater energy becomes available for mature relationships
   Mastery Scale item: 6U Expressions of Emotional Self-Control Over Conflicts

6. Self-control increases as the repetition or acting out behaviors are lessened and new ways of responding in relationships emerges
   Mastery Scale item: 6V Expressions of New Changes in Emotional Responding

7. Self-control increases due to enhancement of the ability to self-analyze conflict
   Mastery Scale item: 6W References to Self-Analysis

1962, 1975) and with patient ratings of change on target complaints (Battle et al., 1966). Other comparative outcome measures used are described below. This research design ascertains whether the Mastery Scale measures the kind of change that is recognized by researchers, clinicians, and patients as being clinically meaningful. In summary, if mastery is a key change variable, it should lead to, and be associated with, broad changes in global mental health and symptomatic improvement.

METHOD

Participants

Forty-one patients (29 women, 12 men, mean age = 25 years, range = 18–48 years) were chosen as a representative sample from 72 patients comprising the Penn Psychotherapy Project (Luborsky et al., 1988). Of these 41 patients, 10 had shown most improvement, 10 had shown the least improvement, and 21 fell somewhere in the middle. The sample has been used in a number of previous psychotherapy research studies (Luborsky & Crits-Christoph, 1990; Luborsky et al., 1988). Twenty-six patients were single, 7 were married, and 6 were divorced or separated. (Two patients had missing data for this variable.) Five had graduated from high school only, 19 were undergraduates, 6 had completed college, and 11 either had completed or were enrolled in graduate school.

The sample had a mixed diagnostic picture according to the criteria of the *Diagnostic and Statistical Manual of Mental Disorders* (3rd ed.; *DSM–III*; American Psychiatric Association, 1980). Fifteen had primary diagnoses of dysthymia and 11 generalized anxiety disorder, whereas the rest of the primary and secondary diagnoses were mainly Cluster A (8 schizoid, 3 schizotypal), Cluster B (4 histrionic, 1 narcissistic), and Cluster C (3 compulsive, 3 passive–aggressive) Axis II personality disorders. (These diagnoses are very similar to those in the 4th edition of the *Diagnostic and Statistical Manual of Mental Disorders*; *DSM–IV*; American Psychiatric Association, 1994.)

Psychotherapy Treatment

Treatment was based on weekly individual time-unlimited supportive–expressive psychoanalytic psychotherapy (Luborsky, 1984) within a mean treatment length of 54 weeks (range = 21–149 weeks). Therapy was conducted by 31 psychiatrists (mean age = 36 years, range = 26–56 years). Of these, 17 were residents, 9 had up to 10 years of postresidency experience, and 5 had more than 10 years of experience. The residents saw their patients in an outpatient clinic, and the postresidents saw their patients in private practice. Thirty of the therapists were married, and 23 had children.

Judges

Four judges scored the Mastery Scale. Two judges were clinical psychologists, one judge was a doctoral-level research psychologist, and one was a doctoral-level psychoanalytic theorist. Payment for judges was based on an hourly rate. Judges were trained on a set of practice transcripts. Each judge scored a transcript independently, and then scores were compared and discussed at a round table meeting. Then the next transcript was scored and compared, and so on through all practice transcripts. This process took approximately 5 1/2 hours to complete. By the end of this process, judges agreed on each scorable clause more than 90% of the time.

Psychotherapy Transcripts

The data consisted of verbatim transcripts of psychotherapy sessions collected during the Penn Psychotherapy Project. The transcripts were made for earlier studies (Luborsky et al., 1988). For each patient, transcripts were available from early-in-therapy (generally Sessions 3 and 5) and late-in-therapy sessions (at the 90% completion mark).

By evaluating transcripts from two time points, it should be possible to detect any changes in self-understanding and self-control in the narratives over the course of therapy. Transcripts from the very first sessions and very last sessions were avoided. Early in therapy, the first couple of sessions are often constrained and involve a good deal of fact finding and information giving. By the third session, patients usually are at the stage where they can comfortably narrate relationship episodes (REs) that contain their conflicts. Late in therapy, patients must come to terms with the termination of the relationship with the therapist, and this can cause a temporary return of symptoms and problems. Therefore, Sessions 3 and 5 and sessions at the 90% mark (and the sessions immediately before this) were used (Luborsky et al., 1988).

Narratives of interactions (REs) served as the scorable units of analysis of mastery. REs had been identified from the transcripts of early and late sessions in an earlier core conflictual relationship theme (CCRT) study (Luborsky & Crits-Christoph, 1989). There were usually 10 REs from early in therapy and 10 REs from late in therapy for each patient.

Scoring Procedure

The REs were cut out from the transcripts and randomized between sessions and patients. This was to prevent judges from having cues as to the progress of the patient in therapy. The aim was for each RE to be scored on its merits, without bias by prior knowledge. A random number code was given to each RE prior to randomization so that the data could be reassembled into the original order after judges had completed scoring.

The REs were divided into grammatical clauses by marking off the claused speech units with a slash (/) according to the conventions described in chapter 4. The following is an example of three marked clauses, with mastery scores in parentheses:

/I'm afraid of myself, (2E)/because it's a father–lover sort of thing. (5Q)/It's also this hangover from when I was real young. (5R)/.

To facilitate the process of scoring, one judge read all the REs and identified all the clauses that could be scored using the Mastery Scale. This technique was also used in CCRT research to control for location or position disagreement (as opposed to scoring disagreement). The judge completed this clausing task after the data had been randomized, so there were no clues as to which patient the RE came from nor whether the RE was from either early- or late-in-therapy sessions. The judge completed this task after having read and claused the entire RE.

These scorable clauses were consecutively marked with a number of the scorable clause next to the slash:

/^{1} I'm afraid of myself /^{2} because it's a father–lover sort of thing. /^{3} It's also this hangover from when I was real young/.

A blank sheet of paper with numbers running down it in columns was used to record each judge's mastery scores. The mastery score was written next to the number corresponding to the clause on the coding sheet.

The usual method of scoring with content analysis is to have judges write the score immediately above the relevant clause on the transcript. However, because each RE was scored twice, this would have meant having two copies of each RE (one for each judge), which proved impractical given the huge size of the data (running to many thousands of pages). Therefore, the numbering method was used because this meant that only one physical copy of each RE was required.

All the REs were scored twice using the Mastery Scale. Each RE was independently scored by two of the four trained judges. Each judge was given a random portion of the total number of REs to score. No individual judge scored the same RE twice. Judges were blind to patient identity, RE time frame, the treatment outcome status, and other clinical variables. The judges assigned 1 of the 23 mastery categories from 1A–6W to each of the codable clauses.

Each of the 23 category choices comes with its own built-in score (1–6) representing one of the six levels on the scale. These scores were used to compile the statistics. Mastery scores were calculated for each RE by summing all the scores and dividing by the number of scorable clauses (for details of this method, see chapter 4). These scores were then used to calculate average levels of mastery for each patient early and late in therapy.

Outcome Measures

Outcome measures were collected at the commencement and termination of therapy as part of the original Penn Psychotherapy Project (Luborsky et al., 1988). Because the original Penn study was concerned with predicting outcomes, numerous variables were collected. The authors made several composite measures, which combined a large number of the predictive outcome measures into single variables. Although this suited the purpose of the Penn study, for the present study it was important to select a few well-known and widely used outcome measures, to facilitate appraisal by reviewers of the research about the findings on the basis of familiarity with these measures. The measures selected were as follows:

1. The HSRS (Luborsky, 1962, 1975) was one of the first scales designed to predict and measure the outcome of psychotherapy. It has had more than 45 years of continuous use since its inception at the Menninger Foundation in Kansas in 1949. It is a clinician-rated measure of mental health based on an interview; assessment is usually made prior to and following the end of psychotherapy. It consists of eight graphic 100-point scales (one global scale and seven specific scales): (a) the ability to function autonomously, (b) seriousness of the symptoms, (c) subjective discomfort and distress, (d) effect on the environment, (e) utilization of abilities, (f) interpersonal relationships, and (g) breadth and depth of interests. The global scale is the most often used in research, and it has been slightly modified to form the Global Assessment of Functioning (GAF; also known as the *Global Assessment Scale* or GAS; Endicott, Spitzer, Fleiss, & Cohen, 1976), which forms Axis V of *DSM–IV* (American Psychiatric Association, 1994).

   The mean of the eight subscales of the HSRS is more reliable than the single-item global scale (Luborsky & Bachrach, 1974). It was therefore decided in this study to use the mean of the eight subscales as the measure of psychological health–sickness (PHS; Luborsky, Diguer, Luborsky, McLellan, et al., 1993). This mean has an internal consistency (Cronbach's alpha) of .87 prior to therapy and .92 posttherapy (Luborsky et al., 1988, p. 88) The HSRS has shown good concurrent validity in a wide range of studies (Luborsky & Bachrach, 1974). For example, a factor analysis of 14 patient predictor variables has shown that the HSRS was related to interpersonal relationships (.93), level of psychosexual development (.89), anxiety tolerance (.82), and ego strength (.79; Kernberg, 1972).

2. The Prognostic Index—Control and Insight ratings (PI–Control; PI–Insight; Auerbach, Luborsky & Johnson, 1972; Luborsky et al., 1988). Because the Mastery Scale incorporates self-control and self-understanding, it was decided to evaluate its relationship with a clinician-rated measure of self-control and insight taken at the beginning and end of therapy. In this measure, a clinician interviews the patient and then rates 29 areas that are believed to be related to outcome. In a factor analysis of the index on 47 patients, insight was found to load .67 with the "patient's aptitude for psychotherapy" and self-control .46 with "general emotional health" (Luborsky et al., 1988, Table 7.5). It was decided to use these two measures, not as predictors of outcome, but as independently rated global measures of insight and control that could help to understand aspects of the Mastery Scale.

3. Therapists' rating of patient satisfaction, success, and improvement (SSI). A rating by the therapist, a primary participant in therapy, is a valuable addition to this validation study. The measure used was a composite of three ratings, all very similar, that the therapist was asked to make at the conclusion of therapy. They were ratings of patient satisfaction (Rogers & Dymond, 1954), success (Rogers & Dymond, 1954), and improvement (Waskow & Parloff, 1975, p. 233).

4. The therapist's rating of the patient achieving insight (TInsight). This was a Likert-scale rating made by the therapist at the same time as he or she made ratings of success, satisfaction, and improvement. It was evaluated for the same reason as the prognostic index rating of insight: It could overlap to some degree with the Mastery Scale rating because an important component of the Mastery Scale is the patient's insight.

5. Target complaints (Target; Battle et al., 1966). In this measure, the patient is asked at the initial interview to name three problems with which he or she most wants help. At termination the patient is then asked to rate the change in severity of these three target complaints. Only the primary problem nominated by the patient is used, because this is usually the central issue that the patient wishes to change through psychotherapy (Deane & Spicer, 1998). Although some have criticized the method for its lack of standardization (Mintz & Kiesler, 1982), it has appeal because it personalizes the patient's own goals in a meaningful way.

6. Symptom Checklist (SCL; Derogatis, Lipman, Covi, Rickels, & Uhlenhuth, 1970). The Hopkins Symptom Checklist (an early version of the more contemporary SCL–90–R; Derogatis, Rickels, & Rock, 1976) was used as a patient-rated measure of overall symptomatic improvement. The scale was administered at intake and termination. It is widely used and has demonstrated adequate reliability and validity in many studies (Derogatis, Rickels & Rock, 1976).

Of the seven measures used, therefore, four target general changes in psychological health–sickness (HSRS, SSI, Target, and SCL), two rate insight (PI–Insight, TInsight), and one rates self-control (PI–Control). There are three ratings made by an observer (HSRS, PI–Insight, PI–Control), two by the therapist (SSI, TInsight), and two by the patient (Target, SCL).

Data Analysis

A variety of data analysis strategies were used to investigate the following 5 features of the scale:

1. *Interrater reliability.* Because the unit of analysis is the RE, the resulting average mastery scores for each RE per judge were compared. Pearson correlation coefficients were computed between each pair of judges.

2. *Test–retest reliability.* To assess the stability of scoring the Mastery Scale, 5 REs that Judges A and C had both scored were randomly selected and presented to them a second time 3 weeks after the initial scoring. A total of 45 individual clauses were scored across the 5 REs. The correlation between their initial and retest scores per clause was calculated as the measure of test–retest reliability. The same procedure was used to assess the test–retest reliability of Judges B and D, using 5 REs scored in common (representing 51 individual scored clauses).

3. *Internal consistency.* Proximities analysis was used to investigate the relationship between the 23 Mastery Scale categories. Of chief interest was whether the categories clustered together in the way hypothesized by the assignation of the scores 1 to 6. This is a test of the internal consistency of the scale, that is, whether the categories actually fit into the purported six levels of mastery. For example, if category 6W, References to Self-Analysis, was regularly found in REs with categories 1A, 1B, 1C, and 1D (the lowest hypothesized level of mastery), then this would cast doubt on whether 6W actu-

ally deserves a mastery score of 6; perhaps it should have a score of 1 (i.e., very low mastery).

The method used to investigate this was as follows. Each RE was investigated in turn, and a score of 1 was given to represent one or more appearances of a category. If the category did not appear (was not scored) in that RE it was given a score of 0. In other words, 1 indicated the presence of a category, and 0 indicated its absence. Hence, this was a binary analysis. It was hypothesized that categories that are similar (proximate) in mastery level should cluster together and that categories that are remote (distant) in mastery level should rarely appear together.

In psychotherapy terms, patients who show low mastery should have many instances of low-mastery categories in their REs and should not have this combined with many high-mastery categories. Although for each individual case there will probably be a diverse scatter of mastery categories, the global trend across all patients and all REs should be for the categories to appear in the hypothesized levels presented in the Mastery Scale.

The similarity measure used was phi, which is the binary form of the Pearson product–moment correlation coefficient (SPSS-X, 1988, p. 831). It is argued that a correlational method is the most appropriate and robust statistic for making comparisons between complex RE patterns. The data were converted into binary form and analyzed using the CLUSTER module (using average linkage between groups) and PROXIMITIES (phi) modules of SPSS-X. Results were presented as a dendrogram (tree diagram) showing the relationships between the mastery categories.

4. *Change in mastery over therapy.* A paired (repeated-measures) *t* test was used to investigate changes in overall mastery from early to late in therapy. An estimation of the clinical significance of this change was made by calculating an effect size estimate.

5. *Relationship between mastery and the outcome variables.* Following the recommendations of various authors (Fiske, 1971; Kazdin, 1994; Luborsky et al., 1988; Manning & DuBois, 1962), residual gain scores were calculated for those measures where there were early and late evaluations (mastery, HSRS, SCL). The residual gain score takes into account the extent to which the gain is related to the severity of the patient's problem at intake. For example, a patient whose problem is very

severe at intake potentially has a long distance to cover to reach optimal functioning. In contrast, a patient who is only mildly symptomatic must improve only slightly to reach optimal functioning. The residual gain score takes this difference in initial conditions into account and is appropriate for correlational designs such as the present study. In other studies that compare treatments using analysis of variance, it is appropriate to control for initial level by using it as a covariate.

RESULTS

Interrater Reliability

The data consisted of 794 REs (an average of 19 per patient). Given that the data were scored twice (1,588 REs), Judge A scored 437 REs, Judge B scored 463 REs, Judge C scored 391 REs, and Judge D scored 297 REs. Interrater agreement was uniformly high; correlation coefficients among the four independent judges are presented in Table 5.1.

These results show an impressive degree of agreement between judges, although there were slight variations between different pairs of judges. However, taking the standard Pearson correlation coefficient, the agreement is significant in all cases at $p < .00001$; in other words, the likelihood of this result being due to chance is less than .001%. Judges' mastery scores were therefore averaged in all subsequent analyses.

Test–Retest Reliability

Test–retest reliability was assessed by selecting 5 REs at random and presenting them to judges again after a period of 3 weeks. Test–retest reliability was good; test–retest correlations were .77 (Judge A), .80 (Judge B), .92 (Judge C), and .89 (Judge D). Although these data were calculated on a relatively small sample of scored clauses (45 for Judges A and C and 51 for Judges B and D), the results are all highly significant ($p < 0.0001$).

Internal Consistency

All scored samples (794 REs) were converted from mastery scores (1–6) into binary scores (1 = category appears in RE, 0 = category does not appear), and these data were subject to a proximities analysis using phi, the binary form of the Pearson correlation coefficient. The result, presented as a dendrogram, shows the way the categories cluster together according to their relationship with each other. The results are presented in Figure 5.1.

TABLE 5.1
Relationship Between Four Judges' Mastery Scores

Comparison between judges	r	r²	REs scored in common N
A vs. B	.75	.56	187
A vs. C	.77	.60	161
A vs. D	.81	.66	89
B vs. C	.79	.63	149
B vs. D	.85	.73	127
C vs. D	.89	.66	81

Note. RE = relationship episode.

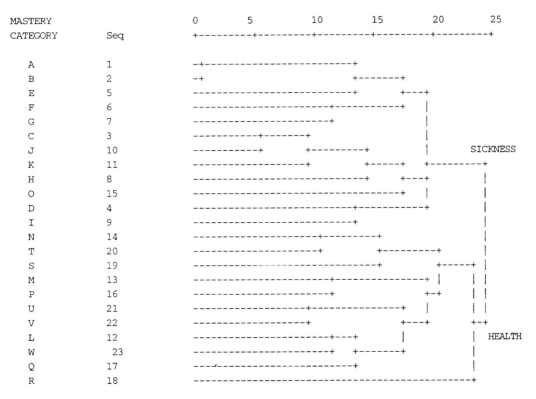

Figure 5.1. The internal consistency of the Mastery Scale. *Note. N* = 41. A dendrogram of similarity between Mastery Scale categories, representing the binary form of the Pearson product–moment correlation coefficient (phi). Seq = Sequence.

Changes in Mastery Over the Course of Therapy

To investigate changes in mastery scores across the 41 patients over the course of therapy, a paired *t* test between early and late mastery scores was calculated. An average mastery score was calculated for each patient early in therapy and late in therapy. The change in mastery was highly statistically significant, $t(40) = 4.94$, $p > .0001$, with a large (1.35) effect size. When compared to the published effect sizes in other psychotherapy studies, the changes detected by the Mastery Scale are clinically significant (e.g., Lambert & Bergin, 1994). The trend in this psychotherapy sample was thus for patients to display greater levels of self-understanding and self-control in their interpersonal relations late in therapy.

To illustrate these typical changes in mastery from early to late in therapy, consider one patient (Figure 5.2). Ms. Sevent, a 24-year-old divorced graduate student with no children, was seen in weekly therapy sessions for 41 weeks with the goal to help change her difficult "personality patterns." Her psychodynamic therapist was a 31-year-old married resident psychiatrist. Early in therapy she expressed suffering (2E) related to conflictual interactions with others, which led to her avoiding relationships (2H). When in close relationships she felt worthless and guilty (2F) and encouraged men to hit her (1D). Toward the end of therapy she could see (5Q) that her global view that "men are evil" was due to unconscious hostility toward an abusing person from her childhood (5R). She therefore began to

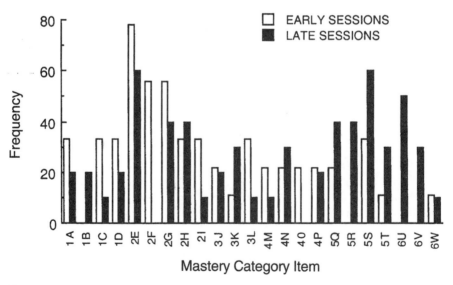

Figure 5.2. Frequency distribution of Mastery Scale categories as a percentage of narratives told early in therapy (open bars) and late in therapy (closed bars) for one patient in the study (Ms. Sevent, age 24)

struggle free from these bonds (4P) and enjoy relationships (5S) in a new way (6V). These conflictual patterns also appeared within the early transference relationship with her therapist. Toward the end of therapy she could express with confidence to her therapist that "you basically seem good to me now" (6V), thus showing some mastery over her interpersonal problem.

In the study, overall changes in mastery categories from early- to late-in-therapy sessions were investigated. Figure 5.3 shows the percentage change in the frequency of Mastery Scale categories appearing in narratives from early to late in psychotherapy for all 41 patients. The data confirm the cluster analysis, in that the first half of the scale represents sickness and the second half health. Dimensions indicative of poor mastery (categories 1A–3L) show a reduction in appearance in narratives late in therapy, whereas interpersonal awareness, self-understanding, and self-control dimensions (categories 4M–6W) show a corresponding increase in appearance late in therapy.

Relationship Between Mastery and the Outcome Variables

The relationship between Mastery Scale residual gain scores and outcome variables was calculated using Pearson correlations and is presented in

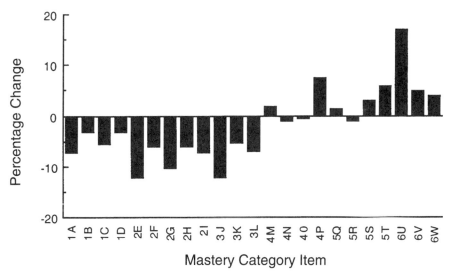

Figure 5.3. Percentage of frequency of Mastery Scale categories appearing in narratives late in psychotherapy, expressed as percentage change from early in therapy narratives. Data are for 41 patients.
Note. Dimensions indicative of poor mastery (categories A–L) show a reduction in appearance in narratives late in therapy, whereas interpersonal awareness, self-understanding, and self-control dimensions (categories M–W) show a corresponding increase in appearance late in therapy. Data at 0% indicate no change in the percentage of appearance of categories from early to late in therapy.

TABLE 5.2
Pearson Correlations Between Mastery Scale Residual Change Scores and
Clinical Outcome Scores

Clinical outcome measure	Pearson correlation
Observer ratings of outcome	
Health–Sickness Rating Scale residual change score	.51***
Prognostic Index Control item	.30
Prognostic Index Insight item	.01
Therapist rating of outcome	
Therapist rating of patient satisfaction, success and improvement	.47**
Therapist rating of patient achieving insight	.12
Patient ratings of outcome	
Rating of change of primary target complaint	.59***
Symptom Checklist residual change score	−.53***

Note. $N = 41$. ** $p < .01$. *** $p < .001$

Table 5.2. Significant relationships were found between mastery change scores and observer, therapist, and patient ratings of outcome, but not for the insight and control ratings. Figure 5.4 shows the data for the HSRS residual change scores plotted against the Mastery Scale residual change scores.

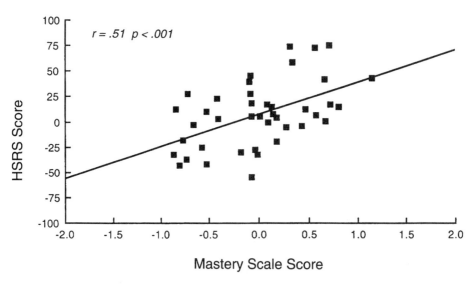

Figure 5.4. Distribution of Health–Sickness Rating Scale (HSRS) and Mastery Scale residual change scores for all 41 patients.

DISCUSSION

This study evaluated the reliability and validity of the Mastery Scale as a measure of therapy process and outcome. The results supported both the reliability and validity of the scale. Each of the three hypotheses tested is discussed in turn.

Can the Mastery Scale be reliably applied by judges working independently with good interrater and test–retest reliability? The results overwhelmingly suggest that it can. Both the interrater and test–retest reliability of the Mastery Scale were impressive. Good interrater and test–retest reliability was probably achieved in part because the judging task was highly structured, obviating the disagreement that can result from unguided complex inferential judgment methods. Judges did not assess levels of mastery per se; the corresponding scores were already built into the category choices. This method of content analysis has proved a very powerful way of identifying underlying constructs (Gottschalk et al., 1969). In addition, judges were well-trained prior to scoring the data.

Does the Mastery Scale have good internal consistency? The results verify that it does. The clusters fall neatly into two large groups split at the middle of the Mastery Scale (between 3L and 4M; see Figure 5.1). One dimension can be conveniently called "sickness" and the other "health." Within the sickness dimension are a number of subclusters. From top to bottom on the graph, these can be labeled *negative symptoms* (categories 1A, 1B, 2E), *conflictual interpersonal relations* (2F, 2G), *cognitive confusion* (1C, 2H, 3J, 3K, 4O), and *helpless dependency* (1D, 2I). Similarly, within the health dimension, a number of subclusters are discernable: *interpersonal sensitivity* (4N, 5S, 5T), *self-assertion* (4M, 4P), *self-control* (6U, 6V), and *self-understanding* (3L, 5Q, 6W).

A number of categories are worth noting. First, two categories do not appear to be in the correct place. 4O: Questioning the Reaction of Self is given a mastery weight of 4 and should fit into the health dimension, yet it appears in the sickness dimension alongside the other cognitive confusion items. Similarly, 3L: References to Positive Struggle With Difficulties is given a weight of 3 and should appear in the sickness dimension, yet it appears among the insight items. It may be that within the dimensions that cluster, these categories represent the extreme. In other words, within the cognitive confusion cluster, 4O represents the mildest form of this (from 1C, 2H, 3J, 3K), and therefore its score of 4 is justified. Similarly, within the self-understanding cluster, 3L may represent the worst form of this and therefore should be scored lower. However, it would be worth examining whether this discrepancy can be replicated on a different sample.

Also of interest is the position of 5R: Making Dynamic Links Between Past and Present Relationships, which fits into the health cluster but does not cluster with any other category. This is a very puzzling result. In fact, it only clusters very abstractly with the rest of the health dimension. Perhaps it is a superordinate category that has special importance in mastery, or alternatively it may simply be unique in its presentation to have consistently clustered with other categories. A final explanation is that this cluster occurs very rarely in REs (only 6.5% of REs had this category), and so the lack of data may have prevented it from clustering unambiguously with any other variable.

This study was designed to test the hypothesis stated in the beginning of this chapter, that patients rated as showing greater gains in mastery have larger gains on measures of general psychological health–sickness and reductions in symptoms than those patients showing fewer gains in mastery. The results support this hypothesis. There were significant relationships between the Mastery Scale scores and measures of change assessed by observers, the therapist, and the patient (Table 5.2). For example, changes in HSRS were significantly related to changes in mastery. This is clearly seen in Figure 5.4. These results are consistent with the view that patients who are more sick are less able than other patients to see the interpersonal dynamics of their predicament and tend to react more helplessly and painfully to problems in getting their needs met.

Perhaps of most interest is that patients' own judgments of changes in their main complaint (Target) paralleled changes in the mastery of interpersonal conflicts found in their narratives. This suggests that changes in mastery are not only related to changes in reported symptoms, but also to the fulfilling of the patients' main goal in therapy.

It is also of interest that both the observer PI–Insight and PI–Control ratings and the therapist's rating of insight did not show a significant relationship with mastery (Table 5.2). The PI–Control item was very close to being significant ($r = .30$) given that the criteria of significance at $p < .05$ is .308. There was therefore a marginally nonsignificant relationship between the measure of control and mastery.

The two ratings of insight (PI–Insight and TInsight) were not related to mastery, although the trend was in the right direction. Researchers have often found it difficult to find relationships between insight and clinically relevant change. For example, in his careful analysis of the case material from 42 patients in the Menninger Psychotherapy Research Project, Wallerstein (1986) found that 45% of patients who had made clinically significant structural changes did not have parallel changes in insight; 7% made large changes in insight but showed no clinically relevant structural change. What is common to the Wallerstein study and the two measures of insight used here is that they are all based on subjective global ratings of insight. They may all have validity problems because of the demands made on judges to make a single global judgment of such a complex construct as insight. In support of this view, research with the PI has demonstrated that considerable variation exists between different judges' scoring patterns

(Luborsky et al., 1988). Guided and well-validated measures of insight are required, but at present they are only in the pilot stage of development (Crits-Christoph et al., 1993).

In addition, the Mastery Scale subsumes insight and control into a single concept, mastery, which is different in important ways from either variable. When the scale was being developed, attempts were made to have judges separate the intellectual (as in insight) from the emotional (as in control). The difficulty in separating these two supported the view that the overall concept being measured was mastery. Nevertheless, one might expect that at least a moderate relationship would be found between mastery and the measures of insight. Further research using different measures of insight (Weiss et al., 1986, p. 387) and control (D. H. Shapiro & Bates, 1990) are needed to further investigate this issue. The categories of self-understanding used in the Mastery Scale might provide a useful starting point for constructing a better rating scale of insight.

It is possible to argue that the results of this study show that mastery may not have sufficient discriminant validity. However, it was purposely designed to encompass broadly the general features of self-understanding and self-control and was not designed to measure a narrow feature of psychotherapy change. As such, it would be expected to overlap with other similar measures such as self-esteem or self-concept. It is significant in that spontaneous narratives told by patients can be scored on 23 categories of psychological constructs linked to a biopsychosocial theory of mastery and that the overall outcome of this analysis provides a meaningful window into patient changes in psychological functioning that previously has proved elusive.

Further inspection of the change data for the individual categories of the Mastery Scale (Figure 5.3) reveals some interesting findings. In general, psychotherapy leads to a diminution in three of the lower levels of mastery: lack of impulse control, introjection and projection of negative affects, and difficulties in understanding and control (categories A–L). This indicates that there is a general reduction in distress and confusion in interpersonal relationships over the course of psychotherapy.

As predicted, certain dynamic variables showed an amplification over therapy, such as expressions of self-control (6U), which showed a large (16.5%) increase. It is of interest that a few dynamic variables showed no change (e.g., 5R: Making Dynamic Links Between Past and Present Relationships). This could be partly attributed to the paucity of appearance of this category, because only 6.5% of narratives in therapy contained scorable clauses for this category. It is possible that this category is dynamically important in therapy but that our method is not sensitive enough to capture it. The superordinate nature of this category is suggested by the internal consistency analysis discussed above.

As indicated by the modest percentage changes in the frequency of Mastery Scale categories appearing in early- and late-in-therapy narratives

(Figure 5.3), there is support for the view that psychotherapy does not completely eliminate relationship conflicts, but rather helps people to gain mastery over them. The case study of Ms. Sevent illustrates the clinical relevance of the scale's categories.

CONCLUSION

This study aimed to evaluate the reliability and validity of the Mastery Scale as a measure of therapy process and outcome. The results support both the reliability and validity of the scale. Interrater reliability for four judges over 41 patients was excellent (range = .75–.89), and test–retest reliability 1 week later was between .86–.97. The Mastery Scale showed excellent internal consistency, as demonstrated by a cluster analysis, which confirmed that the categories fell into the predicted order of levels of the scale. The scale was also shown to be valid. Patients rated as showing greater gains in mastery had larger gains on measures of general psychological health–sickness and reductions in symptoms than those patients showing fewer gains in mastery. Significant correlations were found between changes in mastery and clinical outcome scores. For example, changes over the course of therapy were related to changes in HSRS ($r = .54$). Change in mastery over the course of psychotherapy was high, with a clinically significant effect size of 1.35.

The trend in this psychotherapy sample was thus for patients to display greater levels of self-understanding and self-control in their interpersonal relations late in therapy and for this in turn to be reflected in observer ratings of their HSRS scores. The Mastery Scale is valid and was found to measure the kind of change that is recognized by researchers, clinicians, and patients as being clinically meaningful. This process is described as one of mastering conflicts, with the outcome being a high level of mastery.

The theoretical basis for mastery was established in Part II and a method for measuring mastery was presented and evaluated in Part III. The third and final part of this volume demonstrates how the mastery concept can be applied in a clinical setting. The discussion includes a combination of original case studies and research investigating the application of the mastery concept and measurement tool to understanding patient progress. A set of case studies show the development of mastery from the patients' and therapists' perspectives, with specific guidelines for maximizing mastery.

IV

USING THE MASTERY CONCEPT IN CLINICAL PRACTICE

6

HOW PSYCHOTHERAPISTS HELP PATIENTS DEVELOP MASTERY

How patients change over the course of psychotherapy is something of a mystery. In many instances, the explanation for patient change has been left to theoretical notions, based in part on suppositions arising from case studies. Empirical studies in this area are still in their infancy, as reviewed in chapter 3. Much of the research effort in the history of psychotherapy has been spent on validating treatment outcomes rather than on understanding treatment progress and process, and much work remains to be done. The increasing availability of synchronized digital images and voice, its amenability to computer dissection, and systems for automatic translation of voice into text provide rich and more readily available raw data for analysis than has been available to date. Most studies still require the extremely time-consuming manual transcription of audiotapes and in some cases analysis and coding of videotape. The advances in the understanding of mastery have involved the technology of transcribed audiotape and manual (pencil and paper) coding by trained judges. Although there is clear loss of data from this technique (e.g., voice intonation, real time markers, nonverbal communications), it has served the current project well.

This chapter discusses the changes that patients make in psychotherapy as measured by the Mastery Scale, which illustrates and illuminates the types and degree of changes that psychotherapy can bring about and the way psychotherapists can foster mastery. It presents a systematic way of looking at change and may provide an impetus for the field to look further and deeper into the change process. The chapter first summarizes the change process using the mastery concept and illustrates three different phases of change and the techniques used by psychotherapists to augment mastery. Mastery is conceived as a continuum. Three phases of mastery may be identified: (a) Phase 1, low mastery, characterized by Levels 1 and 2 of the Mastery Scale (see chapter 4 for a description of the scale); (b) Phase 2, medium mastery, characterized by Levels 3 and 4; and (c) Phase 3, characterized by Levels 5 and 6. The progress of a single case over the course of psychotherapy is then traced, and aspects of technique associated with both clinical change and improvements in patient mastery are discussed. Consideration is given to the major implications of the mastery theory and research and how these can be applied in practice.

THE THREE PHASES OF MASTERY

Phase 1. Low Mastery, Dominance of Symptoms and Defenses

In this phase, patients are distressed and unable to cope effectively with their problems. The defining feature in this phase is the dominance of symptoms and defenses, often accompanied by difficulties with interpersonal relationships. The two key levels within mastery for this phase are (a) lack of impulse control, where a person's emotional life is unbound and uncontained, and (b) introjection and projection of negative affects, where distressing emotional feelings are split off into others or are directed internally. Their personality functioning may be primitive, in that their sense of self or feeling of integration may be fractured, split, and perhaps permeable. In terms of diagnosis, patients with severe personality disorders, and other types of disorders such as anxiety, obsessional, addictive, dissociative, melancholic, and psychotic disorders may have a Phase 1 level of mastery. Patients may have built a wall of depression around themselves and become so overcome with their anxiety symptoms that they have very little ability to concentrate on anything other than themselves. They may have a profoundly distrustful view of others because of their own paranoid ideas or feelings of being controlled. The defenses against these kinds of problems can include repression of affect and ideas, numbness, withdrawal from others, or a response that blocks out the impact of the interpersonal through an omnipotent or narcissistic stance. Alternatively, their interpersonal anxiety may be manifest in emotionality, dependency, and hypersensitivity to others.

Patients with low mastery function extremely poorly, are highly distressed by interpersonal relationships, or are isolated from others altogether.

The risks of this phase include suicide, self-harm, and acting out behaviors, which may indicate the need for high level care, often within a hospital.

The following example illustrates this level of low mastery. The patient, 39-year-old Ted, had a 20-year history of mental problems, including a number of failed relationships, polysubstance abuse (cocaine, cannabis, and alcohol), and several hospitalizations, during which he was diagnosed as having paranoid personality disorder. He was being treated by a female psychotherapist. The following exchange occurred during the fifth psychotherapy hour. Within parentheses are the Mastery Scale codes applicable to the sample.

> *Therapist:* I get the feeling you're really, you're really trying to test me out right now—lately either you're asking questions, or thinking about situations to provoke me in some way.

> *Ted:* Well, perhaps that's because I'm getting a little more, um, militant about, more militant about people responding to me. (40)/I get—trying to get back to the whole thing about me feeling that you're a conspirator in this plan to destroy me. (2G)/[pause] Boy, I really think I must be crazy, (1B)/I must be out of my mind. (1B)/When I think of mysel- you know, when I think of you,/and I think, you know, like you're placing me as "this cat is out of his mind" (2G)/and, um, you know, it just, it, it, destroys me. (1A)/The thing is, I don't know you at all [pause], (3J)/and yet I feel there's something missing in you (2F)/because there's something that's, that's going wrong in me. (1D)/It's sort of like I can't, um, [pause] you know, I can't really trust you. (2G)/

This exchange clearly demonstrates that the patient is paranoid (2G) and distressed (1A) about his relationship with his therapist (see Figure 6.1 for Mastery category scores). He is tormented (2G) by the thought of how the therapist views him, and this "destroys" (1A) him. He feels that he cannot trust the relationship because of a serious disorder in himself: "something" is "going wrong in me" (1D). He displays very low mastery; he has neither insight into the problem nor control over it. The overall mastery score, at 32%, illustrates how Ted is functioning within Phase 1 of mastery. The two largest spikes in Figure 6.1 are his paranoid ideas (2G) and feeling of being crazy (1B). Central to the presentation is the difficulty the patient is having in connecting with the therapist on a personal level. This core problem with interpersonal relations is the hallmark feature of low mastery.

Phase 2. Medium Mastery, Struggle to Understand and Control Responses Within an Interpersonal Context

In this phase, marked by Levels 3 and 4 of the Mastery Scale, patients question themselves and others in the struggle to understand their reactions and improve their relationships. The defining feature in this phase is the

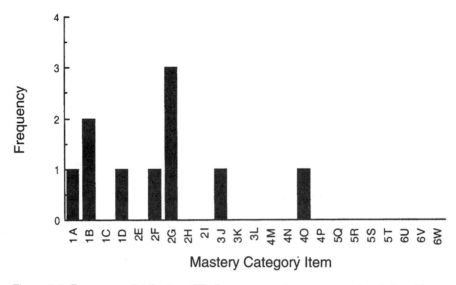

Figure 6.1. Frequency distribution of Ted's mastery category scores in relationship episode narrative from early in therapy.
Note. The mastery score for this sample was 1.9 (32%; sum of mastery scores / number of scorable clauses, i.e. 19/10).

active search for connection with themselves and with others. The two levels of mastery in this phase are (a) difficulties in understanding and control, where individuals are trying to sort out their personal feelings and reactions, and (b) interpersonal awareness, where they begin to look outside themselves to their relationships with others. In this phase, patients attempt to understand the interrelationships between their reactions toward others and others' reactions toward them. This movement or shift in focus, from the singular world of the individual with his or her defenses and symptoms to the interpersonal world of self in relation to others, is a defining moment in psychotherapeutic progress. The shift is a prognostic signal and shows that the person is now ready to ground his or her experience within a social context and to profit from the experience of the therapeutic relationship. This phase in mastery is where much of the hard work of the middle phases of psychotherapy occurs, and it is characterized by the working through of relationship conflicts.

The following example illustrates this level of medium mastery. The patient, 24-year-old Brad, presented with severe depression to his physician, who referred him to a local male psychotherapist. In the early sessions of the psychotherapy, the major work was in Phase 1, dealing with the patient's depression. The following passage was from the 21st psychotherapy hour, where the patient's depression had lifted considerably, and the work now focused on interpersonal relationship patterns and expectations.

> Brad: /I was just thinking about this the other day. (6W)/oh, that, you know, I just expect you know to meet a girl and (5Q)/you know, to

immediately fall into a serious relationship—you know,/serious meaning-ful relationship, without uh, really getting to know her or anything like that. (5Q)/That's sort of what happened with this girl I was going with last year, uh,/sort of neurotically we were just, she initiated it./But we just—you know, immediately, you know, the first night I, I went out with her,/and we went through this heavy necking thing (5S)/and the next weekend I was sleeping with her. (5S)/And al' —you know, even though I had, you know talked to her—(5S)/I had a couple of uh intimate dis-cussions beforehand, I guess, (5S)/but we didn't really know what we were about—(5T)/I didn't know what she was about, (4O)/she didn't know what I was about. (4N)/And I sort of expect the same thing to hap-pen again. (5Q)/I get the feeling that I didn't really learn anything from that relationship, (4O)/uh—you know it that, if I if maybe I was, well, then the way I broke it off (2H)/just totally, completely. (1B)/The way I reacted against it, against her finally. (2H)/Uh, was, uh, really a regres-sion—(5Q)/and you know, I I don't know if I described to you the way it happened/but briefly it was just that, uh, she had a lot of second thoughts about sleeping with me. (4N)/Finally—and she decided that you know to tone down the relationship, especially sexually. (4N)/and I went along with it uh, (2I)/and I guess I really didn't know what I felt at the time (1C)/but uh, finally I I just uh, —what I felt I guess was like uh, I'd been really rejected. (2G)/And so I just broke off the relationship com-pletely—(1B)/like you know I just couldn't handle it. (1A)/You know, it might have been, you know uh, now that I look at it (3K)/as the saner thing to do than to plunge into things the way we were. (4O)/

As illustrated in Figure 6.2, the patient is working hard to understand a dysfunctional relationship so that he might be able to avoid falling into the same trap in the future. He describes aspects of the relationship in which his response was to withdraw (2H) and separate completely (1B) after an intense and premature affair. He recognizes the position of the other person (4N) and realizes it was not dissimilar to his own (4O) in that "we didn't really know what we were about" (5T). He carefully describes the maladap-tive pattern of relating (5Q) and has some insight into how this pattern might be active in his life (5Q). However, he does not show in this sample that he has resolved the problem.

An interesting aspect of this example is how higher (Phase 3) and lower (Phase 1) material coexists and zigzags backward and forward. On the one hand, Brad shows insight into his behavior, yet at the same time he is confused and anxious about his feelings, struggling with the idea that cutting off the relationship totally was preferable to maintaining its intensity. Establishing a middle ground in terms of the development of relationships (neither too deep and intense, nor too shallow and withdrawn) is the principal struggle Brad is dealing with at this stage. He is confused, yet questions both his own reactions and those of the other person, which shows he is working on the principal tasks of Phase 2 and is currently at a mastery level of 60%.

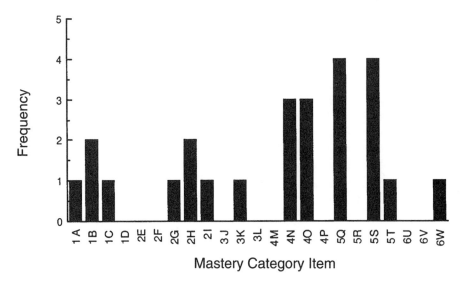

Figure 6.2. Frequency distribution of Brad's mastery category scores in relationship episode narrative from Session 21.
Note. The mastery score for this sample was 3.6 (60%; sum of mastery scores / number of scorable clauses, i.e. 90/25).

Phase 3. High Mastery, Self-Understanding and Self-Control

In this phase, patients are able to connect disparate parts of their life story narrative, to understand themselves and others more fully, and to interact in a way that is less conflictual and more rewarding. The key feature in this phase is the sense of connection with oneself and others. The two key levels within mastery for this phase are (a) self-understanding, where there is a ready and active awareness of typical reactions of self and others within relationships and a consequent ability to be meaningfully close to another, and (b) self-control, where patients are emotionally free and flexible, actively anticipating and clarifying their responses to interpersonal and personal situations. This phase of psychotherapy is significant because it signals readiness for termination. The consolidation of this phase in mastery is protective of future mental health, as patients consolidate skills and insight to be able to manage their own responses to problems.

The following example is from the therapy of Dianne, a 32-year-old librarian who presented to a male psychotherapist following a recurrence of panic attacks. These attacks had coincided with the breakup of a relationship with a man who had left her for another woman. In the early sessions, the focus was on relieving anxiety and developing an awareness of the link between her somatic symptoms of panic and psychological distress. The middle phases of therapy dealt with trying to understand the failure of a number of recent relationships. The following exchange occurred toward the end of therapy (after 41 hours of therapy), when Dianne was able to reflect more clearly on her interpersonal patterns.

> *Dianne:* /I just never really ran up against anyone/that I really felt dominated me/to the extent that I couldn't fight back/or that I couldn't couldn't you know, tell them a thing or two./Which is what I've done [laughs]. (5Q)/And uh—I don't think I've ever—I've never really thought that I've made any enemies because of it,/but—you know yet I'm sure that I-I'm sure that people have felt, (4N)/you know that I've been [pause] a little too big for my britches sometimes./Even with my parents, um/especially now that I've been away from home I go an' [pause]/if they have arguments or something,/and I don't agree with what they say, (4M)/I'll just tell 'em what I think. (4P)/And I feel good about myself, (6U)/and I think that they respect me for it. (4N)/I don't just jump in, (6U)/I think carefully about what I am going to say first. (6W)/.

In this sample, Dianne is showing that she has both awareness (5Q) and control (6U) over her interpersonal pattern of relating. She is both thoughtful (6W) and assertive (4P). She is able to laugh at her own style of asserting herself and reflect on the impact that this style may have had on others. The benefit of being clear-minded in her convictions was that she felt respected. Of particular importance, she is able to moderate and modulate her assertiveness and bluntness through careful contemplation beforehand of the likely impact of her views on others. Her mastery is high (82%) in this passage, and she shows not only self-awareness, but also the ability to control her responses to interpersonal conflicts (see Figure 6.3).

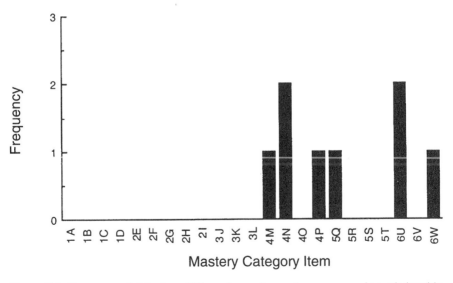

Figure 6.3. Frequency distribution of Dianne's mastery category scores in a relationship episode narrative from late in therapy (Session 42).
Note. The mastery score for this sample was 4.9 (82%; sum of mastery scores / number of scorable clauses, i.e. 39/8).

HOW PSYCHOTHERAPISTS PROMOTE MASTERY

Findings from this mastery model and attendant research point to how therapists might maximize the development of mastery in their patients. There is a frequent misconception, particularly among beginning clinicians, that psychotherapy is about administering techniques. The implication is that with practice, a set of defined techniques can be delivered with greater and greater skill, achieving, presumably, better and better results. This view—that the skills and techniques used are responsible for clinical change—is sometimes promoted by one or more schools of psychotherapy. Hence, for these schools the tendency is to promote more specific forms of skills. Psychotherapy is viewed like a pill made up of specific ingredients that is clinically efficacious when given to a patient for a certain number of sessions. This view is conceptually flawed, and these issues have been discussed and debated in detail elsewhere (Stiles, 1988, 1994; Stiles & Shapiro, 1994).

It is helpful to further illustrate the flaw in the pill dispensing metaphor of psychotherapy. In dynamic therapy, knowledge about the importance of transference has led some to believe that more frequent transference interpretations in a session produce outcomes superior to less frequent interpretations. However, research does not bear this out, at least for some patients (Piper, Azim, Joyce, & McCallum, 1991). The difficulty in the pill metaphor is that to be effective, techniques require a sophisticated understanding of when and when not to apply them. Guiding the use of a technique must be a body of knowledge and theory about how the tool may serve to promote a particular patient goal at that time. Ultimately, anything the therapist does has to come out of an understanding of the patient, and how the patient responds to his or her own interpersonal world.

What the mastery concept therefore offers therapists is a guide and a window into the kinds of specific changes patients can and do make during therapy. By knowing about these changes, detecting them, and organizing them in terms of mastery, the therapist can see where the patient is currently functioning and what is needed to move that patient forward. By observing markers of self-understanding and self-control central to the concept of mastery, the therapist can determine when the patient is ready to end therapy.

Psychotherapy is not only about administering specific techniques, but rather more importantly about providing a setting whereby a special relationship can be fostered between patients and therapists, one that is focused exclusively on helping patients overcome their difficulties (Strupp & Binder, 1984). What is critical is how therapists handle the relationship and whether or not they respond to their patients in ways that are appropriate to the patients' current level of mastery. More important than technique is the model and framework of therapy to which therapists subscribe. This framework guides them through the quagmire of microscopic details and tangents through which patients may lead them.

The Therapeutic Techniques Continuum

It is common to present therapy techniques as falling within a continuum from supportive to expressive (Kaplan & Sadock, 1998, pp. 885–890). For example, Gabbard (1990, p. 78) viewed the following list as a continuum from supportive (1–4) to expressive (4–7):

1. affirmation (e.g., "I understand")

2. advice and praise (e.g., "It is good that you did this," "I think it would be OK to do that")

3. empathic validation (e.g., "It seems this was really tough for you")

4. encouragement to elaborate (e.g., "Tell me more about this")

5. clarification (e.g., "It seems that you felt it right then, is that true?")

6. confrontation (e.g., "It seems you are avoiding doing it")

7. interpretation (e.g., "Your strong feelings toward it today remind me of some situations when you were young").

Interventions at Level 1 are generally empathic, nonthreatening, and supportive, whereas those at Level 7 are considered somewhat more intense, challenging, and expressive. The importance of the supportive–expressive continuum is that it documents different intensities of intervention, which can be tailored to individual patient levels of health and sickness. For very sick patients, it is recommended that therapists provide supportive techniques (i.e., from 1–4 above) to help bolster their fragile functioning, whereas less sick patients may benefit from more expressive techniques, which help engender insight and change (Luborsky, 1984). Therapists should assess the level of mastery of their patients and choose interventions consisting of more supportive or more expressive techniques, so as to match the patients' current functioning. In general, for patients at the Phase 1 level of mastery, therapists should primarily use supportive techniques, such as affirmation, praise, and empathic validation. Trying to pitch interventions at too high a level (such as trying to engender insight through interpretation) could be unhelpful or possibly even harmful to the progress of treatment. In Phase 2, the techniques should be aimed at the middle of the supportive–expressive continuum, that is, elaboration, clarification, and confrontation. During Phase 3, patients may benefit from mainly expressive techniques, which help them understand and control their problems. The psychotherapist should be working with patients at their current mastery level, rather than too far forward or too far back. The three phases of mastery, and the attendant therapy techniques, are illustrated in Figure 6.4.

THE THREE PHASES OF MASTERY

PHASE 1 : LOW MASTERY

Dominance of symptoms and defenses
Includes
• Lack of impulse control and blocking defenses
• Ego boundary disorders
• Introjection and projection of negative affects
• Withdrawal and helplessness.

Predominantly supportive techniques that convey
to the patient that the therapist
• Can tolerate their level of defenses, symptoms,
confusion and ambivalence
• Understands them (through affirmation and empathic
validation)
• Can help, advise, assist to set goals, and promote
hopefulness for improvement.

PHASE 2 : MEDIUM MASTERY

**Struggle to understand and control
responses within an interpersonal
context**
Includes
• Difficulties in understanding and control
• Ambivalence
• Questioning the reactions of the self and others
• Interpersonal self-assertion.

**A mixture of supportive and expressive
techniques** that convey to patients that the therapist
• Can help to elaborate the personal and interpersonal
nature and sources of their difficulties
• Can assist them to clarify these difficulties by exploring
both their and others' responses to conflict
• Is willing to confront them about unhelpful thoughts or
behaviors to promote greater awareness and self-control.

PHASE 3 : HIGH MASTERY

Self-understanding and self-control
Includes
• Insight into interpersonal relations and
repeating personality patterns of self
• Making dynamic links between past and present
relationships
• Interpersonal union
• Emotional self-control over conflicts and new
changes in emotional responding
• Self-analysis.

Predominantly expressive techniques that convey
to patients that the therapist
• Can help promote self-understandings by suggesting
reasons why patients might think, feel, and act in a
certain way to situations
• Encourages confidence in the patient's ability to self-
analyze
• Notices and reinforces gains in self-control and
relationship improvements
• Supports them through the ending of therapy.

Figure 6.4. Patient functioning and therapy techniques in the three phases of mastery.

Case Study

The therapeutic progress of a successful case over the course of psychotherapy illustrates how these levels signal shifts in therapist focus. Jenni, a 22-year-old with generalized anxiety disorder with psychosomatic symptoms (back pains, nausea, vomiting), was treated for 3 months by a female psychotherapist. Jenni was referred to psychotherapy by her physician, who was prescribing antidepressant and anxiolytic medication for her distress. Prior to referral, her symptoms had been assessed by several specialists who had not identified a physical disorder.

Working With Patients in Phase 1 (Low Mastery): The Beginning of Therapy

When working with patients in the first phase of mastery, the therapist must be able to tolerate high levels of patient defenses, symptoms, confusion, and ambivalence. This is particularly the case when patients are manifesting ego boundary disorders or extreme impulse control disorders; are denying, blocking, or avoiding thinking or feeling; or are projecting or introjecting negative affect or paranoia. The mastery research shows that patients in the early stages of mastery express a lot of negative affect, including helplessness and guilt, and are often confused or ambivalent about their feelings and thoughts. Therapists working with such patients are mainly concerned with conveying that they understand them (through affirmation), are able to help them, can provide direction and hope for the future (through advice and praise), and can bear and understand their feelings (through empathic validation).

When patients are very sick, they often feel that no one has ever felt this way in the past, and therefore the therapist could not possibly understand them. They may believe that nothing can help them; they may have very low self-efficacy about the effectiveness of treatment. Some believe that the therapist couldn't be strong enough to cope with the level and intensity of their affect. A good therapeutic alliance promotes and predicts gains in mastery (chapter 7) and can be built, in part, by conveying empathy and understanding of their problems. Therapists must also promote hope in their patients and a sense of direction by negotiating therapeutic goals and developing a therapeutic formulation. In this case study, the first task of therapy was to be supportive of Jenni in her distress and to show that her problems could be understood.

Jenni had presented for psychotherapy on the recommendation of her physician. She had no insight into the origins of her anxiety and psychosomatic symptoms, thinking that she was suffering a biomedical disorder. The relationship between biological, psychological, and social problems was dissociated:

> *Therapist:* How much do you think that all that has got to do with your physical complaints?
>
> *Jenni:* Well, all the doctors have been telling me for 6 months that it was stress. And I didn't believe them. I went from doctor, to doctor, to doctor, and I didn't, I've always thought that I could handle it but . . . things like this have happened in my life and I didn't let it get to me, I didn't let it change me or make me depressed. Or, —I got on, I . . . and even now I'm finding it hard . . . to accept that . . . I'm stressed. I, I honestly think that my mother has got nothing to do with it . . . .

Here the therapist is seeking elaboration about the patient's insight into the link between her symptoms and her history. Jenni had had a difficult childhood. She was sexually abused by a family friend at age 11 and was emotionally abused by her mother until she ran away from home and left school, at age 14 years. Her mother was cruel, neglectful, and punished her regularly (both physically and emotionally) and made unreasonable and capricious demands on her. One of the first themes dealt with in therapy was her feelings of anger, which presented itself in tandem with helplessness. Her current functioning indicated very low mastery. The mental pain of confronting her previous history created a sense of panic and terror, which she defended against by numbness:

> *Therapist:* So you've got a feeling of being alone, and helplessness; and on the other side a feeling of anger and frustration. I wonder what is in the middle?
>
> *Jenni:* [pause] I don't know. Nothing I suppose. A feeling of nothingness. Sometimes when I get really upset I just—I don't know what I feel sometimes.
>
> *Therapist:* Is it numbness, or emptiness?
>
> *Jenni:* Emptiness, I suppose. Sort of just, sometimes you just don't feel anything, you feel too—like I get really cranky—and and cry or—or then I have a tantrum or something—afterwards you always feel . . . empty.

By affirming Jenni's current mental state, the therapist shows support and invites her to further elaborate. Jenni shows blocking defenses (Mastery Scale Item 1C) and uncontrolled emotional functioning, vacillating between helplessness (2I) and anger (2F). Her defense against the overwhelming anger and anxiety she feels over the abuse leads her to frequently repress it. Her feeling of shame had prevented her from being able to confide in others. When discussing the abuse, she reveals that in her mind, she felt that it was her fault because her mother frequently gave her the message that she was naughty and did bad things. She is starting to see that the anger she feels toward her mother is an important factor to consider. However, her multiple abuse experiences have reinforced a very strong flight–avoidance–dissociation response (with its attendant psychological and psychosomatic symptoms), rather than a fight–confrontation response.

> *Jenni:* [pause] . . . well I . . . I don't know. um . . . [pause] . . . [slowly:] I always felt . . . not quite good enough, um . . . that I was a bad person because what had happened when I was eleven . . . um . . . with that man . . . and . . . I always thought, well—my mother—she was right, and that I had to be like a better person. Um . . . [pause] . . . I, I, really . . . it's hard to sort of . . . think back on it now . . . um . . . [pause] . . .
>
> *Therapist:* I know it's painful

Jenni: but . . . [pause] . . . I really—I don't even know myself sometimes I just think —well that was like another life. That happened but . . . I don't know—it wasn't really me. It feels now like it didn't happen. Was so long ago. It's sort of hard to . . . to think like, I suppose you make yourself forget . . . a lot of things

Therapist: Like you shut yourself from feeling so that you wouldn't get too much pain.

Jenni: mm . . . [pause] . . . my doctor thinks that my biggest problem is what happened to me when I was eleven. But, like I've said to Aunty Janis, it's like it happened to someone else. Now, I don't . . . think about it. She's been really worried about that side of it more than Mum—the Mum side of it. So is Greg. And the doctor. I really . . . well I don't. My doctor wants me to tell Grandma and Grandpa . . . and . . . well I don't, I don't want to dwell on it . . . I don't want to to feel like [teary voice:] ashamed or . . . or um [teary voice:] I don't want them to pity me! [cries] mm- mm- you know? . . . I, I'm . . . because it doesn't hurt me now.

Therapist: But you still blame yourself?

Jenni: [pause] . . . yeah, sort of . . . um . . . he thinks that I should go and face this person. And . . . tell him what he did was wrong. But I sort of got a fear of seeing him like I fear seeing Mum.

The therapist mainly uses supportive techniques, affirming Jenni's mental state ("I know it's painful") and seeking clarification of her feelings ("But you still blame yourself?"). At the end of the first phase of psychotherapy, her psychosomatic and anxiety symptoms are linked in her mind to her mother's harsh neglect and her sexual abuse. With these links coming together, she is able to begin looking at how she needs to work on her current interpersonal world to elicit more support. In addition, she does not need to rely to the same extent on blocking defenses and repression, because she is beginning to clarify the real and imagined aspects of her history through the telling of narratives while putting the past into the context of her current life. These changes are brought about because she feels that the therapist not only supports her but also is showing her a way to come to terms with her problems and alleviate her distress.

Working With Patients in Phase 2 (Medium Mastery): Middle Phase of Psychotherapy

The key feature of the middle phase of mastery is the patient's struggle to understand and control responses within an interpersonal context. The therapist needs to maintain an interpersonal focus in order to advance the patient beyond a reliance on defenses or a preoccupation with symptoms and toward greater mastery. In particular, patients need to explore how interpersonal conflicts or problems are received, both by the self and by others. Interpersonal and intrapersonal conflict around issues of identity, autonomy, intimacy, and generativity is often at the core of patients' difficulties. Using the related core conflictual relationship theme (CCRT) method (see chapter 3), therapists can guide their formulations and interpretations to address these conflicts and promote mastery of them (for a complete discussion of using the CCRT in clinical practice, see Book, 1998).

A particularly salient focus of therapeutic work probably involves analysis of patients' relationships with their parents and recent lovers, which may be especially helpful in promoting mastery (see chapter 7). During this phase, the key techniques of the therapist are geared to promoting interpersonal and personal awareness of the sources of conflicts, through the telling of narratives. The therapist should use a combination of supportive and expressive techniques, focusing on the techniques of elaboration, clarification, and confrontation. The link between the symptoms and the interpersonal problems should be made. As patients are still struggling to understand themselves and the reactions of others, supportive techniques must be maintained as the bedrock of therapy, to continue fostering the therapeutic alliance.

In the case of Jenni, the roots of her anxiety lie in a problematic relationship with her mother, which is also affecting her present relationships. Because of the abuse she had experienced and her feeling of not being protected and cared for when she was younger, she has become estranged from her immediate family and now realizes the importance of seeking the support of relatives (aunts, uncles, grandparents). She married her boyfriend Greg who had helped her run away, and their relationship is stable. It is often observed that patients only come to therapy when their lives are sufficiently stable, and they have the support to allow them to bear the pain and the hard work involved in therapy.

After a considerable number of psychotherapy sessions, she decided to confront her Aunt Dee about the abuse, after which she related the following narrative:

Therapist: And the incident with Auntie Dee has compounded things.

Jenni: /Oh um, we haven't heard from her for a couple of days/and Grandma went around this morning/and told her to come around and talk to me/and get it sorted out./Because I didn't want to go around there, (2H)/because Janis was there . . . probably *xxx* flew off again . . ./so Auntie Dee came around/and we had a bit of a talk/but—it's not, it's not resolved really. (3J)/It's not back the way it was before we had the argument./But, we talked about it (5S)/and . . . she doesn't like to talk about things, (4N)/she just likes to forget about it. (4N)/I, I do too, to a certain extent, (5Q)/but I can't pretend that it never happened. (3L)/She is the type of person—she hasn't rung (5T)/or come around since it has happened./She is the type of person that would leave it a fortnight (5T)/and then come around as if nothing had happened./

Therapist: This is what Janis said on Wednesday, isn't it?

Jenni: /Yeah yeah,/so she hasn't been around or rung./Rung anyone, not even the rest of the family./And Grandma just went around there this morning,/because she has been really worried (4N)/and upset the last couple of days./So she went around and told her to come around./When she came around she just walked in and sat down./She didn't want to say anything (4N)/—I had to talk to her/and I—and when I started she said "I'd rather just forget about it"/and I said "I would too, I'd rather forget that thing happened (5Q)/but we sort of got to talk about it a bit, (3J)/and then once we have talked about it then we can leave it."/That was very frustrating, (2E)/not—waiting these last couple of days/—not knowing what was going on, (3J)/what was happening./And I felt really, I don't know, at loose ends I suppose. (3K)/

Therapist: You felt angry?

Jenni: /Mm, angry, (2F)/I was more upset at first (2E)/but as . . . the last few days have gone on,/I've got more and more angry about it. . . . (2F)/I was cranky at her—for not coming around (2F)/and talking to me about it./

Therapist: Not giving you the opportunity to say what you wanted to say

Jenni: /Yeah, yeah,/I was getting madder at her, (2F)/thinking—"she's she's got no right to . . . to start something (2F)/and then just—to start a fight and then walk away and leave it"/and I was . . . oh . . . I didn't, when we had the fight/I really didn't get to say anything (2I)/because I was too upset. (2E)/And those two were yelling./And, well I—even when the fight happened I didn't really say anything. (2I)/And, she came around/and had her say/and I didn't really get to—to say my say, (2I)/and the last . . . first I was upset because it happened (2E)/and I just wanted to fix it (3L)/and the last two days . . . sh . . . you know, her not coming around—/it's sort of building up and building up (2E)/and when she came around this morning,/and she was gone,/I was glad that we had done it. (6U)/And got it over with./And now we can sort of . . . just try and go on. (3L)/

Therapist: So what did you get over? How did it help you?

Jenni: /Well, I was scared about talking to her. (2E)/

Therapist: Because?

Jenni: /I don't know, (3J)/I just was . . . I felt/

Therapist: That you would be rejected or was it - was that what it is?

Jenni: /Well, a bit of that/and bit of—that we'd have like another fight./And *xxx* trying to smooth it over./And . . . well I'm, I'm not really that type of person either. (5Q)/I don't like confrontations. (5Q)/I'm a bit like Auntie Dee, (5Q)/and I can understand how she feels, (4N)/sometimes I'd rather just forget about things . . . (5Q)/but something that big you just can't leave. (3L)/Otherwise things—well they just won't be the same./You have to . . . I need to talk about things (3L)/but I'm scared about doing it (2E)/and I find it hard to do it . . . (5Q)/I know myself— (5Q)/if I don't—if I didn't ⌐ . . . even though I was scared,/I knew that it was . . . I had to do it, (3L)/and I had to make myself do it . . . (3L)/

Therapist: So what were you scared that might happen?

Jenni: /Well, that we would have another fight,/or, or she wouldn't believe what I was saying . . . (2G)/

Therapist: Wouldn't believe what I was saying, because she wasn't believing you last time, was she? [no] If people don't believe you, what do you feel?

Jenni: /[very quietly:] [pause] um, that like I am lying or *xxx* /

Therapist: You feel that you are lying because—

Jenni: /—what they would think— (2G)/that I was lying [spoken together with therapist]/

Therapist: —that you were lying yeah.

Jenni: /and . . . I know that I wouldn't lie over something like that, with Auntie Dee,/and . . . just the fact that you are being really honest—/and they, they don't believe you— (2G)/

Therapist: So what is the feeling you have, when you are in that situation?

Jenni: /Frustration. (2E)/[pause] Upset, (2E)/and just . . . feel . . . I don't know, (3J)/like you can't . . . can't cope or . . . [pause] (1A)/

Therapist: Cope with what?

Jenni: /With her not believing me. (2G)/.

In this passage the therapist is focused on helping Jenni elaborate her narrative (e.g., "so what is the feeling you have, when you are in that situation?") and clarify her responses to the conflicts (e.g., "you felt angry?"). The therapist both encourages an elaboration of the other protagonists' role (Dee and Janis) in the conflict and probes Jenni's own reactions. The principal focus is kept at the level of the interpersonal narrative. As presented in Figure 6.5, the overall picture is of the client struggling (3L) with her interpersonal tendency to avoid the confrontations (2H), which are so obviously distressing (2E). She is angry (2F) at how the other person is avoiding the issues but recognizes that she has a similar pattern of reacting to interpersonal difficulties (5Q). Although she has some insight into both her and the other person's pattern of relating (5T), she does not feel in control of the situation (1A). She clearly struggles to master her feelings (3L) but nevertheless is persecuted by her own perception that other people harbor negative thoughts toward her (2G).

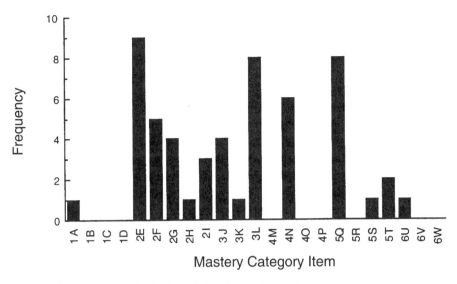

Figure 6.5. Frequency distribution of Jenni's mastery category scores in relationship episode narrative from middle in therapy.
Note. The mastery score for this sample was 3.1 (52%; sum of mastery scores / number of scorable clauses, i.e. 165/53).

This passage shows evidence of quite a range of mastery levels. Adequate mastery is shown by the following:

- her understanding of her own repetitive tendency to avoid confrontations,
- her awareness of the interpersonal nature of difficulties,
- her consideration of the other person's point of view and weaknesses in the situation, and
- her struggle to improve the situation.

Instances where she shows lower levels of mastery include the following:

- her interpersonal avoidance,
- her feelings of being persecuted, and
- her inability to think or assert herself during one episode.

As is typical of the middle phase of psychotherapy, Jenni is struggling to understand her reactions and responses within interpersonal situations, but she is also becoming aware that other people's responses contribute to, and help explain, the outcome of interpersonal conflicts. The therapist promotes the development of this mastery by working with her to elaborate and clarify the interpersonal difficulties, as they are presented in the narratives. Seeing the contribution of the other person is a crucial gain in the development of mastery. Jenni has moved on from a preoccupation with symptoms, prevalent in Phase 1, and is now actively working on the current interpersonal context of her problems.

Working With Patients in Phase 3 (High Mastery): Self-Understanding and Self-Control

In this phase, the therapist uses predominantly expressive techniques, including the judicious use of interpretation and confrontation. The mastery research has shown that patients tend to zigzag through different mastery levels (in the sense that within a single patient narrative, contrasting mastery levels are often present), so even in the final phases of psychotherapy there is always a place for very supportive techniques, particularly in response to termination anxiety. When the therapist maintains an interpersonal therapeutic focus over time, patients are able to develop insight into the origins of their difficulties, begin to control their emotional responses to conflicts, and maintain these gains through self-analysis. In this phase, patients are able to connect disparate parts of their life story narrative, to understand themselves and others more fully, and to interact in a way that is less conflictual and more rewarding.

In this case study, as therapy progressed Jenni was able to confront her avoidance–flight–dissociation defense, begin to assert herself in interpersonal situations, and begin to understand how her characteristic reactions to situations were caused by her past history. This led her to understand and begin to control these responses, while recognizing her characteristic ways of dealing with interpersonal conflicts. She also ceased all anxiolytic and antidepressant medication. During the final phases of psychotherapy, she presented the following narrative to the psychotherapist, which demonstrates not only her characteristic pattern of relating (avoidance and distress), but also her increasing ability to understand and control this response, allowing new more adaptive ways of approaching conflicts to be put to use.

Therapist: So it is hard to get that middle ground [mm]

Jenni: /I know because we have got someone living with us at the moment, David,/and it's a very—he works with Greg,/and a lot of our friends—they all work together./And, he's just started having, I don't know, an affair,/what you could say, with one of the girls in the, in the like group—the group of friends./And, another one was always really attracted to David./And we found out,/because he was living with us,/well we didn't say anything/because it wasn't our problem. (4P)/And the other one that liked David/—I was pretty close with. (5S)/And just before I came,/about—oh, 3 or 4 weeks before I came down here,/she found out/and it all blew up./And she wouldn't speak to me/because—I, um, well I knew/and I didn't tell her./And I tried to explain to her that it wasn't my place to tell her. (4P)/And, that really hurt me (2E)/and upset me, (2E)/and Greg said "well—you should learn to forget about it—she's the one with the problem"/and um "she's got to snap out of it,/you can't do anything about it."/And well it really hurt (2E)/because I didn't think I'd done anything wrong. (6W)/And that, sort of, I suppose knocks the wind out of me. (2E)/Things like that./[mm] She's, she's come around now,/but I don't know how to cope with, with things like that. (3J)/And, Greg sort of says "oh well if she's not talking to me—fine—that's her problem"/and he gets on with it I suppose/and I—that sort of hurts a lot. (2E)/

Therapist: That's a bit like what happened when you were a kid—you got punished for doing nothing wrong. And then that gets into blaming yourself and feeling— "oh well, I'm not much good anyhow—I'm not really worthy of it or something like that". So Greg is telling you that it's the girl's problem— What are your feelings about her and the way she reacted?

Jenni: /Well, I was disappointed that she would be angry with me./Um and that she, she couldn't see that (4N)/—I understood that she was hurt, (4N)/but she wasn't talking to me/but she was talking to David./And I thought that, well, it should be the other way around. (4M)/She should be cranky with David if she's going to be cranky with someone. (4M)/And . . . [pause] um . . . [pause] I'm not sure . . . (3J)/

Therapist: So how do you interpret her behavior like that?

Jenni: /I understood that she was hurt, (4N)/but I thought she was being childish about it. (4M)/That I knew that she was hurt (4N)/and that she wanted to sort of lash out at someone. (4N)/And, but I, I, was trying to be there for her. (5S)/And, sort of be nice and help her. (5S)/But she didn't—I suppose she didn't want my help./

Therapist: So does that make you wonder about your friendship with her?

Jenni: /Yes. Because I thought we were closer than that. (5T)/

Therapist: And what do you think of it now?

Jenni: /Well apparently Greg says she has been coming around to visit,/and asks about me and everything,/so hopefully when I go home I'll be able to like be the same as we were before. (3L)/I hope we can. (3L)/

Therapist: Do you think that's a good thing?

Jenni: /. . .well I think that the problem really wasn't with us two, (5T)/because with Dav- if it had been something that I'd done,/or there was a problem that had caused it between us two,/it probably would be different./But, I really like her/and I think she's a nice person,/and it was probably her way of dealing with something hurtful. (4N)/

Therapist: So what do you think you need to do with that friendship with her?

Jenni: /. . . [pause] I suppose, just, stand back (6U)/and see how things go./Not fix it, just see what happens. (6U)/

Therapist: Can you also re-define the friendship, have different rules for behavior in it? So that she is treating you the way that you are treating her?

Jenni: /Yes. Now I realize that if someone wants to be like that—well—/I'm not, I feel—I don't know, (3J)/whereas before I would be upset (5Q)/and it would really upset me—/I'm not as strong as Greg (5Q)/in the sense that I can forget about it,/I'm sort of a half way. (5Q)/

Therapist: Oh to say "forget about it" is very dismissive of your feelings.

Jenni: /I do look at her differently now, (6V)/an I realize that I do have a lot of other friends if she wants to be like that— (6U)/well she can./Um . . . and and it won't worry me as much. (6V)/I'll I'll let her go her own way. (6U)/That sort of thing./.

In this passage, the therapist is predominantly using expressive techniques, such as interpretation, confrontation, and clarification. For example, at one point the therapist states, "That's a bit like what happened when you were a kid—you got punished for doing nothing wrong. And then that gets into blaming yourself and feeling—'oh well, I'm not much good anyhow—I'm not really worthy of it or something like that'." Here the therapist uses interpretation to link the present problem to Jenni's past. This involves pointing out to her how the transference of feelings from the past (where her mother blamed her) is associated with her current symptoms of dysphoria and withdrawal arising in the present conflict. The therapist also confronts her about her reactions; for example: "oh to say 'forget about it' is very dismissive of your feelings." By so doing, she pushes Jenni to continue to engage with her feelings and not to avoid them by the low mastery blocking defenses, which she relied on at the beginning of therapy.

As illustrated in Figure 6.6, Jenni has achieved a sense of control (6U) over the conflict with her girlfriend by emotionally separating (6U) and putting into perspective the negative reactions expressed toward her (5T). She is seeing how her own ways of reacting contribute to her feelings of distress (5Q). Although the conflict is upsetting (2E), she is now "sort of half way" toward resolving her feelings (5Q). She has achieved this by not only understanding (4N) and challenging (4M) the way that her girlfriend responded to the problem, but also by seeing that she can control her own feelings and "look at her differently now" (6V).

These ways of negotiating and re-evaluating her responses to conflicts are a significant gain over her early functioning. Although much of her characteristic tendency toward avoidance is still present, she has considerably more mastery over it and is now able to modulate her feelings and, in turn, find more adaptive ways of dealing with such conflicts. At the end of therapy, she reflected on the changes wrought over the course of psychotherapy.

Therapist: How do you think you can achieve what you want?

Jenni: By talking to people, um . . . - um . . .Yeah. [pause] And just to think about things myself and try hard. . . . I will have to be honest and

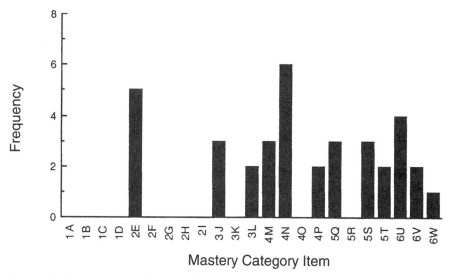

Figure 6.6. Frequency distribution of Jenni's mastery category scores in relationship episode narrative from late in therapy.
Note. The mastery score for this sample was 4.2 (70%; sum of mastery scores / number of scorable clauses, i.e. 151/36).

say that at first I was very scared about the idea of psychotherapy, but after the first few visits my attitude changed and I realized that I did have to deal with some issues in my life. I have really sat down and thought about myself as a person for the first time—who I was before I got sick, what my life was like, and what it all means. Now I look back and wonder why it was so hard and why it took me so long! [laughs] Now I realize that that is very important because the person that came down here sick and running away wasn't what I wanted to be. . . . Talking to someone was the first step to overcoming all this stuff. Just talking to someone is a big relief in itself.

Therapist: And talking . . . it's like it's your safety valve

Jenni: Yeah. I know now that I did have to talk about and face a few things concerning my mother, my abuser, and my relationship with Greg. It is like I have opened my eyes for the first time and thought about things that I continually pushed aside and refused to acknowledge. . . . At first talking and thinking about these things was very painful and hard, and even though there are things that we still need to work on . . . it's getting easier each time. I do realize that all those things can't be changed overnight, and that I have to work hard, but if I really want it to happen I can do it. I need to have a bit of patience, I suppose when things go a bit wrong.

In this passage, Jenni eloquently discusses the process of achieving mastery through psychotherapy. Through the telling of narratives, she is able to move beyond being dominated by her symptoms and defenses toward confronting the interpersonal context of her difficulties. She not only has worked on her past trauma but has also started to see how that trauma has affected her current functioning. Although the characteristic ways of responding are still there, she has now developed some self-understanding and self-control over them. She finds that "it's getting easier each time" and that rather than reacting blindly, with "a bit of patience" she is able to work through her difficulties. Although her psychotherapy was quite short (3 months), it provided enough support and understanding for her to be able to move onto the next phase of her life. The therapist reinforces these changes and encourages her to continue to talk about her problems after therapy is over. By talking about her feelings rather than blocking them, these affects are less likely to manifest themselves in the psychosomatic anxiety symptoms that brought her to therapy. The therapist is therefore reinforcing the changes brought about through the telling of narratives in therapy and is helping Jenni to avoid a relapse.

CONCLUSION

This chapter presents a view of the changes that patients make in psychotherapy, coded using the Mastery Scale, which illustrates and illuminates the types and degree of changes that psychotherapy can bring about. Actual patient cases are presented to illustrate how patients develop mastery and how therapists help augment mastery. Mastery is conceived as a continuum, but generally three phases of mastery are discernable. The mastery concept offers therapists a guide and a window into the kinds of specific changes patients can and do make during therapy. By knowing about these changes, detecting them, and organizing them in terms of mastery, therapists have a way of seeing where patients are currently functioning and what is needed to move them forward. Therapists are then able to assess the mastery level of their patients and choose interventions consisting of more supportive or more expressive techniques, so as to match patients' current functioning.

Phase 1, low mastery, is characterized by a dominance of symptoms and defenses. In this phase (which generally is equivalent to Levels 1 and 2 of the Mastery Scale), patients are distressed and unable to cope effectively with their problems. The key features in this phase are the dominance of symptoms and defenses, often accompanied by difficulties with interpersonal relationships. With patients in this first phase, therapists must be able to tolerate high levels of defenses, symptoms, confusion, and ambivalence in their patients and provide a supportive alliance. Therapists are mainly concerned with conveying to the patients that they understand (through affirmation), are able to help them and provide direction and hope for the future (through advice and praise), and can bear and understand their feelings (through empathic validation).

Phase 2, medium mastery, is characterized by a struggle to understand and control responses within an interpersonal context. In this phase (which generally is equivalent to Levels 3 and 4 of the Mastery Scale), patients question themselves and others in their life in the struggle to understand their reactions and improve their relationships. The key feature in this phase is the active search for connection with themselves and others. The two levels within mastery for this phase are difficulties in understanding and control, where patients try to sort out their personal feelings and reactions, and interpersonal awareness, where patients begin to look outside themselves to their relationships with others, to understand the interrelationships between their own reactions toward others and others' reactions toward them.

This movement or shift in focus (from the singular world of individuals with their defenses and symptoms to the interpersonal world of self in relationship to others) is a defining moment in psychotherapeutic progress, perhaps the most important moment. The shift is a prognostic signal that patients are now ready to ground their experiences within a social context and are prepared to profit from whatever was learned during the therapeutic relationship. The therapist must maintain an interpersonal focus to help patients move beyond a reliance on defenses or a preoccupation with symptoms and toward greater mastery. In particular, through the telling of narratives, patients should be encouraged to explore and elaborate the reactions of others and to clarify their own responses to their interpersonal conflicts or problems.

This phase in mastery is where much of the hard work of the middle phases of psychotherapy occurs. It characterizes the working through of relationship conflicts.

Phase 3, high mastery, is characterized by self-understanding and self-control within interpersonal context. In this phase (which generally is equivalent to Levels 5 and 6 of the Mastery Scale), patients are able to connect disparate parts of their life story narrative, to understand themselves and others more fully, and to be able to interact in a way that is less conflictual and more rewarding. The central feature in this phase is the sense of connection with themselves and others. The two key levels within mastery for this phase are self-understanding, where there is a ready and active awareness of typical reactions of self and others and a consequent ability to be meaningfully close to another, and self-control, where patients are emotionally free and flexible, actively anticipating and clarifying their responses to interpersonal and personal situations. In working with patients in Phase 3, the therapist is able to use predominantly expressive techniques, including judicious use of interpretation (such as linking the past and the present), confrontation (such as challenging defenses), and working with the CCRT.

The significance of this third phase of psychotherapy is that it heralds the arrival of readiness for termination. Gains in self-understanding and self-control should be reinforced, and the meaning of termination should be discussed with patients to avoid a relapse. The consolidation of this phase in mastery helps foster future mental health, as individuals develop skills and insight so they may manage their own responses to future problems.

7

MASTERY AND INTERPERSONAL RELATIONS: THERAPEUTIC ALLIANCE, TRANSFERENCE, AND CORE RELATIONSHIPS WITH PARENTS AND LOVERS

Interpersonal relationships are central to both mastery and mental health in general. Jaspers (1951) has written that "man's supreme achievement in the world is communication from personality to personality" (p. 147). According to Sullivan (1953), isolation and loneliness are central problems of society. Reaching out to others and engaging in deep communication with them are complex and difficult endeavors that require high mastery. The ability to understand oneself and to take the perspective of the other person are important steps toward gaining mastery. As Marcel (1960) observed, "when somebody's presence does really make itself felt, it can refresh my inner being; it reveals me to myself, it makes me feel more fully myself than I should be if I were not exposed to its impact" (p. 13). The patient's relationship with the therapist is an opportunity for developing an intimate, trusting relationship, which can be formative for understanding oneself and one's responses to others. Forming a good, productive, and trusting relationship with the therapist should therefore be considered fundamental to effective psychotherapeutic progress; research overwhelmingly bears this out. My first aim in this chapter is to explore the relationship between the therapeutic alliance and gains in mastery. Understanding and controlling habitual patterns of relating to others that are problematic and conflictual are often at the core of psychotherapy. My second aim is to

141

explore how these transference-like patterns relate to mastery. My third aim is to look deeper into the types of relationships that people have and the role of mastery in them. People in psychotherapy often discuss many different types of relationships—with friends, family, work colleagues, lovers, acquaintances, and therapists. The impact of these different types of relationships and their differential contribution to mastery is then explored.

STUDY OF MASTERY AND THE THERAPEUTIC ALLIANCE

The collaborative relationship between the client and therapist consists of an emotional bond as well as a shared understanding about the goals and tasks of therapy (Bordin, 1979; Greenson, 1967). The therapeutic alliance has been consistently shown to be an important and significant predictor of change (Connors, DiClemente, Carroll, Longabaugh, & Donovan, 1997; A. O. Horvath, 1994; A. O. Horvath & Symonds, 1991; Krupnick et al., 1994; Krupnick et al., 1996). One striking finding in alliance research is that the perception of the alliance by the patient, rather than the therapist, is most strongly predictive of change (Horvath & Symonds, 1991). This suggests that patients' feelings are central to good psychotherapy, no matter how well or how poorly the therapist may think the therapy is proceeding.

Ratings of the alliance early in therapy are most predictive of outcome (Hartley & Strupp, 1983; Luborsky et al., 1983; Luborsky et al., 1985). Although the alliance early in therapy is known to be associated with improvement, the mechanism by which this occurs is not clear. Freud (1913/1958c) always distinguished between the so-called real relationship of therapist with patient and the relationship that involved unconscious transference and countertransference processes. However, distinguishing between the alliance and the transference has proved elusive. Gelso and Carter (1985) proposed that the therapeutic relationship has three dimensions—the real relationship, the working alliance, and the transference relationship—and developed 19 speculative propositions about how each relates to the other (Gelso & Carter, 1994). What seems clear is that negative transference reactions can impair the alliance, as can too many transference interpretations (Piper et al., 1991). Moreover, a working alliance can display a high-low-high pattern, with a "tear and repair" cycle (Bordin, 1994). Good alliances can be ruptured at different stages of therapy, usually when transference feelings are aroused by changes in the therapy frame. For example, a therapist who announces vacation dates may invoke powerful feelings of abandonment that can weaken the alliance. In successful therapy, the careful analysis of these feelings can help to repair and strengthen the alliance. Patients who improve in psychotherapy tend to obtain more positive responses from others and from themselves: "the therapeutic alliance reflects the positive bonds with the therapist; these bonds tend to fluctuate in tandem with positive expectations from others" (Luborsky, 1994, p. 47). A supportive helpful relationship with the therapist should provide a significant sense of security so that the interpersonal conflicts and problems can be mastered.

Much research has focused on tools to measure the therapeutic alliance (Tichenor & Hill, 1989). The majority of measures have consisted of questionnaires; however, a few researchers have used other methods, such as Q-sort (Price & Jones, 1998) and content analysis applied to transcripts of psychotherapy (Luborsky et al., 1983). The latter measure has the advantage that what is being measured is the actual process rather than a post hoc subjective perception rating as in the questionnaire method.

Although many studies have compared the therapeutic alliance to traditional measures of outcome, few have investigated its relationship with process measures of the internal workings of therapy. The importance of this task, as reviewed in chapter 1, is in furthering our understanding of why the therapeutic alliance appears to be such a potent therapeutic ingredient. The current effort to study the alliance has been almost entirely devoted to developing measures of the alliance and evaluating its relationship to outcome (for a comprehensive review, see Horvath, Gaston, & Luborsky, 1993). The field is therefore ready to extend this research with studies that look in more detail at how the alliance relates to other key process variables.

The study reported below examined the extent to which changes in mastery can be predicted from an early measure of the therapeutic alliance. The theoretical importance of this question lies in the fact that what is mastered in therapy are the interpersonal transference-related conflicts. A supportive helpful relationship with the therapist should provide the bedrock for the interpersonal conflicts to be worked through. The alliance was measured early in therapy because measuring the alliance later in therapy can lead to confounding the outcome with the alliance (e.g., if the therapy is going well in terms of a reduction in distress, then the patient tends to consider and respond to the therapist more favorably). Early-in-therapy alliance measures mostly avoid this difficulty. It was predicted that those patients who go on to show the most significant gains in mastery are the ones who had developed a good alliance with their therapist early in treatment. The hypothesis was that the strength of the patient's therapeutic alliance early in therapy is positively related to the patient's gains in mastery.

Participants and Treatment

The same 41 patients (29 women, 12 men, mean age = 25 years) from the Penn Psychotherapy Project (Luborsky et al., 1988; described in chapter 5) were used in this study. Treatment was based on weekly individual time-unlimited supportive–expressive psychoanalytic psychotherapy (Luborsky, 1984) within a mean treatment length of 54 weeks.

Therapeutic Alliance

The Penn Helping Alliance Counting Signs Method was used (Alexander & Luborsky, 1986; Luborsky, 1976; Luborsky et al., 1983) to measure the therapeutic alliance. The data used in the following analyses were the average scores of two raters; they were taken from an earlier published study, which reported acceptable interrater reliability between judges (Luborsky et al., 1983). This method involves finding literal, or nearly literal, cues of the quality of the helping alliance from the content of patients' speech in transcribed therapy sessions. This method is therefore similar to other content analysis methods, such as the Mastery Scale (chapter 4) and the Gottschalk–Gleser scales (Gottschalk et al., 1969). The specific content considered to be a "sign" of the helping alliance falls into two broad types. The first is the patient's perception of the therapist as being helpful, supportive, and facilitative of the treatment goals. The second is the sense that the therapist and patient are working together as a joint team with a positive bond. Both of these two types are rated as either positive, meaning that the characteristic is present, or negative, meaning that the opposite is true (signs that the therapist is unhelpful and the relationship is poor). Full details are given in Alexander and Luborsky (1986).

In this method, an external judge reads the transcripts, searching for instances in the dialogue that can be scored for therapeutic alliance. Each instance is then rated for intensity on a 5-point Likert scale (1 = *very low*, 5 = *very high*). The sum of the positive intensity scores is subtracted from the sum of the negative intensity scores to arrive at a difference score. In each analysis reported here the difference score was used as the measure of the helping alliance. The first 20 minutes of Sessions 3 and 5 were scored.

Mastery

The Mastery Scale, which is described in chapter 4, was used to measure mastery; the reliability and validity of the scoring of this sample are presented in chapter 5. The mean early-in-therapy mastery scores and the residual gain scores were used in the analyses in this study.

Two analyses were performed. A Pearson correlation coefficient was calculated to assess the relationship between early-in-therapy mastery scores and early-in-therapy alliance scores. The second analysis addressed the question of whether the helping alliance scale predicts gains in the mastery of interpersonal conflict. A simple regression analysis was performed. One patient's scores on the Helping Alliance were not available (total $N = 40$, $df = 39$).

Results

The relationship between the early-in-therapy helping alliance score and the early-in-therapy mastery score was significant ($r = .32$, $p < .05$). The helping alliance accounted for 10% of the variance of early mastery.

The ability of the early-in-therapy alliance scores to predict gains in mastery was represented by the regression equation $y = -.073 + (.049 * x)$, with the relationship between the variables found to be significant ($F = 16.46$, $p < .0002$). In all, 30% of the variance of the gains in mastery could be accounted for by early helping alliance. The relationship between the variables is shown in Figure 7.1.

Summary of Mastery and the Therapeutic Alliance Study

The study investigated the degree to which changes in mastery can be predicted from an early measure of the therapeutic alliance. The alliance was measured early in therapy because measuring the alliance later in therapy can lead to a confounding of outcome with alliance. The hypothesis of this study was that the strength of the patient's therapeutic alliance early in therapy is positively related to gains in mastery. The results strongly support this hypothesis.

Patients who had a better relationship with their therapist early in therapy went on to make larger gains in the mastery of their interpersonal conflicts. Patients who have higher initial levels of mastery were also able to form better relationships with their therapists. This result is hardly surprising: Individuals who have serious and pervasive interpersonal conflicts would be expected to have difficulty forming positive relationships with others, including their therapist. Overall, 30.2% of the variance of gains in mastery can be accounted for by the helping alliance. This highlights the importance of being able to form one good relationship (i.e., with the therapist) to

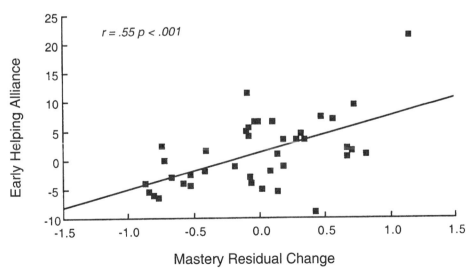

Figure 7.1 Relationship between early Penn Helping Alliance and mastery residual change scores. ($N = 40$)

master more pervasive and maladaptive relationship conflicts. It is probably also the case that support from the relationship with a therapist helps patients understand and control their long-term interpersonal difficulties. How these longer term transference-related difficulties are mastered is the subject of the next study.

STUDY OF MASTERY AND THE TRANSFERENCE PATTERN

One of Freud's (1914/1958e) great discoveries was that the patient's unconscious wishes and previous vivid or defining experiences repeat themselves in behavior, in the sense that they attach or transfer into relationships with others, including the therapist. This phenomenon of transference is an example of the compulsion to repeat, which is the tendency to repeat sequences of behaviors and reactions that have been formed out of early experiences: "the transference is itself only a piece of repetition, and . . . the repetition is a transference of the forgotten past not only on to the doctor but also on to all the other aspects of the current situation" (p. 151; see chapter 2 for a fuller discussion). What is transferred or repeated in current relationships, then, is the expectation about relationships formed out of early experiences. If early experiences are traumatic and frustrating, then one may have problems with effectively getting needs and wishes met. Ineffective and maladaptive methods of satisfying wishes within relationships are commonly found in psychotherapy patients, and it is one central task of psychotherapy to master (understand and control) the tendency to repeat these core conflictual relationship themes (CCRT; Luborsky & Crits-Christoph, 1998). Because symptoms arise directly out of these maladaptive transference-related patterns (Freud, 1926/1959), it is predicted that increases in mastery evidenced in more positive CCRT narratives should be associated with greater feelings of well-being and health and that more negative CCRT patterns in narratives should be associated with lower mastery and poorer mental health. The study reported below examined this relationship between mastery and the transference pattern.

Measurement of the Repetition Compulsion

Measuring the action of the repetition compulsion had proven elusive until Luborsky (1977) noticed that this pattern could be found within the narratives of relationship episodes (REs) that patients typically discuss with their therapists in psychotherapy. The basic transference pattern could be extracted into three CCRT components: the wishes, needs, or desires (W) expressed implicitly or explicitly by the patient toward the other person; the response from the other (RO) person to these wishes; and the corresponding response of self (RS) that the interaction evokes (see chapter 3 for further details).

When a person's relationship narrative is of the form "I wish (W) to be loved, and the other person (RO) is affectionate, and I (RS) feel close," we say that the outcome of the RO and the RS are positive (i.e., that their need to be loved is satisfied). Luborsky (1998a) defined positive responses as where "there is noninterference or expectation of noninterference with the satisfaction of wishes or a sense of mastery in being able to deal with the wishes" (p. 30).

On the other hand, if the RE is "I wish (W) to be loved, but the other person (RO) rejects me, and I become (RS) frustrated," then clearly the outcome of satisfying the wish in this interaction is negative: The person feels frustrated at being rejected. Luborsky (1998a) defined a negative response as "one in which, to the patient, interference with satisfaction of the wishes has occurred or is expected to occur" (p. 30).

Quantification of Positive and Negative Narratives

Several studies have compared levels of positive and negative narratives across different samples. In one study, narratives were obtained from 18 children who were interviewed at ages 3 and 5 years using a guided and prompted story completion task about a doll family (Buchsbaum & Emde, 1990). The children's narratives were scored with the CCRT, and the percentage of positive and negative components were computed. At age three, 69% of the ROs were positive, and at age five 71% were positive. For the RS component, 63% were positive at age 3 and 77% were positive at age 5. Thus, most of the doll family narratives told by the young children contained positive ROs and positive RSs.

These findings with children are in strong contrast with those typically found in adult patients in psychotherapy. For example, in the Penn depression study (Diguer, Barber, & Luborsky, 1993), only 21% of combined RO and RS components of the 30 participants were positive. Similarly, patients with major depression seen on an outpatient basis at Penn (N = 20) had only 19% of combined RO and RS positive components (Eckert, Luborsky, Barber, & Crits-Christoph, 1990). These results are similar to those found in patient reports of dreams versus waking narratives told during psychotherapy (Popp et al., 1998; Popp et al., 1996). It was found that in both dreams and waking narratives told late in therapy, negative components ranged from 67% to 76% for RO and 65% to 80% for RS. An interesting finding was that the RS in waking narratives was significantly more negative than in dreams, which might suggest the influence of striving toward wish fulfillment in the dreams.

For further contrast, two studies provide data on normal nonpatient adult controls. In Ulm, Germany, 36 young women (mainly medical students; mean age = 23.8 years, range = 20 to 30 years) were asked to provide narratives about their relationships, and the resulting narratives were CCRT scored (Dahlbender et al., 1992). Thirty-seven percent of RO components were positive, and 43% of the RS were positive. In another German study with 30 adult nonpatients, 35% of RS components were positive (Cierpka et al., 1992).

In summary, children's narratives appear to be far more positive in both RO and RS components, whereas the adult nonpatient narratives appear to be more negative, and those of psychotherapy patients considerably more negative. The different conditions under which each set of narratives was collected may partly explain the results. With the children, actual interactions were not prompted; rather, the children completed a fictitious doll family story. In this respect, some of their answers may be heavily infused with wish-fulfillment fantasies. Furthermore, the narratives collected from the patients were told in the context of psychotherapy, where presumably they are focusing on their most troublesome problems through the telling of negative and problematic relationship narratives.

It also appears that contextual factors within psychotherapy may have an influence on the magnitude of the positive versus negative dimensions in psychotherapy. For example, in one study patients told REs about the therapist that were less negative than REs told about others: For the RO and RS components, 55.8% and 61.5% respectively were negative for the therapist REs compared with 81.5% and 88/5% respectively for other REs (Fried, Crits-Christoph, & Luborsky, 1998). This suggests either that patients had difficulty telling negative REs about the therapist in the therapists' presence or that their relationship with the therapist was in fact less negative. Despite these possible confounds, it still remains plausible that there are genuine developmental differences in the emotional valence of relationship narratives from childhood through adulthood, with adults being "sadder yet wiser" in appraising their own and others' motives.

Interpretation of Narratives

Positive and negative narratives can be interpreted on a number of levels. On the surface is the interpersonal dimension, which assumes that the narrative is an account of an actual interaction. The outcome of the interaction may be a positive or negative one for the narrator. A more fundamental level is the object relations dimension, where one can more clearly see internal dynamic conflicts distorting the way the relationship interaction proceeds. Freud discussed (1912/1958a) how in relation to the therapist both positive and negative transference patterns are likely to emerge: "we must make up our minds to distinguish a 'positive' transference from a 'negative' one, the transference of affectionate feelings from that of hostile ones" (p. 105). The wishes are expressions of drives, which may or may not have clear unconscious roots (e.g., sexual drives may be manifest in affiliative wishes). Positive responses of others and self usually refer to successful gratification of drives, whereas negative responses refer to unsuccessful gratification of drives, as predicted by the biopsychosocial drive theory (chapter 2). The importance of this for mental health is that undischarged drive energies manifest in negative symptoms such as anxiety, which eventually lead the sufferer to seek psychological treatment.

In relation to the positive transference, Freud (1913/1958c) commented that typically (though not always) at the beginning of treatment "the patient's happy trustfulness makes our earliest relationship with him a very pleasant one" (p. 126). The only danger with the positive transference is in the case of transference-love: the propensity of the patient to fall in love with the therapist and similar figures (Freud, 1915/1958b). Because the therapist is seen as being helpful by the patient, we can say that the relationship is a positive one, and a good therapeutic relationship is known to predict a successful psychotherapy outcome and improvements in mastery.

By and large, the major focus of treatment interventions within psychotherapy is on the negative transference. Negative transference is generally considered to mean the projection of hostile and paranoid feelings into relations with the therapist and others in the patient's life or of depressive and helpless feelings onto the self. The expectation of a negative outcome in terms of the wish leads the patient to project this negative expectation into relationships with others. Luborsky, Barber, Schaffler, and Cacciola (1998) found that the most frequent negative ROs were that the other "rejects or criticizes me" (33% of patients), "dominates or controls me" (27%), is "distant" (18%), or is "unhelpful or unreliable" (12%). The most common positive ROs were that the other is "close to me" (21%) and "likes me" (6%). For the response of self, the most common negative RS was that the person becomes "angry" (36% of patients), "withdrawn or distant" (24%), feels "inadequate or helpless" (21%) or engages in "self-blame" (18%). The most common positive RS was to feel "close to the other" (15%) and "assertive" (9%) and that they "like the other" (9%). Clearly, then, positive RO and RS CCRT components are linked to mental health and positive outcomes, negative components being linked to mental illness and distress.

Psychoanalytic theory posits that symptoms arise directly out of these maladaptive patterns. Accordingly, it was predicted (a) that more positive CCRT narratives should be associated with greater feelings of well-being and mastery and (b) that more negative CCRT patterns should be associated with greater distress and lower mastery.

On this last point, it was hypothesized that people who exhibit greater levels of positive CCRT components are more often able to fulfill their needs and wishes through their interpersonal relationships and that this would be reflected in associated increases in mastery. For these patients, narratives typically contain more positive interactions than patients in psychotherapy who are experiencing greater difficulties. Two studies were conducted. The first (Study A) investigated changes in the positive–negative dimension using the original CCRT scores from the Penn Psychotherapy Project (N = 41), and the second (Study B) rescored a representative portion of the sample (N = 20) using a more rigorous and finer detailed positive–negative scoring method than was used in the first study.

Study A: Mastery of Positive and Negative Transference Patterns

The participants in this study were 41 mixed-diagnosis patients from the Penn Psychotherapy Project (Luborsky et al., 1988; see chapter 5). The mean Mastery Scale scores from early- and late-in-therapy and residual gain scores were used. Two CCRT components from early and late in therapy were used: the response of self (CCRT-RS) and response of other (CCRT-RO). The sum of the negative responses was subtracted from the sum of the positive responses and divided by the total number of responses to obtain a score early and late in therapy reflecting the overall degree of positivity–negativity for each of the two CCRT components for each patient. A residual change score for positivity–negativity was then calculated to capture change across the course of therapy.

Percentages of positive and negative components were calculated to facilitate the description of the data. The relationships between the two sets of variables (mastery and CCRT) were investigated by calculating Pearson correlations. The average of two judges' scores were used for both the mastery and CCRT measures.

The first task was to describe the proportion of negative to positive CCRT components for both ROs and RSs. The results appear in Table 7.1. In general, four-fifths of CCRT components were negative, with little change over the course of therapy.

The relationships between the mastery and CCRT scores were calculated; the results are presented in Table 7.2. There were few significant relationships between the positive–negative CCRT scores and mastery. Of most

TABLE 7.1
Percentages of Positive and Negative Components in the CCRT(N = 41)

Response	% Positive	% Negative
Of others		
Early in therapy	20	80
Late in therapy	25	75
Of self		
Early in therapy	21	79
Late in therapy	24	76

Note. N = 41. CCRT = core conflictual relationship theme.

TABLE 7.2
Relationships Between Positive and Negative CCRT and Mastery Scores

Response	Mastery		
	Early	Late	Change
Of others			
Early	.58**	.37*	.26
Late	.02	.06	.06
Change	.08	.03	.03
Of self			
Early	.32*	.22	.21
Late	.16	.27	.37*
Change	.13	.08	.14

Note. $N = 41$. CCRT = Core conflictual relationship theme. * $p < .05$. ** $p < .01$.

interest, late-in-therapy scores on the RS component were significantly related to changes in mastery ($r = .37$, $p < .05$). This suggests that one improvement in mastery over therapy is in the patient's ability to cope with his or her responses to transference-related interpersonal conflict.

Consistent with earlier studies, narratives from both early and late in therapy were overwhelmingly negative. There was only a slight (approximately 4%) reduction in the negativity of narratives from early to late in therapy.

The analysis of the relationships between the RO and RS dimensions and mastery revealed some interesting findings. Early positivity–negativity was significantly related to early mastery levels for both the RO and RS dimension. Late-in-therapy RS was significantly related to the change in mastery over the course of therapy. This suggests that increases in mastery are reflected in the late-in-therapy RS, with only a slight increase in more positive responses.

Several problems with the above data lead to a small revision of the analysis. These CCRT data were the result of the first application of the CCRT to a large sample, and as such the methods used were not as rigorous as the recent CCRT method. First, each judge scored the REs freely and independently, and therefore combining their scores is not always meaningful. Second, judges were not instructed to evaluate carefully the positive–negative dimension, so some of the data may not be as valid as one would hope. Third, judges (inconsistently) used a "neutral" category in addition to the positive and negative dimension. The neutral category is no longer recommended in scoring the CCRT, for both theoretical and empirical reasons. Freud (1912/1958a) considered that transference reactions in theory could be either positive or negative with respect to wishes and that only gratification or frustration was possible; in other words, a "neutral" outcome was not, in fact, neutral. Recent research by Bargh and colleagues suggested that all perceptions are emotionally tinged with a positive or nega-tive valence, which appears to be automatic and instantaneous (Bargh, Chaiken, Govender, & Felicia, 1992). For these reasons, a subsample of the data were rescored using the most up-to-date CCRT scoring procedures. This comprises Study B, described in the following sections.

Study B: Mastery of Four-Category Positive and Negative CCRTs

Luborsky's (1977) original proposal was to divide responses to the wishes into one of two dimensions: positive (P) and negative (N). The agreement between two judges using this bipolar distinction is high: 95% for both the ROs and RSs (Luborsky et al., 1998). Popp et al. (1998) found that the reliability of scoring the negative dimension of the RO and RS was .76 and .79, respectively ($p < .00$).

The current rating method stipulates that each RO and RS compo-nent extracted should be rated using one of the following four categories: NN = strong negative, N = moderate negative, P = moderate positive, and PP = strong positive. For research purposes, these correspond to scores of –2, –1 and + 1, + 2, respectively. Although positive and negative scores are only applied to the RO and RS components, it is important for the scores to be evaluated in the context of the expressed or implied wishes. This is because the RO or RS is only positive or negative depending on the success in rela-tion to gratification of a wish.

When studying the positive–negative CCRT dimension, it is impor-tant to investigate the degree to which judges are able to reliably identify the positive–negative dimension using this new four-category distinction. The reliability of this scoring method was therefore assessed by having two independent judges rate the degree of positivity–negativity for the RS and RO components across 20 patients from the Penn Psychotherapy Project. The sample of the Penn Psychotherapy Project consists of 41 patients, and the set of 20 selected for this study was representative of the 41. Five of the patients were among the original 10 who had been classified as "improved," 5 patients who had been classified as "nonimproved," and 10 were from the original 21 in the middle group. In this way we ensured that we had a sample that covered the full range of positive and negative CCRT scoring possibili-ties. Transcripts from early in therapy (Sessions 3 and 5) and late in therapy (at the 90% completion mark) formed the database, and REs (generally 10 early in therapy and 10 late) were extracted and CCRT scored. Before the judges began the rating task, an independent judge located all scorable CCRT components to ensure that judges scored the same thought units. The two judges were both doctoral-level psychoanalytic researchers. A total of 386 REs were scored using the CCRT.

Of the 20 patients, 1 was married, 2 were divorced, and the remainder (17, or 85%) were single. The average age was 23 (range = 18–35), with 10 women and 10 men, none of whom had children. In terms of education, 2 had finished high school only, 7 were in college, 3 had completed college, 5 were pursuing higher degrees, and 2 had completed a postgraduate degree. All were undergoing supportive–expressive psychoanalytic psychotherapy, with a mean duration of 48 weeks (range = 27–102 weeks). There were 19 therapists, with a mean age of 35 (range = 26–47 years). All therapists were married psychiatrists; 12 had children, and 13 were residents at the time.

Interrater Reliability

The reliability of the judges' scoring was examined in two ways. First, reliability was assessed by taking the RE as the unit of analysis. The interrater reliability over 386 REs using Pearson's correlation coefficient was high. For the RO dimension, $r = .64$, $p < .0001$, and for the RS dimension, $r = .72$, $p < .0001$. Second, instances of scoring showing perfect agreement between judges were examined. For the RO, 278 of the 386 REs were scored identically between judges (72%), and for the RS, 274 were scored identically (71%).

Interrater reliability was then investigated taking participants ($N = 20$) as the unit of analysis rather than REs ($N = 386$). Average positive and negative scores were calculated for each judge per participant. For the RO component, the interrater reliability was .77 ($p < .001$); for the RS, it was .93 ($p < .001$).

Changes in Positive and Negative Dimensions Over the Course of Psychotherapy

The distribution of positive and negative scores for the RO and RS dimensions was investigated using this new scoring method. Given the high interjudge agreement, we pooled the data from the two judges. Overall, for the RO there were 8% NN scores, 51% N, 19% P, and 2% PP scores. For the RS, there were 10% NN, 46% N, 19% P, and 5% PP scores. These results are very similar to the distributions of positive and negative components found in other psychotherapy samples, as reviewed above, and are in accordance with those found for all 41 patients as reported in Study A (see p. 150, this chapter). In general, the bulk of transference CCRT narratives told by patients in psychotherapy are negative, that is, wishes and needs are often unsatisfied.

Percentages of positive and negative components were measured early and late in therapy to investigate changes in the proportion of each over the course of psychotherapy. The data of the 5 most improved and the 5 least improved patients were separated. This was done to graphically illustrate some of the patterns of change in the positive–negative dimensions. The results for the RS dimension appear in Figure 7.2; those for the RO dimension are presented in Figure 7.3.

For the 5 most improved (best) patients, there are large reductions in the number of RS negative (N and NN) components (around 35% reduction

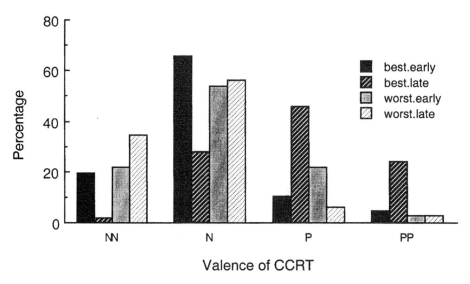

Figure 7.2 Percentages of the response of self component of the core conflictual relationship theme (CCRT) for five highly improved patients (best) and five least improved patients (worst) measured early and late in psychotherapy.
Note. NN = very negative, N = negative, P = positive, PP = very positive.

for N) and a parallel increase in the number of positive (P and PP) components from early in therapy to late in therapy (a 35% increase for P). This indicates an increase in the satisfaction of wishes and needs. For the 5 least improved (worst) patients, the pattern is in the reverse direction: There are

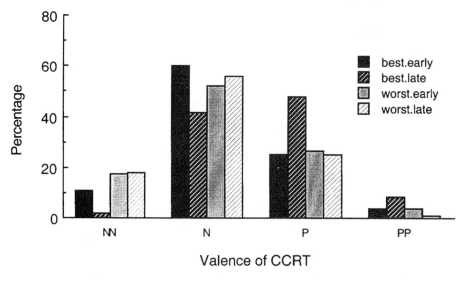

Figure 7.3. Percentages of the response of other component of the core conflictual relationship theme (CCRT) for five highly improved patients and five least improved patients measured early and late in psychotherapy.
Note. NN = very negative, N = negative, P = positive, PP = very positive.

actually increases in the NN component late in therapy and parallel reductions in the P component. For the worst patients, there appear to be increases in the perception of others as blocking the gratification of wishes, with their general perception of others found to be very negative throughout therapy. As the CCRT judges commented, these patients actually seemed to be getting worse; their relationship narratives were more conflictual and negative toward the end of therapy, compared with their initial level.

The pattern for the RO dimension (Figure 7.3) is similar to the RS dimension, but the changes are less striking. The best patients again reduced their negativity and increased their positivity within relationship conflicts, and for the worst patients the reverse trend occurred (albeit slightly). Overall, the RO dimension did not change as much over the course of psychotherapy for the most improved or the least improved patients. It appears in general that there is a slight reduction in the perception of others as blocking the gratification of wishes; however, the overall perception of others in the REs is negative throughout therapy.

Relationship of Transference Valence to Mastery

The final aim of the mastery of the four-category positive and negative CCRTs study was to investigate the relationship of the positive–negative dimension to the Mastery Scale and a commonly used psychotherapy outcome measure, the Health–Sickness Rating Scale (HSRS; Luborsky, Diguer, Luborsky, McLellan, et al., 1993). The HSRS, a 100-point scale of degrees of mental health–sickness, is rated by a trained observer on the basis of data collected from a clinical interview. Table 7.3 presents the results of the analyses.

Like the results reported in "Study A: Mastery of Positive and Negative Transference Patterns," in this study the RS component appears to be related in an important way to clinical changes. There was significant concordance between the RS components and the Mastery Scale scores both early and late in therapy. The RS late-in-therapy measure appeared to be a particularly good index of psychological mastery. A strong relationship was observed between RS late and residual change and late-in-therapy Mastery and HSRS scores. In addition, residual change in the RS component was significantly related to residual and late mastery scores and termination HSRS. After using the new scoring conventions, the RO component was not related to mastery, either at intake or termination. The RO component showed a weak relationship to the outcome variables. Early-in-therapy RO was related to early-in-therapy mastery scores, and changes in the RO over therapy were related to termination HSRS scores.

Consistent with other studies reviewed, the adult patients in this study appear to have very negative relationship narratives, particularly when compared with children and with other adults who were not in therapy. Judges were able to agree very well on the scoring of the positive and negative dimensions of the CCRT, probably because of the simplicity and clarity of the scoring method for these dimensions. The revised four-category scoring

TABLE 7.3
Pearson Correlations Between Positive and Negative CCRT Response
of Other (RO) and Response of Self (RS) Scores With the Mastery
Scale and Health–Sickness Rating Scale (HSRS)

Measure	RO		RS		Change	
	Early	Late	Early	Late	RO	RS
Mastery						
Early	.67*	−.15	.68*	.15	−.47	−.00
Late	.26	.35	.24	.82*	.30	.57*
HSRS						
Intake	.18	.45*	−.12	.38	.29	.39
Termination	.03	.47*	−.19	.64*	.47*	.46*
Change						
Mastery	.09	.31	.12	.70*	.38	.51*
HSRS	−.20	.19	.02	.49*	.32	.16

Note. Scores are for early in therapy, late in therapy, and residual change over therapy ($N = 20$). CCRT = core conflictual relationship theme. *$p < .05$.

method appears meaningful, adds further specificity to the measurement, and is recommended for future studies.

It appears from the data in this study that the RO dimension is only indirectly related to clinical changes. Although some relationships were found in Study A (see page 151, this chapter), these are not considered to be as reliable or valid as the findings from Study B on the mastery of four-category positive and negative CCRTs, for which a more rigorous method was used. However, the latter study had only a modest sample size, so the results can only be considered preliminary until the study is replicated. The lack of a relationship between the RO dimension of the CCRT could in part be because the Mastery Scale specifically limits scoring only to self-statements and self-reflections on others, whereas the CCRT is more broad in that statements made by others are scored. For example, direct quotations of others in narratives can be scored in the CCRT but not in the Mastery Scale.

Changes in the positivity and negativity of transference patterns found in psychotherapy patient narratives were small but clinically meaningful in that they relate to changes in mastery (Grenyer & Luborsky, 1998a, 1998b). With a revised, finer detailed method of scoring the CCRT valence, however, these findings only related to the changes in the RS dimension of the CCRT, which shifted in clinically meaningful ways.

Summary of Mastery and the Transference Pattern Studies

The major finding of the research reported in this section is that the valence of the transference is an important correlate of mastery. Patients with very negative transference patterns appear to be lower in mastery, and the emergence of more positive transference patterns over the course of therapy appears to be very important for improving mastery. Learning to master problematic transference-related conflicts appears to be very important for clinical change. Improvements in transference valence point to the importance of focusing on relationship conflicts and problems to achieve mastery over them. Given that the valence of transference patterns even at the end of therapy was predominantly negative, the process of psychotherapy does not appear to cure or resolve all intrapsychic conflicts. In fact, earlier research has shown that by and large, the same CCRT patterns found early in therapy remain late in therapy (Crits-Christoph & Luborsky, 1998a). In other words, the transference template appears to be pervasive and resistant to change.

What occurs over the course of psychotherapy is a person's mastery of his or her transference patterns. In CCRT terms, the thing that is mastered is the RS: the response of the self to the pressure of the wishes and the obstructiveness of the RO. The RO component, in psychoanalytic terms, relates very much to the projection of the transference conflicts into relationships with others. It makes sense, therefore, that if the transference template remains relatively unchanged, the projected RO components should also remain less malleable to change. It appears from this research that the factor that leads to clinical change is the development of mastery, whereby individuals master their own responses to the CCRT pattern.

STUDY OF MASTERY OF CORE RELATIONSHIPS: PARENTS AND LOVERS

Whether certain types of relationships are particularly important to focus on in therapy has long puzzled psychotherapists. The study reported in this section was designed to investigate the significance of changes in mastery of different types of relationships. Some regard the core nuclear relationship—the relationships with the parents—to be particularly important (Malan, 1963). Those who subscribe to the interpersonal school reason that only active, current relationships should be the major focus (Klerman et al., 1984). Those with a strict psychoanalytic leaning maintain that the relationship with the therapist should be the central concern of clinical work (Joseph, 1985/1988). Although all therapists would consider the three relationships to be important, they differ on degree of emphasis. Some practitioners interpret all narratives told by patients as being related, connected, and originating from feelings evoked in the current transference relationship with the therapist. An alternative view is that certain relationships people have in their life are more "core" or fundamental, and this view is supported by the common clinical observation that patients' perceptions of people are often polarized. For example, one 24-year-old patient, John, idealized his grandmother, to whom he was close in his early years, but hated his mother and had similar problems forming close relationships with other women.

In a naturalistic study of short-term therapy, Malan (1976; Marziali & Sullivan, 1980) reported that when there is a focus on linking patients' feelings about the therapist to their feelings about their parents, patients are observed to have significantly better outcome in therapy. Marziali (1984) attempted to replicate this finding and obtained mixed results. Both studies were methodologically flawed; Malan's study was of case notes, Marziali rated frequency of interpretations rather than proportions, and the ratings of interpretations suffered from low reliability ratings. Another replication of the Malan study, with more rigorous method, was reported by Piper, Debbane, Bienvenu, Carufel, and Garant (1986). Again the focus was on therapist interpretations (not patient activity) that emphasized therapist–parent, other–therapist, and other–parent links, expressed as a proportion of total interpretive activity by the therapist. Relationships between these proportions were compared to a large number of outcome variables, with almost no significant results. This may be due to the focus being on therapist activity, rather than on the patient's response to the therapist's activity. A high proportion of well-constructed parent-transference interpretations does not necessarily improve patient functioning if the patient does not construe them as helpful and useful.

Freud (1914/1958e) discussed how in the final analysis the real effort in therapy occurs in the present relationship with the therapist. He stated:

> we must treat his illness, not as an event of the past, but as a present-day force. This state of illness is brought, piece by piece, within the field and range of operation of the treatment, and while the patient experiences it as something real and contemporary, we have to do our therapeutic work on it. (pp. 151–152)

Furthermore, not only must the contemporary nature of the patient's problems be the focus of analysis, but these must be welded into the immediate relationship with the therapist.

> The doctor tries to compel him [the patient] to fit these emotional impulses into the nexus of the treatment and of his life-history, to submit them to intellectual consideration and to understand them in the light of their psychical value. This struggle between the doctor and the patient, between intellect and instinctual life, between understanding and seeking to act, is played out almost exclusively in the phenomenon of transference. It is on that field that the victory must be won—the victory whose expression is the permanent cure of the neurosis. (Freud, 1912/1958a, p. 108)

If changes in the relationship with the therapist through the transference are so signal, as Freud maintained, then these changes should be manifest in the narratives told by the patient about the therapist (which includes therapist–patient enactments). Improvements and changes in the transference relationship between patient and therapist over the course of therapy should predict gains in mastery and parallel improvements in mental health. It was hypothesized in the current study that patients rated as having larger gains on measures of general functioning and symptoms show the greatest gains in mastery of their relationship with the therapist.

Luborsky and colleagues (1998) investigated the kinds of people who are commonly the subject of patient narratives. Studying a sample of 33 patients from the Penn Psychotherapy Project, they found that 76% of patients tell narratives about their therapist, 85% about their family, 73% about their intimate relationships, 60% about friends, 45% about authority figures, and 36% about coworkers and people in general. This suggests that the three most important relationships in patients' lives at the time of analysis are with their family, therapist, and intimate partner.

The major aim of this study was to specifically investigate changes in narratives about different people across the course of therapy: (a) to investigate the changes in mastery across the course of therapy in narratives told about the therapist; (b) to investigate changes in narratives told about significant others in the patient's life, including narratives about their partners or lovers, parents, family, friends, and acquaintances; and (c) to investigate whether narratives of early childhood memories change in mastery over the course of therapy. Early memories hold a special place in the theory of psychoanalysis and probably contain the core nuclear conflict that drives the repetition compulsion (see chapter 2). Changes in the mastery of early memories should be clinically important and should also parallel improvements in mental health.

Participants and Analysis of Data

The participants in this study were 41 mixed-diagnosis patients from the Penn Psychotherapy Project (Luborsky et al., 1988; see chapter 5). The mean Mastery Scale scores from early and late in therapy were converted into residual gain scores using the procedure described below. A few measures used in the validation study (described in more detail in chapter 5) were chosen to conduct the initial analyses. These were (a) an observer-rated measure, the HSRS; (b) a therapist-rated measure, the composite therapists' rating of patient satisfaction, success, and improvement (SSI; Luborsky, Crits-Cristoph, Mintz, & Auerbach, 1988), measured at the end of therapy; and (c) a patient-rated measure, the patient's rating of change on their primary target complaint (Target).

There were five steps in the analysis of the data.

1. Each RE by each patient was classified according to the object of the narrative (i.e., whether it was a narrative about the

therapist, the patient's sister, etc.). Unlike the earlier Luborsky et al. (1998) study discussed above, narratives were classified and collected in such a way as to simplify the coding, to maximize the cell size of each category, and to make the categories more dynamically precise. For instance, instead of collapsing narratives told about the parents and other members of the family into one category labeled *family*, it was decided to divide these into narratives about parents and narratives about family. The family category included narratives about members of the patient's family and extended family but excluded narratives about the parents. The intimate relations category was tightened into a category specifically about *lovers*, defined as the central person in the patient's life toward whom the patient formed an erotic attraction. This was usually the spouse or steady girlfriend or boyfriend, but sometimes included unconsummated desires expressed toward a particular person.

All narratives were individually read to ensure that the best categorization was made for each. Narratives about all other people considered close to the patient but not holding a primary position as a lover, parent, or family member were coded as friends. The authority figures category was dropped because these judgments were difficult to make; the category was collapsed into an others category, which was made up of people who were more remote (e.g., neighbors, work colleagues, and acquaintances).

In summary, then, five categories were used: therapist, parents, lovers, friends, and others. In the Piper et al. (1986) study reviewed above, the categories derived were mother, father, sibling, therapist, other real person, undirected person, and unspecified family member. Although it would be possible to further divide the sample with parents into mother and father and to distinguish between siblings and other family members, as did Piper et al., this would lead to a critical loss of narrative pairs early and late in therapy and render the research untenable.

In the study reported in this section, a sixth phenomenologically different category was also analyzed: early memories. This was defined as any RE about an event that happened before the patient turned 13 (i.e., became a teenager). Where a memory narrative was clearly from the remote past but was impossible to date within the patient's chronological age, it was accepted into the analysis as being an early memory. Narratives that were recent or within at least the past 10 years, or that recounted an episode when the patient was clearly an adult or a mature teenager, were not accepted. The aim was to analyze early childhood memories.

2. For each patient, instances where categories of narratives were discussed both early and late in therapy were highlighted for further analysis. For example, a narrative about the therapist told by a patient early in therapy but not late in therapy (or vice versa) was not included in the analysis. This is because it was the change in narrative about a particular object (e.g., therapist, parents, lovers) that was of primary interest. The patient must have told one or more narratives within each category both early and late in therapy for the narrative to be accepted into the analysis. If a patient had early and late narratives in one category but not another, only those categories where there were both early and late data were used.

3. For narratives that were accepted into the analysis from each patient (as described in Step 2), the mastery scores for each category were averaged to derive one mean mastery score for each category included (therapist, parents, etc.) early and late in therapy.

4. Residual gain scores were calculated for each patient for each included category to quantify the degree of change in mastery for each specific object relations type.

5. The relationship between the mastery residual gain scores for each object relation and the nominated clinical outcome measures (HSRS, SSI, Target) were examined by Pearson correlations, to investigate the specific importance of changes in each object relations dimension to clinical outcome.

Relationship Narratives

Table 7.4 shows the number of patients who had narratives both early and late in therapy for each of the five object relations categories. Also included is the mean number of narratives told per patient per category.

As can be seen from these data, 61% of patients (25 out of 41) told one or more narratives about their therapist both early and late in therapy; 80% told narratives about others throughout therapy, but only 27% told narratives about their family (excluding their parents). Only 20% continued to tell early memories both early and late in therapy. It must be cautioned here that generally only two early-in-therapy and two late-in-therapy sessions were sampled; there were probably many more narratives told by patients within these categories at other times in the therapy that were not included in this study.

TABLE 7.4

Number of Patients and Mean Number of Relationship Episodes (REs) for Each of the Five Categories of Object Relations

Object relation category	No. of patients included	No. of REs included	
		M	SD
Therapist	25	4.04	1.77
Parents	22	4.64	1.56
Family	11	3.55	1.44
Lovers	29	8.07	4.50
Others	33	7.30	2.88
Early memories	8	5.25	3.62

Of those patients who told narratives early and late in therapy (within one or more of the relationship type categories), the majority of narratives were about their lovers (M = 8 narratives per patient) or others (M = 7.3). Patients also told narratives about their family (M = 3.6), therapist (M = 4), and parents (M = 4.6 narratives per patient).

Table 7.5 presents the results from the Pearson correlations between the mastery residual change scores for each object relation versus the three clinical outcome measures.

The results from this analysis reveal a surprising finding: the strongest consistent relationship across all three outcome measures was with the changes in the mastery of the relationship with the parents. The second strongest relationship was with changes in the relationship with the patient's lover, with a significant correlation with two of the three outcome variables (and almost significant for the third variable). The only other variable of note was a relationship between others and HSRS, which was not

TABLE 7.5

Relationship Between Changes in Mastery of Different Relationships and Three Measures of Clinical Outcome

Object Relation	HSRS	SSI	Target
Therapist	−.17	−.19	−.25
Parents	.58**	.54**	.62**
Family	.21	.43	.51
Lovers	.39*	.48**	.36
Others	.37*	.27	.22
Early memories	.38	.12	.59

Note. HSRS = Health–Sickness Rating Scale; SSI = therapist's rating of success, satisfaction, and improvement; Target = patient's rating of change in the primary target complaint.
*$p < .05$. ** $p < .01$.

TABLE 7.6

Regression Analysis Investigating Mastery of the Parents and Lovers
Narratives in Relation to Health–Sickness Outcome Status

Variable	HSRS B	Signif t
Mastery of Relationship Episodes with Parents	23.57	.03*
Mastery of Relationship Episodes with Lovers	15.15	.15

Note. HSRS = Health–Sickness Rating Scale. R^2 = .45. Adjusted R^2 = .35. F = 4.54, p = .04. *p < .05

found in the SSI and Target measures. Contrary to the main hypothesis, changes in mastery of the patient–therapist relationship were unrelated to any of the clinical outcome measures. It was therefore decided post hoc to separate out the data on the parents and lovers and enter these into a multiple regression analysis to see whether the ability to encapsulate outcome, using the HSRS, could be improved by combining the two object relations variables. The results are in Table 7.6.

Tables 7.5 and 7.6 demonstrate that the single most important variable that accounts for outcome is the change in the mastery of relations with the patient's parents. The parents' data significantly contributed to the model (p < .03), whereas the lovers' data did not. The regression equation was then repeated with SSI as the dependent variable instead of HSRS and then with Target as the dependent variable; the resulting summary of the significance of beta is presented in Table 7.7.

These further analyses confirm what was found in the HSRS multiple regression: The changes in the relation with the parents is the single most important variable accounting for clinical outcome in this sample. For both the SSI and Target, the contribution of the parents' data was significant (p < .02 and p < .04, respectively), but not the contribution of the lovers' data. The relationship between the mastery of relations with the parents and psychological health–sickness is shown in Figure 7.4.

TABLE 7.7

Regression Analysis Investigating Mastery of the Parents and Lovers
Narratives in Relation to Change in Target Symptom (Target) and Therapist
Rating of Success (SSI)

Measure	Significant t	
	Parents	Lovers
Target	.02*	.18
SSI	.04*	.07

Note. Only significance of β is shown for each comparison.
* p < .05.

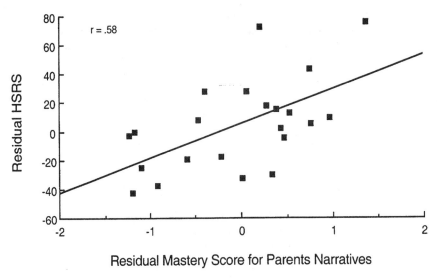

Residual Mastery Score for Parents Narratives

Figure 7.4. Relationship between changes in the mastery of patients' narratives about their parents and their scores on the Health–Sickness Rating Scale (HSRS; *N* = 22)

This study investigated in more detail the types of people who form the object of relationship narratives told by patients in psychotherapy and the significance of these for clinical change. The results were surprising: The strongest consistent relationship across the outcome variables was with changes in the mastery of the relationship with the parents. The second strongest relationship was with changes in the relationship with the patient's lover. Changes in mastery of the patient–therapist relationship were unrelated to any of the clinical outcome measures, perhaps because the relationship with the therapist was almost uniformly positive. It was hypothesized that patients rated as having larger gains on measures of general functioning and symptoms would show the greatest gains in mastery of their relationship with the therapist. This hypothesis was not supported, because no relationship was found between changes in the mastery of narratives about the therapist and clinical outcome scores. This appears to contradict Freud's (1914/1958e) assertion that the transference relationship with the therapist affords the most clinically relevant changes. It may be that patients more often concealed their feelings in discussing their relationship with the therapist and that this obscured clinically meaningful changes in mastery. Alternatively, the transference relationship with the therapist may act as the medium or "container" by which the work on the other relationship problems proceeds (Winnicott, 1956). Research also supports the view that a good quality relationship with the therapist predicts good outcomes, particularly early in therapy (Horvath, 1994).

Considerable caution, however, should be placed on the interpretation of these data. Only 22 of 41 patients told narratives about their parents both early and late in therapy during the two early and two late sessions sampled.

It may be that all 41 patients told narratives about their parents early and late during sessions that were not sampled. On the other hand, it may be that for only 50% of the sample was the mastery of the relationship with their parents clinically important. The sample consisted of relatively young people (mean age = 25 years) and most were still in college, so perhaps separation and individuation from their parents were developmentally important goals at that time in their lives; older patients might have other concerns (Cohler & Galatzer-Levy, 1990). The results of this study clearly require replication with another set of patients, preferably using a much larger number of sessions from early and late in therapy. Nevertheless, these preliminary findings are fascinating and have implications for our knowledge of the potent change mechanisms in psychotherapy. To my knowledge, this is the first study to investigate changes in different kinds of relationships over the course of therapy within the spontaneous narratives told by patients.

As discussed in the introduction to this chapter, some thinkers view the whole therapeutic situation as being related to transference, triggered by the therapist–patient relationship. Such a view is at odds with the strategy adopted here of dividing the narratives into five categories (therapist, parents, family, lovers, and others), because it holds that all narratives are manifestations of the patient–therapist transference relationship. However, the fact that clinically meaningful differentiations were found in this sample between the objects of the narratives argues against this broad view of transference. Freud (1912/1958a, p. 100) acknowledged that there may be "several" characteristic transference patterns. It was possible in this study to differentiate statistically between mastery levels of each object within the narratives, which suggests that the "repetition compulsion" may act differentially depending on the prevailing relationship conditions. It would certainly appear from these results that changes in the relationship with the parents is central to mastering these conflicts.

The relationship between children and their parents has been the subject of intense study in the attachment and bonding literature (Bowlby, 1988). Given that it is the primary and central bond that helps children to learn to integrate their personality, it is hardly surprising that ruptures or difficulties in patients' relationship to their parents should be associated with psychopathology. The finding that the nuclear family and romantic relationships are important in achieving mastery parallels research into adult attachment. Two traditions in attachment research come from research into nuclear families, focusing on adults' memories of childhood experiences with their parents and research focusing on attachment with contemporary peers or romantic partners (Simpson & Rholes, 1998). There is also some evidence that the valence of these relationship patterns is transmitted intergenerationally (A. Jones, Henry, & Grenyer, 2001).

These findings are consistent with another study of transference (Gelso et al., 1999). In that study, 11 psychodynamic therapists were interviewed separately about a patient they had successfully treated within the previous 12 months. They were asked to reflect on the source of typical enactments that emerged when the patient transferred thoughts and attitudes onto the therapist. All therapists traced these enactments to either the mother (most frequently), the father (also typical), and (occasionally) to others. The most common theme emerging in this transference was fear or mistrust; also prominent was the wish for approval and for good treatment. This research highlights the centrality of feelings about the patient's parents in the origins of the transference template.

Summary of the Mastery of Core Relationships Study

The results from this study suggest that a potent change mechanism is the mastery of patients' relationships with their parents and (to a lesser degree) with their lovers, which is reflected in narrative telling during psychotherapy and the benefits of their resultant mastery. It is probably the case that the relationship with the therapist is a vehicle for this change to occur, but it appears that the mastery of the relationship with the therapist does not change in a clinically meaningful way through therapy, as Freud had previously suggested. The research reported here suggests that therapists would profit from focusing on the "primary nuclear scene"—how patients construe and experience the relationship with their parents—to enhance mastery. These results suggest that the deepest and core relationships—with the parents and lovers—are fruitful areas of clinical investigation and mastery augmentation.

CONCLUSION

The results of the studies reported in this chapter reinforce the importance of interpersonal processes in psychotherapy and in mental health. A supportive therapeutic alliance between patient and therapist early in treatment helps considerably in the patient's task of achieving greater mastery. As therapy progresses, issues of transference or core maladaptive relationship patterns often emerge, and mastery of these becomes an issue. Modifying the negative valence of the patients' reactions to others and their own responses to interpersonal conflicts appears especially related to mastery gains. In terms of the kinds of relationships with which patients have problems, mastering the relationships with their parents and with the current lover appears to be particularly helpful. Three different levels of interpersonal functioning require the therapist's attention: (a) patients' current, ongoing relationship with the therapist; (b) patients' pattern of responses toward others, which may be problematic and require modification; and (c) patients' core relationships, typically with their parents and lovers.

Addressing these three levels helps maximize the mastery gains that patients can make through treatment.

The next chapter of the book considers specific clinical problems and how mastery changes in these different client groups. Consideration is given to how to give more specific help for people with different disorders, in particular depression, personality disorders, and substance dependence from the perspective of enhancing mastery.

8

MASTERY AND DIFFERENT CLIENT POPULATIONS: DEPRESSION, PERSONALITY DISORDERS, AND SUBSTANCE DEPENDENCE

Although mastery is a common desired outcome of all therapies, it may be that patient problems determine how patients master their problems and the kinds of self-understandings and tools for control they gain. Symington (1996) has said that "we are not trying to protect our patients from the pain of life—we are trying to strengthen them, so that they can manage the worst" (p. 115). Clinical wisdom suggests that what requires strengthening varies depending on the particular problems encountered. This chapter investigates three groups of patients: (a) those who experience primarily major depression, (b) those who have a personality disorder, and (c) those with a substance dependence problem. It aims to trace changes in mastery across the course of therapy and to investigate differential paths of change depending on diagnosis. The chapter is divided into three parts, each focusing on a different patient group. Case studies illustrate changes in mastery for each group, and outcomes using the Mastery Scale with each sample are presented.

MASTERY AND DEPRESSION

The World Health Organization has estimated that major depression is the single largest cause of disability worldwide and will be epidemic by the year 2020 (cited in Murray & Lopez, 1996). The estimates for depression are

169

that about 5%–12% of all men and 10%–26% of all women will experience a major depressive episode that lasts at least 2 weeks at some time during their lives. The point prevalence of depression is 2%–3% of men and 5%–9% of women (American Psychiatric Association, 1994). It has been estimated that mood disorders account for three quarters of all psychiatric hospitalizations (Sartorius, 1979).

The symptoms of depression can be divided into two major types, cognitive and vegetative. Cognitive symptoms are marked by feelings of helplessness and worthlessness, often with pathological guilt. Vegetative symptoms include weight fluctuation (typically weight loss), loss of appetite, weakness, fatigue, sleep disorders (such as early morning awakening), and loss of interest in sex. Suicide is a significant risk in a subsample of people with major depression. About half of people who commit suicide had major depression (Robins & Kulbok, 1988). Unlike the etiology of bipolar disorder, for which there is considerable evidence for a genetic predisposition (with roughly 80%–90% of people with bipolar disorder having a family history of some mood disorder), for major depression the contribution of genetics is far weaker, with only half of people with depression having some family history of the disorder (American Psychiatric Association, 1994).

The high prevalence of untreated depressive disorders that are socially disruptive and medically costly has been established as a major public health problem (Klerman, 1989). Depression is a highly relapsing and chronic disorder. Two near-identical 15-year follow-up studies of people with depression in London (Lee & Murray, 1988) and Sydney (Kiloh, Andrews, & Neilson, 1988) found that only 20% of patients recovered and remained continuously well whereas 20% remained incapacitated throughout the 15-year follow-up or committed suicide. In Australia, 22% of deaths in the 15–24 age range in 1991 were suicides (Australian Bureau of Statistics, 1994).

The largest and most important controlled trial to date in the psychotherapy literature for evaluating treatments for depression is the National Institute of Mental Health Treatment of Depression Collaborative Research Program study (Elkin et al., 1989). This study found that interpersonal factors, in particular perfectionism and the therapeutic alliance, were especially salient in predicting outcome (Blatt, Zuroff, Quinlan, & Pilkonis, 1996). In the depression literature, many have attacked the cognitive theory as being circular in reasoning, focusing on the symptoms of depression but not addressing the causative factors involved (Brewin, 1985; Coyne & Gotlib, 1983, 1986; Teasdale, 1983). These commentators cited how interpersonal problems are highly prevalent prior to depression and therefore may stand in relation to depression as a genuine cause that treatments should address (Brown & Harris, 1978; Weissman, Klerman, Paykel, Prusoff, & Hanson, 1974).

Previous research suggests that some people with depression have characteristic traitlike interpersonal patterns that make them particularly prone to having unsatisfactory and conflictual relationships with others.

These patterns may include a pervasive internalization of anger at others, engendering helplessness (and interpersonal avoidance) and subsequent vulnerability to suicidal ideation and intention (Freud, 1917/1957b; Luborsky et al., 1995). Perfectionism, in particular, has been found to predict outcomes for depression, with two main types of concern: (a) anaclitic depression (associated with socially prescribed perfectionism), which is based on feelings of helplessness (2I) and a desire to gain the love of others (5S) even though the other is perceived to be critical and hold high expectations (2G), and (b) introjective depression (associated with self-oriented perfectionism), characterized by self-criticism (2E) and independence from others (2H), caused by the expectation that rejection (2G) follows interpersonal closeness (Blatt, 1995; Blatt, Quinlan, Chevron, McDonald, & Zuroff, 1982; Blatt, Quinlan, Pilkonis, & Shea, 1995; Blatt, Zuroff, Bondi, Sanislow, & Pilkonis, 1998; Blatt, Zuroff, et al., 1996, Reis & Grenyer, 2001).

The study reported in the sections that follow investigated the way in which patients who are very depressed are helped by psychotherapy and how the pathways to mastery are followed. Changes in mastery are related to changes in depression and overall functioning, and developing self-understanding and self-control over these problematic patterns should provide an alternative way of meeting wishes and achieving self-esteem and psychological health.

Participants and Treatment

The study included 30 psychotherapy patients (23 women, 7 men), mean age 38 (range = 22–60 years), who formed part of the Penn Study of Supportive–Expressive Dynamic Psychotherapy for Depression (Penn SE; Diguer et al., 1993). To be selected for the study patients had to meet the criteria for major depression after a *DSM–III–R* (American Psychiatric Association, 1987; equivalent to *DSM–IV*, American Psychiatric Association, 1994) evaluation, which included the following: Axis I, Axis II, Global Assessment Scale (GAS; Endicott et al., 1976), Health–Sickness Rating Scale (HSRS; Luborsky, 1962), Beck Depression Inventory (BDI; Beck, Ward, Mendelson, Mock, & Erbaugh, 1961), and Hamilton Rating Scale for Depression–17 items (HRSD-17; Hamilton, 1967; Hamilton, 1960). Certain diagnoses were excluded: current substance abuse, antisocial personality, agoraphobia, schizophrenia, and organic brain disorder. Twelve patients were single; 10 were married; and 7 were divorced, separated, or widowed. Sixteen were employed full-time, 6 were unemployed, 5 had part-time work, and 2 were students. Nine had finished only high school, 12 had completed college, and 8 had completed a graduate degree.

Each psychotherapy session was audiotaped with the patient's and therapist's informed consent. The four therapists (three women and one man) were trained in supportive–expressive dynamic psychotherapy using a special manual, and adherence to the techniques was monitored. The treatment consisted of 16 sessions of time-limited supportive–expressive dynamic psychotherapy for depression administered according to a specific manual (Luborsky et al., 1995) based on the general supportive–expressive psychotherapy manual (Luborsky, 1984).

Mastery Scale

The data set consisted of verbatim transcripts of psychotherapy sessions collected during the Penn SE Depression Project (Diguer et al., 1993). The transcripts came from early therapy sessions (generally Sessions 3 and 5), and two or three transcripts from late in therapy (at the 90% completion mark). Transcripts from the very first sessions and very last sessions were not scored. The first two sessions are often more constrained and involve a deal of fact finding and information giving. By the third session, patients usually reach the stage where they can comfortably narrate relationship episodes (REs) that contain their conflicts. Late in therapy, patients arrive at the stage where they have to come to terms with the termination of the relationship with the therapist, and this can bring forward a temporary return of symptoms and problems. Therefore, Sessions 3 and 5 and sessions at the 90% mark (and the sessions immediately before this) were used. REs served as the scorable units of analysis of mastery as discussed in chapter 4. There were usually 10 REs from early in therapy and 10 REs from late in therapy for each patient.

The REs were extracted from the transcripts and randomized among sessions and patients. This was to prevent judges from having other cues as to the progress of the patient in therapy. The aim was for each RE to be scored on its merits, uncontaminated by prior knowledge. The REs were then divided into grammatical clauses by marking off the claused speech units with a slash (/) according to the conventions described in chapter 4. To facilitate the process of scoring, one judge read all the REs and identified all the clauses that could be scored using the Mastery Scale, to control for location or position disagreement (as opposed to scoring disagreement). This judge completed this task after the data had been randomized, so there were no clues regarding the identity of the patient or whether the RE was from either early or late in therapy. The judge completed this task after having read and claused the entire RE.

Other Outcome Instruments

An independent assessor collected outcome measures at the commencement and termination of therapy. Three measures were used in the study:

1. HSRS, an observer-rated assessment scale of psychiatric severity and overall psychological functioning (Luborsky, 1962, 1975). The version of the HSRS used was the average of the seven cri-

terion subscales, which is the best and most reliable assessment of overall functioning and is superior to the single global HSRS rating or the GAF. The GAF form of the HSRS forms Axis V of *DSM–IV* (American Psychiatric Association, 1994).

2. The BDI, a self-administered scale for the assessment of clinical depression.

3. The HRSD–17, an observer-rated scale of depression that is considered the gold standard in assessing depression severity (Rabkin & Klein, 1987).

The relationship between Mastery Scale residual gain scores and residualized outcome variables was calculated using Pearson correlations. Residual gain scores take into account the extent to which the gain is related to the severity of the patient's problem at intake, and these scores are appropriate for correlational designs (Fiske, 1971; Kazdin, 1994; Luborsky et al., 1988; Manning & DuBois, 1962). Pre–post effect size estimates of individual mastery categories, scored using the Gottschalk–Gleser method (chapter 4), were used to profile gains in aspects of mastery.

Results

Interrater Reliability

Two doctoral-level psychoanalytic researchers scored the data. Interrater reliability per RE scored in common ranged from .79 to .90. Judges' scores were therefore pooled for all subsequent analyses.

Changes in Mastery

The pre–post mastery effect size was .57, which is a medium effect. The changes in mastery were significant ($t = 2.70, p = .01$). Because members of the sample were very depressed, changes in mastery after 16 sessions were more modest than would be expected from a less severe sample; at the commencement and termination, scores were 3.56 ($SD = .42$) and 3.80 ($SD = .41$), respectively. Individual effect size estimates per mastery category were calculated; the results are depicted in Figure 8.1. Most of the effect sizes were quite small (< 2), with some notable exceptions: Changes in 4P, 4M, and 5Q showed more medium effect size gains.

Mastery and Depression Changes

The mean depression score, measured using the HRSD–17 at the start of treatment, was 17.73 ($SD = 3.60$), and at termination it was 6.83 ($SD = 5.69$). A paired t test was significant ($t = 8.23, p = .00$), indicating significant improvement over the course of psychotherapy. Pre–post effect size score

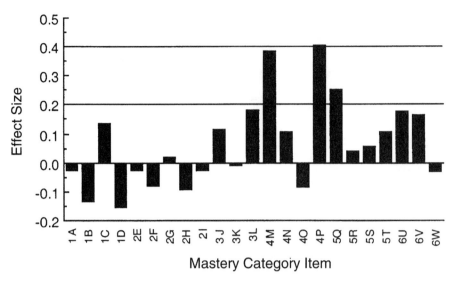

Figure 8.1. Pretreatment versus posttreatment effect size estimates of change in individual Mastery Scale categories.

change was very large (3.03). Residualized gain scores were entered into a Pearson correlation to determine the relationship between changes in mastery and changes in depression. Changes in mastery were significantly related to changes in depression ($r = .57, p = .00$), with 31% of the variance in depression being predicted by mastery. The scatter plot showing the relationship between the HRSD–17 and mastery appears in Figure 8.2.

Residual changes between mastery and an alternate self-report measure of depression, the BDI, were also highly significant ($r = .40, p = .03$). Depression scores measured by the BDI at the start of therapy averaged 28.47 ($SD = 6.76$); at the completion of therapy they had dropped to 13.97 ($SD = 11.27$).

Mastery and Changes in General Functioning

At the start of treatment, the mean HSRS score was 51.25 ($SD = 5.71$); at termination it was 66.40 ($SD = 12.33$), which indicates a significant improvement ($t = 8.73, p = .00$). HSRS scores of 51 at intake and 66 after 4 months indicate that this sample was quite severe in psychopathology and that gains were relatively modest. Nevertheless, the changes made were clinically meaningful; pre–post effect size for the HSRS was very large (2.65). A Pearson correlation was calculated between HSRS residual change and mastery residual change scores to assess the relationship between changes in HSRS and mastery. The relationship was significant ($r = .56, p = .00$) and accounted for 31% of the variance.

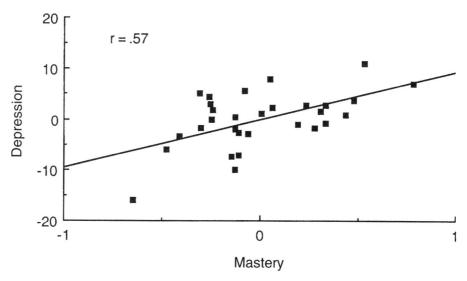

Figure 8.2. Relationship between residual gain Hamilton Rating Scale of Depression scores and residual gain Mastery Scale scores (*N* = 30).

Discussion: Fostering Mastery in People Who Are Depressed

Changes in mastery during psychotherapy predicted changes in depression. Those who had the highest gains in mastery were the least depressed at the end of therapy, and those who achieved little mastery were still symptomatic at termination. Improvements in mastery predicted not only reductions in depression but also gains in overall health–sickness.

The pattern of changes in individual mastery scale categories was striking. The most notable gains were in 4P (expressions of interpersonal self-assertion) and 4M (references to questioning the reactions of others), which evidenced medium effect sizes. Also noteworthy were improvements in 5Q (expressions of insight into repeating personality patterns of self), which showed a small but clinically meaningful gain. In general, the pattern of gains (Levels 4–6) and reductions (Levels 1–3) followed the predicted pattern of the Mastery Scale, offering further support for its validity. For this depressed sample, clinical change appeared to be particularly important in the interpersonal domain. The picture that emerges is of a person becoming less hopeless and helpless and more interpersonally assertive and questioning of others. A willingness to challenge, rather than blindly accept others' views and opinions (4M), seems to be associated with clinical improvement in people with depression. Tied with this increase in interpersonal assertion (4P) are gains in insight about habitual ways of relating. Depressed individuals appear to become aware that their interpersonal style (5Q) has been related to their depression, and this awareness helps them to become more psychologically healthy.

The finding that self-assertion and interpersonal questioning were associated with good outcomes is consistent with other research that suggests that perfectionism is a crucial predictor of outcome in depression. In patients who are depressed, the aspects of perfectionism most associated with poor outcomes are (a) socially prescribed perfectionism, which is characterized by the feeling that self-worth is defined by others and that pleasing others is never satisfactorily achieved; and (b) self-oriented perfectionism, characterized by self-critical attitudes and withdrawal as a result of an expectation of rejection (Blatt, 1995; Blatt et al., 1998; Reis & Grenyer, 2001). Overcoming these feelings, and recovering autonomy and control, is consistent with the kinds of changes seen here. Of particular importance, socially prescribed perfectionism has been found to be associated in particular with psychopathology and is directly linked to depression (Hewitt, Flett, & Ediger, 1996). Socially prescribed perfectionism is characterized by a perceived lack of control over the environment, with an external locus of control, so the changes found here, in assertion and self-control, are in accord with the kinds of changes required for resolving depression in patients with this type of transference-related interpersonal pattern.

A case study illustrates these processes of change. Fiona, age 22, had very severe depression following a number of breakdowns in her personal and work life. Her progress in therapy was very good, and at the follow-up evaluation her depression had remitted. In psychotherapy, it emerged that a common theme for her was an expectation of being rejected by others, which was reinforcing her helplessness and leading her to withdraw from others and social situations. Through her work in therapy, she learned to recognize how her current depression and interpersonal withdrawal was linked to her past and her fear of others' evaluations, and she began to see the way she was enacting this in the present. Toward the end of therapy, she narrated the following:.

> *Fiona:* /On Saturday—first I went to dinner with, at Peter's apartment/and it was very pleasant/but, you know, it completely proved to me in the context of the situation that I really had resolved it in my mind. (6W)/It's like every, everything I used to do to break contact I didn't do anymore, you know. (6U)/I met somebody there and had a really good time./I really spent time with this person. (5R)/I didn't start into a conversation and then back away like I found myself doing so many times before. (6V)/And I felt open enough to the possibility of either acceptance or rejection, you know. (6U)/.

> *Therapist:* So you think this person has the qualities that would be complementary to yours?

Fiona: / Yeah, definitely/. . .And he's also physical in a sense that you know that we're not standing there like this,/that it was, um, you know, however we were talking, we were also we were in—/I just felt like we were in synchrony, you know. (5R)/I had a flash of a study I had read while doing a paper on body language,/because I noticed we were sitting exactly complementary to each other, you know./And uh it wasn't particularly physical it was very synchronized/and I felt that was really interesting that there wasn't—some people you see couples, you see them at odds with each other [laughs]/.

Here Fiona recognizes her transference-related pattern of withdrawing and breaking off contact (5Q), and she demonstrates self-control over this pattern (6U). In so doing, she initiates a more positive relationship (5R) that is open emotionally to any outcome, either acceptance or rejection, without preempting prematurely the outcome (6V). In this way she is finding that she can monitor her own emotional processes and not feel that others have the power to judge or reject her in a way that leads her to withdraw. She is therefore demonstrating her solution to the problem of depression, both through an increased sense of self-control and through self-understanding, which is helping her become closer to others.

Summary of Mastery and Depression

This study investigated how patients with depression are helped through psychotherapy and the kinds of changes in mastery that predict improvement. Mastery gains predicted not only reductions in depression but also gains in overall health–sickness, which also replicates the validity study in chapter 4. The most notable gains in individual Mastery Scale categories were in (a) expressions of interpersonal self-assertion, (b) references to questioning the reactions of others, and (c) expressions of insight into repeating personality patterns of self.

This suggests that overcoming depression requires self-understanding and self-control of relationship patterns, and in particular, overcoming feelings of helplessness and the tendency to withdraw associated with expectation of rejection arising out of past experiences. Challenging, rather than blindly accepting others' views and opinions, and becoming more interpersonally assertive, seem to be associated with clinical improvement in people with depression. Developing insight into the interpersonal pattern of relating to others, such as rejection expectancy and subsequent interpersonal withdrawal, is important to overcome depression.

How the mastery of these long-term interpersonal problems might be exacerbated by an ongoing diagnosed personality disorder has been a topic of debate in psychotherapy circles and is the subject of the next study.

MASTERY AND PERSONALITY DISORDERS

Effectively treating patients with personality disorders remains a challenge, typically because of their very low levels of mastery. Patients with personality disorders present particular difficulties; defects in the developmental psychosocial integration of the personality make forming and maintaining a helping supportive therapeutic relationship with the patient particularly challenging. A principal deficit in these patients is in initiating and maintaining mature interpersonal relationships, so developing mastery should be of significant benefit. Many patients with personality disorders have very little understanding or control over their emotional world.

For example, one patient, Janice, who was admitted three times within 6 months to the local inpatient psychiatric hospital with major depression, borderline personality disorder, multiple suicide attempts, and serious self-harm, was struggling to understand and control her internal world. Coming from a neglectful family, which included a jailed father, an alcoholic mother, and an abusive brother, Janice left school when she was 13 to live with her 29-year-old boyfriend. At 26, after many years of unemployment and unstable, failed relationships, she is currently under the care of a psychiatrist and sees a female psychotherapist three times a week at a local clinic. In psychotherapy her major difficulty is in dealing with the therapeutic frame; she believes that the psychotherapist is both an idealized savior who provides her with comfort and guidance to renew her life and a cruel and uncaring individual who is intent on frustrating and rejecting her. Her difficulty in fusing and reconciling these two extreme images of her psychotherapist in her own mind and coping with the defined nature of treatment contact are major themes in the therapy. In terms of mastery, her functioning is generally at Levels 1 and 2 (see chapter 4 and 6): She has marked ego boundary disorders, is emotionally overwhelmed, frequently projects paranoid ideas from others, and has explosive anger and self-hate. The immediate goals of treatment are to make her safe from harm, relieve her serious depression, and instill in her the hope of improvement through fostering the therapeutic relationship.

Patients with personality disorders bring multiple areas of difficulty into the treatment context. The expert consensus from a meta-analysis of treatments in psychiatry (Quality Assurance Project, 1990, 1991) is that long-term psychotherapy is the treatment of choice for most personality disorders. Research on dynamic psychotherapy for borderline personality disorder offers objective and empirical evidence that this form of treatment is beneficial for the severely personality disturbed (Meares, Stevenson, & Comerford, 1999; Stevenson & Meares, 1992, 1999). Treatment often proceeds on many different problems at the same time; multimodal approaches, as advocated for example by Linehan (1993), are also effective (Linehan, Armstrong, Suarez, Allmon, & Heard, 1991).

In the *DSM–IV* (American-Psychiatric Association, 1994), Axis I includes the typical clinical disorders such as anxiety and depression, and Axis II is reserved for the personality disorders. An Axis II personality disorder combined with an Axis I clinical disorder is associated with worse prognosis and poorer outcome (Docherty, Fiester, & Shea, 1986). In particular, research has focused on the relationship between depression and personality disorders (Klein, Kupfer, & Shea, 1993). Personality disorders have a high comorbidity rate with depression and other Axis I disorders and can be associated with aggression (Barlow, Grenyer, & Ilkiw-Lavalle, 2000). Estimates of major depression in borderline personality disorder range from 40% to 69% (Gunderson & Elliott, 1985; Stone, Stone, & Hurt, 1987). A study investigating factors associated with the comorbidity of personality disorders in major depression (Diguer et al., 1993) found that those with personality disorders were more severe in psychiatric disturbance and less improved than depressed patients who did not also have personality disorders. Consistent with other studies (Shea et al., 1990), dynamically oriented psychotherapy was found to be beneficial for those with comorbid personality disorders.

Some researchers have criticized the diagnosis of individual personality disorder types, because there appears to be an obvious overlap between the symptoms considered to be central to many personality disorders (Morey, 1988). For example, anger is part of borderline, histrionic, narcissistic, and antisocial personality presentations. This has led some researchers to eschew the typical symptom checklists in favor of a more dynamic interpersonal focus (Benjamin, 1993), one more in line with an interpersonal psychoanalytic theory (Sullivan, 1953).

Introduction to the Study

Contemporary psychoanalytic theory of personality emphasizes that a central goal and marker of change for patients with personality disorders is the ability to form and maintain mature interpersonal relationships (Kernberg, 1984). Mature interpersonal functioning presupposes the development of a coherent sense of self and identity and adequate control over emotional impulses (Erickson, 1963; Galatzer-Levy & Cohler, 1993). This study investigates whether dynamic therapy leads to changes in the mastery of interpersonal problems for a subset of patients with personality disorders (personality disorder alone, or in combination with an Axis I disorder) compared to patients without personality disorders.

Despite clinical wisdom, expert consensus, and research evidence that interpersonal, relationship-based psychotherapies are particularly effective and suitable in the treatment of patients with personality disorders, very few studies have attempted to measure the mechanism underlying treatment effectiveness. It is hypothesized that patients with a personality disorder, because of the pervasiveness of their problems, are more resistant to change and therefore do not benefit from psychotherapy as much as those without a personality disorder. It is also hypothesized that (a) initial levels of psychiatric functioning are worse in the Axis II personality-disordered groups than the Axis I clinical-disordered group, (b) initial levels of interpersonal mastery are worse in the Axis II personality-disordered groups than the Axis I clinical-disordered group, (c) changes in interpersonal mastery and psychiatric functioning over the course of therapy are greater for Axis I clinical disorders than the Axis II diagnostic groups, and (d) changes in mastery are significantly related to gains in psychiatric functioning in both groups.

Participants

The participants in this study were 41 patients with a mixed diagnosis from the Penn Psychotherapy Project (Luborsky et al., 1988), as described in chapter 5. The mastery scores were from the reliability and validity study (chapter 5) and were made on the early- and late-in-therapy sessions. The HSRS (Luborsky, 1962) was used to measure psychiatric severity. On the basis of the sample's *DSM–III* diagnoses (American Psychiatric Association, 1980), patients were divided into three groups: 17 with an Axis I diagnosis, 13 with an Axis II personality disorder, and 11 with diagnoses on both Axis I and Axis II. (The categories would be the same if based on *DSM–IV*.) Diagnoses were made by a psychiatrist based on a structured prognostic interview during the course of the original project. Diagnoses were originally made according to *DSM–II*, but these were converted into *DSM–III* categories some years later after re-examination of the interview materials (Luborsky et al., 1988) and would be largely equivalent to *DSM–IV*. Details of the range of diagnoses for each group are presented in Table 8.1.

Results

The resulting demographic data and clinical measures across the three groups are presented in Table 8.2. Three-way analyses of variance (ANOVAs) with planned comparisons were calculated to test hypotheses a and b; with factors of Diagnosis (Axis I, Axis II, or Dual), Demographic or Clinical measure (e.g., Age, Mastery), and Time (early- vs. late-in-therapy REs). Following the recommendations of various authors (e.g., Kazdin, 1994), differences between the groups were tested on the demographic and clinical measures by adopting a criterion of 20% difference ($p < .2$) as representing a significant variation between groups. This acknowledges that a difference of 20% is clinically meaningful. Adopting the usual, strict statistical criterion of a 5% difference may prevent clinically relevant differences between groups from being shown, because finding differences between groups is more unlikely using this stricter criterion. As shown in Table 8.2,

TABLE 8.1
Clinical Diagnoses of the Three Groups

Diagnosis	*n*
Axis I Clinical Disorder Group (*n* = 17)	
Dysthymia	8
Generalized anxiety disorder	7
Obsessive–compulsive disorder	1
Ego-dystonic homosexuality	1
Atypical eating disorder[a]	1
Inhibited sexual excitement[a]	1
Axis II Personality Disorder Group (*n* = 13)	
Schizoid personality disorder	5
Schizotypal personality disorder	3
Passive–aggressive personality disorder	2
Histrionic personality disorder	1
Mixed personality disorder	1
Atypical personality disorder	1
Dual Axis I and Axis II Disorder Group (*n* = 11)	
Dysthymia	7
Generalized anxiety disorder	4
Schizoid personality disorder	3
Compulsive personality disorder	3
Histrionic personality disorder	3
Passive–aggressive personality disorder	1
Narcissistic personality disorder	1

Note. [a]Secondary diagnosis with dysthymia.

the only difference between groups was between Axis II and Dual I and II in initial early-in-therapy mastery, with the Dual group having lower mastery.

Groups were equivalent in age and length of treatment. The first hypothesis was that initial levels of psychiatric functioning would be worse in the Axis II personality-disordered groups than in the Axis I clinical-disordered group. No such relationship was found on the measure of psychiatric functioning (HSRS), disconfirming the first hypothesis.

The second hypothesis was that initial levels of mastery are worse in the Axis II personality-disordered groups than in the Axis I clinical-disordered group. Once again, no such relationship was found. However, levels of mastery were significantly worse for the Dual Axis I and II group compared with the Axis II only group ($p < .2$).

TABLE 8.2
Demographic and Clinical Measures for the Three Diagnostic Groups

Variable	Axis I (n = 17)		Axis II (n = 13)		Dual I and II (n =11)	
	m	*SD*	*m*	*SD*	*m*	*SD*
Age (in years)	25.10	5.56	25.10	4.91	24.70	8.28
Treatment length (in weeks)	53.20	29.44	49.10	23.28	61.70	36.86
Health–Sickness Rating Scale						
At intake	481.50	50.01	457.70	53.19	482.00	46.20
At termination	532.80	45.36	485.20	75.78	531.90	76.30
Mastery Scale						
Early in therapy	3.11	0.31	3.15[a]	0.38	2.87[a]	0.39
Late in therapy	3.64	0.64	3.59	0.54	3.35	0.65

Note. [a] The group pairs were significantly different ($p < .2$) in the planned comparisons.

The third hypothesis was that changes in interpersonal mastery and psychiatric functioning over the course of therapy are greater for Axis I clinical disorders than the Axis II diagnostic groups. Correlations between early- and late-in-therapy mastery scores were taken into account by performing a Mastery × Diagnosis analysis of covariance (ANCOVA), with early-in-therapy mastery scores as the covariate and late-in-therapy mastery scores as the dependent variable. A similar but separate analysis was also performed for the HSRS.

There were no significant effects for diagnosis on the mastery measure, $F(2, 37) = 0.36$, *ns*. The results for the HSRS analysis were similar to the mastery score analysis, $F(2, 37) = 1.26$, *ns*, again with no significant effects of diagnosis. This suggests that the Axis I group experienced no greater improvement than either Axis II group in either mastery or health–sickness.

The fourth hypothesis was that changes in mastery are significantly related to gains in psychiatric functioning in both the Axis II and the Axis I groups. The specific relationship between changes in mastery during psychotherapy and HSRS outcome ratings of gain were investigated using Pearson correlations for each diagnostic group. Like the ANCOVA used above, residual gain scores were calculated to control for the correlations between early and late scores (Manning & DuBois, 1962). Changes in mastery across psychotherapy were highly significantly related to gains in health–sickness for the dual diagnostic group ($r = .74$, $p < .01$), significant for the Axis I personality-disordered group ($r = .63$, $p < .05$), but most surprisingly not significant for the Axis I clinical-disordered group ($r = .27$, *ns*). The distribution of scores is presented in Figure 8.3.

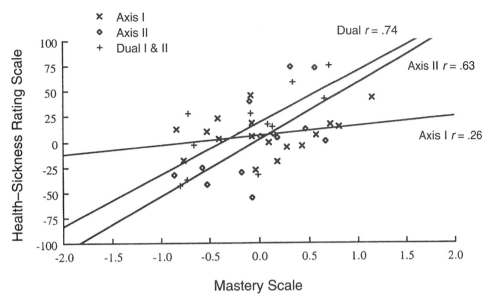

Figure 8.3. Relationship between Mastery Scale residual change scores and Health–Sickness Rating Scale residual change scores for the three diagnostic groups.

Discussion: Mastery and Personality Disorders

The aim of this study was to investigate process–outcome links in dynamic psychotherapy for personality disorders using the new measure of mastery. This began with the assumption, derived from previous research and clinical wisdom, that patients with personality disorders are generally more severe in psychiatric functioning and do not evidence as large gains from psychotherapy compared with those with only an Axis I clinical disorder. The results of this study as a whole do not support this pessimism. Patients with personality disorders (even those with dual Axis I and II diagnoses) were equivalent in initial psychiatric severity (even using a very generous criterion of significance) and showed equivalently large gains from dynamic psychotherapeutic treatment. This finding is at odds with previous research (Diguer et al., 1993; Docherty et al., 1986).

It appears that the patients diagnosed with a personality disorder in this sample were not as severe in psychiatric status as in other samples, although the dual diagnostic group did have significantly worse levels of mastery early in therapy. It is not clear how important this difference in severity is for the interpretation and generalization of these results. There are also several other limitations in this study. First, the sample size in each group was small, so the results may not generalize to the larger patient population. Second, the ranges of diagnoses were reasonably heterogeneous. It would have been preferable to have focused either on one diagnostic group in the comparisons (e.g., dysthymia vs. schizoid personality disorder) or at least have a larger sample with more equal representation of diagnostic groupings (or clusters of personality disorders). The following concluding remarks should be treated cautiously until further research is undertaken, particularly given the small and somewhat idiosyncratic sample size.

One goal of this study was to investigate the differential effect of diagnosis on changes in mastery. Significant relationships were found between changes in mastery and health–sickness ratings in the personality-disordered groups, but not in the Axis I clinical-disordered group (Figure 8.3). This result could be tentatively interpreted as follows. Gains in mastery and the development of self-understanding and self-control in the context of interpersonal relations are particularly salient and important mechanisms of change in patients with a personality disorder (or, at least, for patients in this sample). Because dynamic psychotherapy is intimately concerned with interpersonal functioning both inside (through the analysis of transference) and outside of the therapy, these results imply that it may be a particularly helpful form of treatment for patients with personality disorders.

Moreover, mastery improved over the course of dynamic therapy in the Axis I group (Table 8.2), but it showed only a nonsignificant trend toward being related to clinical outcome. This suggests that the principal mechanism of change in the Axis I group probably lay elsewhere and that mastery, although important, may not be the central mechanism. It may be, for example, that the emergence of symptoms of helplessness and anxiety may be a more potent change mechanism for this group. Nevertheless, this result is puzzling and requires replication with a larger sample. Other samples with predominantly Axis I disorders (i.e., the study with depressed patients, above, and the study with patients with substance abuse, in the sections that follow) did show a significant relationship between mastery and symptom change, which further suggests that this sample may be atypical with regard to Axis I.

In summary, these results provide reason for cautious optimism in treating patients with personality disorders, particularly when using a treatment that focuses on improving mastery through self-control and self-understanding in interpersonal relationships. Changes in the mastery of patients with a personality disorder were predictive of good outcome. When compared to Axis I disorders, for this sample, the augmentation in self-understanding and self-control appeared to be particularly predictive of improvement. Early in treatment, patients with personality disorders often function at low levels of mastery (Levels 1 and 2; see chapter 4 and 6), and a central goal of treatment is to address the difficulties they experience in trusting the therapist and the therapeutic process; addressing these problems early in the process helps move them to explore areas of interpersonal functioning that foster higher mastery.

The study that follows investigates mastery in patients with another severe and often relapsing clinical problem: substance dependence.

The aim of this study was to investigate changes in mastery in patients with substance dependence and to investigate the nature of these changes in relation to changes in drug use and general functioning. People with substance abuse typically have considerable difficulties in changing or ceasing their addictive behavior. From a biopsychosocial theoretical perspective, understanding drug addiction requires the consideration of the physical–biological rewarding mechanisms underlying addiction, the maintaining psychological conditions, and the social context that nurtures the addiction. Many people with substance dependence problems seek psychotherapeutic help. This is in recognition of the often observed phenomenon that drug abusers often have significant interpersonal and social problems that maintain their drug-using lifestyle. Mastering these interpersonal problems can often be central to making long-term changes in substance abuse behaviors. In this investigation of substance dependence problems, patients in the sample were addicted to cannabis. Cannabis use is a good example of substance abuse in general because it is the most widely used illegal drug, has a clear dependence syndrome, and usually requires psychotherapy to treat.

Introduction to the Study

From a clinician's point of view, one of the quandaries in the field of addictions is why only a very small percentage of people who use or try drugs go on to become habitual users. The phenomenon of self-initiated cessation has begun to receive some research attention (Cunningham, Sobell, & Sobell, 1998). In the case of cannabis, it is estimated that only 10% of people who try the drug go on to use it habitually over an extended period of time (Hall, Solowij, & Lemon, 1994). These are the ones who typically come to the attention of counseling and psychotherapy services, because their ability to control or cease their use has become too hard a task to achieve without professional assistance. Early in a drug using career, users of cannabis may enjoy its general pleasurable effects, but with frequent and prolonged use symptoms of depression, anxiety, paranoia, and insomnia may appear, which the user attempts to alleviate with continued use of cannabis. This may simply serve as an avoidance of life's problems (Solowij & Grenyer, 2001).

Cannabis users seeking treatment have reported smoking as an avoidance technique (Solowij, Grenyer, Chesher, & Lewis, 1995), as have even short-term users, with research showing that these motives for use are good indicators of problematic consequences and lifetime consumption (Simons, Correia, Carey, & Borsari, 1998). Chronic use may also interfere with motivation, in particular with setting and achieving long-term aspirations or even short-term goals (Kouri, Pope, Yurgelun-Todd, & Gruber, 1995; Reilly, Didcott, Swift, & Hall, 1998; Solowij et al., 1995). The idea of an amotivational syndrome caused by cannabis use has long been proposed, although evidence for such a syndrome has been equivocal. Chronic users may become apathetic, lethargic, withdrawn, and unmotivated, but these symptoms are probably attributable to depression, cognitive impairment, and chronic intoxication (Hall & Solowij, 1997; Hall et al., 1994). The use of cannabis on a daily or near daily basis can also result in dependence, and its discontinuation is associated with withdrawal symptoms. Greater numbers of cannabis users are now seeking help, and appropriate treatments are being developed for their specific needs (Grenyer et al., 1995; Grenyer, Solowij, & Peters, 1996; Stephens, Roffman, & Simpson, 1993, 1994).

In accordance with the biopsychosocial drive theory developed in chapter 2, drug use can be understood only within the context of the person's life. In particular, problems may emerge from the inability to satisfactorily meet wishes and needs, an inability that often arises because maladaptive ways of relating to people have formed out of problematic experience and have become ingrained personality traits. Because these maladaptive cognitive and behavior patterns do not lead to a satisfactory negotiation of the needs of the person, they are accompanied by symptoms of distress such as anxiety and helplessness. According to this theory, drug use may be seen as an unsatisfactory attempt to relieve the helplessness, anxiety, and depression resulting from problems in meeting needs and fulfilling wishes. In treating drug dependence, attention increasingly turns to underlying feelings of depression and helplessness arising from maladaptive interpersonal ways of relating. Change is brought about through mastering (understanding and controlling) core conflictual relationship themes and the role of drug use within these problems. The therapist establishes a firm, consistent, and predictable therapeutic framework to strengthen the helping alliance with the patient by focusing on the patient's goals and fostering understanding of relationship conflicts and drug addiction (Grenyer et al., 1995).

The relationship between cannabis use and depression, anxiety, and other affective states is unclear. Individuals often report using cannabis for therapeutic or self-medicating purposes to alleviate symptoms of depression, anxiety, and stress; alter consciousness; and facilitate social and sexual relations, relaxation, and sleep (Gruber, Pope, & Brown, 1996; Gruber, Pope, & Oliva, 1997; Reilly et al., 1998; Solowij, 1998). Some have found it helpful for mania (Grinspoon & Bakalar, 1998), and cannabidiol, a component of cannabis, may even have antipsychotic effects (Zuardi, Morais, Guimarães & Mechoulam, 1995). Nevertheless, there is evidence that prolonged heavy use of cannabis in itself is associated with depressive states and increased symptoms of psychological distress. Depressive symptoms are predictors of cessation of cannabis use (Chen & Kandel, 1998). Sometimes users have little insight into the possibility that their cannabis use may cause their depression and anxiety and claim only that it relieves these symptoms. Both perceptions and affective states can change dramatically after cessation of use, when users feel that they have come out of a fog and have clearer, less muddy thinking (Gruber et al., 1996; Gruber et al., 1997; Lundqvist, 1995; Reilly et al., 1998; Solowij, 1998).

If the development of mastery is a central goal of therapy for substance dependence, then increases in self-understanding and self-control should be associated with reduction in drug use. Because depression commonly occurs with drug abuse (including cannabis abuse), changes in mastery should also be reflected in changes in depression, as a person becomes less helpless and hopeless about the addiction and more in control. The self-control facet of mastery should be particularly important in substance abuse treatment: Although it is important for the patient to understand and have insight into the problem, change requires effective self-control. The study reported in the following sections was designed to assess the role of mastery within substance abuse treatment. An aim was to clarify the changes in mastery between those who receive active psychotherapy treatment and those in a control or brief treatment group and to answer the question: Does mastery increase in those who get little or no treatment?

Participants

Forty-three long-term cannabis users (33 men, 10 women, mean age 31, range = 22–48 years) were recruited to participate in a controlled trial of psychotherapy or brief intervention for their substance abuse. All participants met the *DSM–IV* (American Psychiatric Association, 1994) diagnostic criteria for cannabis dependence, had used cannabis on a near-daily basis for a minimum of 5 years, and had no history of other drug abuse. The 43 users studied were a representative subset of a larger group of 100 cannabis users studied (Grenyer & Solowij, in press). Allocation between groups was stratified on the basis of previous history of cannabis use and other variables. Twenty-seven participants were married or in committed relationships, and 16 were single; participants had an average of 15 years of education. Participants had been using cannabis on average for 13 years (range = 5–27 years). Twenty-three participants were randomized into a psychotherapy group and 20 into a brief treatment group.

Treatment Groups

Psychotherapy consisted of 16 sessions of weekly individual time-limited supportive–expressive psychotherapy (Luborsky, 1984) based on a special manual for cannabis dependence (Grenyer et al., 1995). Therapy was conducted by 5 female and 3 male trained psychotherapists (mean age 40, range = 29–48 years) who were recruited from private practice and had on average 11 years of experience (range = 7–20 years).

The brief (control) treatment consisted of a single session of assessment and advice on quitting cannabis and the provision of self-help materials (Grenyer et al., 1996).

Measure of Mastery

The Mastery Scale was used to measure the level of patient mastery; the scale is described in chapter 4 and the reliability and validity of the scoring are presented in chapter 5. This study used 5-minute speech samples collected during intake and after treatment completion (at 4-month follow-up). Participants were asked to speak for 5 minutes about "your life at the moment—the good things and the bad—what it is like for you," following the instructions by Viney (1983). Although the instructions specify 5 minutes (as a guide), many spoke longer than 5 minutes.

Other Outcome Variables

The GAF (Axis V of *DSM-IV*; American Psychiatric Association, 1994) is a rating scale for measuring the overall functioning of an individual on a continuum from psychiatric or psychological sickness to health; it is based on the HSRS and was administered prior to treatment and at follow-up (Luborsky, 1962, 1975; Luborsky, Diguer, Luborsky, McLellan, et al., 1993). The BDI (Beck et al., 1961), a standard inventory used to assess depression in clinical and nonclinical samples, was administered prior to treatment and at follow-up. It has good reliability and validity and has been shown to relate meaningfully to other clinical ratings of change (Beck & Steer, 1987). Self-reported abstinence from cannabis was used as the measure of change in drug use at 4 months, and urine analyses were available to confirm abstinence for four fifths of the sample that claimed abstinence.

Changes in mastery between the psychotherapy and the brief intervention (control) group were assessed through ANCOVAs between final scores of the two groups, with the initial scores as the covariant to control for differences in initial levels between participants and groups. Effect size estimates were calculated by subtracting termination psychotherapy from brief intervention scores divided by the pretreatment standard deviation (Jacobson & Truax, 1991). Clinical significance is considered a more meaningful index of change than statistical significance in psychotherapy outcome studies. To investigate changes in the individual categories of mastery, scores were corrected for the length of the speech sample using the method of Gottschalk and colleagues (1969; see chapter 4).

Changes in Mastery Over Psychotherapy

Two experienced, trained independent judges scored the Mastery Scale data; interrater reliability was .79 or higher. Discrepancies in scoring were discussed and a final agreed set of scores was then derived for analysis. Because these were relatively short speech samples (average 700 words, range = 226–1,996 words), it was considered more valid to reach agreement

TABLE 8.3
Mastery Scale Scores and ANCOVA *F* Test for Psychotherapy
and Brief Intervention for Cannabis Dependence

Group	Pretherapy		Posttherapy			
	m	*SD*	*m*	*SD*	*F*	*p*
Psychotherapy	2.98	.92	4.61	.77	24.60	.00
Brief intervention	3.18	.71	3.13	.92		

Note. ANCOVA = analysis of covariance.

about the final scores rather than simply average the two judges' ratings. Initial scores between the two groups were not significantly different (F = .17, p = .68). Outcome analyses of the psychotherapy and control group termination scores were calculated using an ANCOVA (controlling for initial levels); the results are presented in Table 8.3. Gains in mastery for the psychotherapy group were significantly greater than for the brief intervention group, with the psychotherapy group making large gains and the brief intervention group not changing over the 4-month evaluation period. To ascertain the clinical significance of the changes in mastery, treatment control effect size estimates of change were calculated for individual mastery score categories. Figure 8.4 shows the effect size changes.

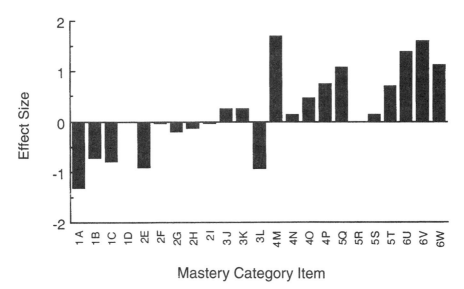

Figure 8.4. Effect size estimates of individual Mastery Scale categories (1A–6W) for psychotherapy versus control after 4 months of evaluation.
Note. Negative effect size scores indicate that control group scores were greater than psychotherapy group scores.

As can be seen in Figure 8.4, the psychotherapy group improved considerably in mastery in Levels 4 (interpersonal awareness), 5 (self-understanding), and 6 (self-control) in comparison with the control (brief intervention) group. Conversely, the psychotherapy group had reductions in lower levels of mastery scores compared to the control group, as indicated by the negative effect size estimates in Levels 1 (lack of impulse control) and 2 (introjection and projection of negative affects) and in one Level 3 (difficulties in understanding and control) category.

Mastery and Depression, General Functioning, and Changes in Drug Use

Depression scores at the start of treatment were equivalent between groups, $F(1, 41) = .09$, $p = .77$, with the average BDI score of 13.74 ($SD = 9.21$). At the completion of treatment, there were significant differences between groups with significant gains in the psychotherapy group ANCOVA, $F(2, 40) = 9.30$, $p = .00$; average follow-up BDI scores were 5.26 ($SD = 6.15$) for the treatment group and 11.10 (SD 8.81) for the control group.

Depression scores were divided into two groups: depressed and nondepressed levels (split at a BDI score of 9, according to the recommendations of Beck & Steer, 1987). Participants who were still depressed at 4 months had correspondingly lower mastery scores ($M = 3.38$, $SD = 1.15$) compared to nondepressed participants ($M = 4.24$, $SD = .98$), and this difference was statistically significant, $F = 6.81$, $p = .01$.

The GAF scores of the psychotherapy and control group at the start of treatment were equivalent; the treatment group had an average GAF score of 63.78 ($SD = 8.34$), and the control group had a score of 64.40 ($SD = 10.45$). At the 4-month follow-up, the GAF score for the treatment group was 76.72 ($SD = 6.78$); for the control group it was 68.45 ($SD = 10.78$), which was significantly different using ANCOVA ($F = 39.21$, $p = .00$). A Pearson correlation between final GAF and mastery scores was calculated; the relationship was significant ($r = .56$, $p = .00$).

At the 4-month follow-up, 80% of the treatment group were abstinent, compared with 20% of the control group. For those who were abstinent, their mastery scores were significantly higher compared with the nonabstinent group ($M = 4.52$, $SD = .76$ vs. $M = 3.09$, $SD = 1.00$), $F = 28.14$, $p = .00$.

Discussion: Mastery of Substance Dependence

Changes in mastery levels were significantly greater for the psychotherapy group than for the brief treatment group. The benefits of these gains in mastery are reflected in significant improvements in general functioning, reductions in depression, and a greater likelihood of being abstinent from the abused drug.

Mastery does not appear to improve without psychotherapy: The very brief intervention did not lead to any changes in mastery, as evidenced from the speech samples provided at 4-month follow-up. In contrast, the psychotherapy group improved significantly. It is interesting to investigate where most of the changes occurred (Figure 8.4). In terms of changes in mastery, the self-understanding items as a group did not change as much as the self-control items. Very large change (effect size > 1) was achieved for the self-understanding item 5Q (insight into repeating personality patterns of self) but not for the self-understanding items 5R (no change) and 5S (.14). Very large improvements in the psychotherapy group (compared to the control group) were observed across all the self-control items (6U. Expression of emotional self-control over conflicts; 6V. Expression of new changes in emotional responding; and 6W. References to self-analysis). This supports the idea that the development of self-control is particularly important for substance abusers.

Large decrements were observed in 1A (expressions of being emotionally overwhelmed) for the psychotherapy group, as compared to the brief intervention condition, with other large changes of note, including reductions in 3L, 2E, 1C, 1B, items related to problems with impulse control, internal negative states, and the difficulties in changing and controlling problems. This suggests that compared to others, drug users who were successful in their treatment were better able to reduce their feelings of being out of control and distressed.

Not only did changes in mastery predict changes in general functioning, but perhaps more significantly in relation to substance abuse, the mastery changes were related to significant reductions in depression. Depression is often observed in drug users, and overcoming the helplessness, hopelessness, and feelings of lack of control appear to be a particularly important key to treatment success. Using the mastery concept, it is possible to understand how these changes come about. The biggest single change (4M) was in "questioning the reactions of others," which relates to developing an interpersonal awareness of the person's problem. It may be that assessing, challenging, and probing others' responses, rather than blindly accepting them, is particularly helpful in treatment. It also implies that this helplessness may have interpersonal roots and that a therapeutic focus on interpersonal understanding of issues may be associated with change.

The following case study illustrates the kinds of changes that the psychotherapy treatment brought about. Frederick, a 32-year-old computer technician, is currently doing a graduate diploma in business systems. He has been smoking cannabis continuously since he was 16, and he came to treatment after finding that his life was stagnated, his relationships were beginning to suffer, and he was worried about the effects it was having on his memory and his ability to complete his studies. At the follow-up assessment following psychotherapy, he stated,

Um, well I would say that um having been on this program/and having 16 sessions of psychotherapy/has been a very kind of um exposing /and um revealing ah process for me./It ah has been very, very difficult. (3L)/But by the same token/it's one in which I have really wanted to go on.(3L)/Perhaps one of the most ah important decisions that came out of my psychotherapy,/and I think particularly as a result of my um counselor—learner/and feeling so sort of safe with her (5S)/was sort of the realization as I went through counseling (5Q)/that um there was sort of a lot of work that I wanted to do about my own spiritual/and emotional development. (5R)/And that marijuana was an issue that was perhaps masking,/and keeping veiled various issues that I found too painful to deal with. (5R)/But one very kind of positive thing that has happened,/I would say that I, in terms of my marriage/Um [pause], my marriage is in good shape. (5S)/I'd say generally from a family point of view things have improved. (6V)/And the particular relationship I had with my mother,/and I suppose still do have with my mother./And um I feel a bit more positive about my relationship with my mother (6V)/ although [pause] I have to consciously hold her at a distance. (5T)/I'm looking forward to going back to studies next year./But because I'm not stressed out/ con- confronting you know major hundred percent exams in the next week,/it's taken a while,/but I do feel more relaxed now (6U)/and I feel healthier now./I feel as if my immune system is ah come back to normal.(6U)/And I'd say generally it's been very good for me to, to make me stop. (6U)/And not to think or smoke dope /.

Frederick is clearly articulating the process of psychotherapy and its benefits. Therapy was a difficult and challenging experience; the strong therapeutic alliance he developed with his therapist helped him to see that he used cannabis to avoid serious spiritual and emotional issues in his life. His response reflects the biopsychosocial model, with improvements in the bio- (his health), psycho- (his emotions), and social (his marriage) dimensions. Interpersonal issues were seen as a central benefit, particularly in the core relationship problem with his mother. The development of mastery is seen not just in relation to reductions in drug use, but also was tied to improvements in functioning across his life. This is in contrast to some treatment approaches for substance abuse, which focus almost exclusively on changing drug use behaviors. The mastery research suggests that drug use can be seen as a symptom of a larger problem in living, prompting a broader biopsychosocial approach to psychotherapy.

This study investigated changes in mastery in patients receiving treatment for substance abuse. The biopsychosocial theory of mastery posits that understanding drug addiction requires the perspective of both the physical–biological rewarding mechanisms underlying addiction, the maintaining psychological conditions, and the social context under which the addiction flourishes. This study has found that gains in mastery predicted significant improvements in general functioning, reductions in depression, and a greater likelihood of abstinence from the abused drug. Improvement in self-control appears to be a particularly important change mechanism for substance abusers.

Mastery does not appear to improve without psychotherapy: The very brief intervention did not lead to any changes in mastery compared to the psychotherapy group. The biggest single change in mastery was in developing an awareness of one's interpersonal problem. Focusing on the drug user's interpersonal world and helping them understand others' reactions appears to be associated with significant improvement. Overcoming the depressive hopelessness common in drug users through an interpersonal focus may be more associated with change than a more exclusive focus on drug use behaviors.

CONCLUSION

The mastery research presented here suggests that different problems might require a different therapeutic focus depending on the patient's presenting difficulties. For example, patients with depression appear to benefit the most from fostering self-assertion, questioning other people's reactions within interpersonal situations, and developing insight into their own repeating personality patterns. In contrast, patients with substance dependence benefit the most from a focus on self-control. Developing an awareness of one's interpersonal problem appears to be one of the keys to overcoming the depressive helplessness and hopelessness common in drug users. Patients with personality disorders also appear to benefit from a focus on interpersonal functioning. The mastery concept can therefore also help clinicians distinguish and differentiate different pathways to clinical change depending on their clients' presenting problems.

The final chapter of this book summarizes the overall clinical implications of this mastery research and future research directions of mastery through psychotherapy.

V

CONCLUSION

9

THE PROCESS OF MASTERY: PRESENT STATUS AND FUTURE DIRECTIONS

The fundamental finding of this study is that established maladaptive patterns for meeting needs and wishes are amenable to mastery (i.e., being understood and controlled) through successful psychotherapy. Mastery was theorized to be part of the change process and has been shown to be an essential dimension of improvement in psychotherapy. Although some of the examples used in this study are derived from psychodynamic therapy, mastery has been shown to be essential in many, if not all, psychotherapies. The evidence suggests that theoretically relevant and central psychological variables can be directly and reliably measured from patient narratives told in psychotherapy. The major findings of the research presented in this book are summarized in this chapter, followed by a comment on the implications for future research and for the practice of psychotherapy.

This book has consolidated a biopsychosocial theory of change using the mastery concept; demonstrated how mastery helps to explain patient gains and can assist the therapist in practicing psychotherapy; and applied a new reliable and valid tool, the Mastery Scale, to verbatim transcripts of therapy. Patients move through predictable steps in mastery acquisition, and these gains are related to improvements in their symptoms and life functioning. Indeed, psychotherapy can be understood as a process that assists in the development of mastery.

A major strength of the research presented here is that important process variables have been systematically scored from the content of patients' verbal communications and linked to central outcome variables in therapy. Variables that have been reliably scored include central dynamic concepts such as insight into repeating personality patterns; dynamic links between past and present relationships; self-analysis; emotional self-control; and psychological defenses such as projection, forgetting, and withdrawal.

Content analysis was chosen to avoid other more subjective, complex, and possibly unreliable, methods of scoring. With this method, judges do not have to make sophisticated global judgments resting heavily on their personal predilections and theoretical persuasion to score the Mastery Scale. Anyone with a reasonable grasp of the language and some emotional sensitivity should be able to score the scale reliably. Patient statements were largely taken at face value, although the scale is not applied mechanistically, as it would be if transcripts were scored by a computer. The method relies on the human integrator (the Mastery Scale judge) who brings emotional capacities into the process of scoring. The method devised is robust and captures an important dynamic change variable.

The empirical research arose out of a comprehensive theory of clinical change. A biopsychosocial theory, founded on established principles, has been translated into a modern psychotherapy research context without loss of these core principles. Links were drawn between the theory and the empirical results, and the data were used to test the theory. The theory, however, is not considered impervious to change, and accordingly, the results are used to suggest modifications to the theory where necessary.

The thrust of this study fits into and contributes to an ongoing effort by researchers across the world to understand how psychotherapy works. The empirical approach was derived from well-established methods of conducting research of this type. The particular concerns of this study arose out of previous research and were designed to further the understanding of how interpersonal processes play a role in psychotherapy.

ESSENTIAL FINDINGS

This book arose in part out of a quandary: the finding that although there are many kinds of psychotherapy, most have equivalent outcomes. The search for factors common and central to change has led researchers to investigate the therapeutic alliance and the related transference or schema processes. Another important common variable, mastery, conceptualized here as self-understanding and self-control, has not received the same theoretical or empirical attention (see Part II of this volume). The studies reported in this book have been designed to overcome this omission, through a comprehensive study of the practical, research, and theoretical implications of the mastery concept. In particular, attention is drawn to patients: how they understand and control their problems through telling narratives to their therapists and how this promotes gains in mastery and a lessening in distress and symptoms (chapter 1).

Mastery and a Comprehensive Biopsychosocial Theory

The attempt to open up this new area of investigation, the development of patient mastery, has required some important synthesizing work regarding the theoretical foundations of mastery. *Mastery* is defined as the acquisition of self-control and self-understanding in the context of interpersonal and social relations, to better meet fundamental needs, wishes, and desires. The biopsychosocial theory adopted here arose out of fundamental propositions about psychology as a science that were first enunciated by Freud (1895/1966). The theory begins with biological motivators or drives, which profoundly influence psychological processes. These are in turn expressed within interpersonal and social relations. The mastery theory thus coherently links biological, psychological, and social processes (chapter 2). The development of problems in mastery can be understood by integrating findings from attachment, self psychology, cognitive, behavioral' and object relations theories and studies. Using the mastery concept helps to advance these theories by extending and integrating an understanding of patient functioning and how it changes through psychotherapy (chapter 3).

Contribution of the Mastery Scale

The advance in the understanding of how mastery operates through psychotherapy was only possible through the development of a new tool to measure mastery: the Mastery Scale (Grenyer, 1994b). The content analysis scale was designed with 6 levels (from low to high mastery) embracing 23 individual content categories, which were applied to verbatim transcripts of patient speech (chapter 4). Analysis of the scale's properties showed that it may be scored reliably and that it has validity (chapter 5).

In science it is important not only to discover new findings but also to ascertain whether they are robust (i.e., that the same results can be replicated on other samples). One strength of this mastery research is that three independent samples of patients have been studied: a mixed diagnosis group of 41 patients, a group of 30 depressed patients, and 43 substance abusers (chapter 8). In each study group, the same essential pattern of results was found: (a) judges were able to identify and score mastery reliably, and (b) gains in mastery predicted improvement in patient functioning and lessening of symptoms. Analysis of the individual mastery categories helped to articulate patient change over treatment. In addition, across these three samples, more than nine independent judges were successfully trained to use the Mastery Scale, with high interjudge agreement.

Mastery and Clinical Practice

The mastery research provides a foundation for understanding the process of psychotherapy from the perspective of both the patient and the therapist. From the perspective of the patient, mastery can be conceived of as a continuum, with three discernable phases. In Phase 1 (low mastery), patients are dominated by their symptoms and defenses and are unable to cope with their problems. In Phase 2 (medium mastery), patients are questioning themselves and others in their life in the struggle to understand and improve their relationships. In Phase 3 (high mastery), patients are able to understand and control their reactions to problems with gratifying needs and wishes and to seek better ways of responding within their interpersonal relationships. Understanding these three levels provides therapists with a guide or window into patient progress. Therapists need to match their approaches with the current functioning of the patient. Patients with low mastery require mainly supportive techniques, those with medium mastery require a sustained interpersonal focus, and those with high mastery benefit from in-depth exploration of sources of self-understanding and self-control (chapter 6).

Mastery and the Interpersonal Interior of Psychotherapy

It was possible to probe further into the interpersonal processes underlying mastery through investigating how mastery relates to the therapeutic alliance, transference, and different types of relationships (chapter 7). The strength of the therapeutic alliance was shown to have an important predictive impact on the subsequent development of mastery through psychotherapy. Support from the therapist probably helps patients to bear the task of understanding and controlling their long-standing problematic transference-related personality patterns. Narratives told in psychotherapy were predominantly negative, yet over the course of successful therapy it was found that patient responses to conflicts became more positive, paralleling mastery improvement. Thus, it appears that an important benefit of therapy is mastering pervasive transference-related responses. In particular, clinical improvement was found to be predicted by patients' ability to master problems in their relationships with their parents and to a lesser extent with their current lovers.

Treatment of Different Patient Populations

Different groups of patients appear to improve in mastery through parallel mastery-related processes (see chapter 8). Patients with depression were found to improve in particular through a focus on enhancing self-assertion, questioning others' reactions within interpersonal conflicts, and developing insight into repeating personality patterns of self. Individuals with personality disorders appeared to benefit from focusing on interpersonal self-understanding and control. For patients with substance dependence, developing an interpersonal awareness of the context of their problem seemed to be beneficial. Challenging the reactions of others appeared to be particularly useful to overcome helplessness in the face of the addiction. Overall, it was found that for different clinical populations, maintaining an interpersonal focus, by assessing not only patient feelings but the responses of others to them in their interpersonal world, was especially helpful in promoting mastery. Patients who were less able to come to terms with their interpersonal conflicts and problems were those who made fewer gains and less improvement by the end of therapy.

Ongoing International Studies Using the Mastery Scale

It is important not only to replicate findings using different samples but also to ascertain whether other research groups, working independently, can achieve the same level of reliability and validity using the Mastery Scale. Several international studies using the Mastery Scale are currently under way. The Mastery Scale has been translated into German (Grenyer, Dahlbender, & Reichenauer, 1998) and Italian (Grenyer, 1994a). For example, a study at University of Ulm, Germany, of 44 young female psychotherapy patients found that mastery was not only scored reliably but also showed important associations with other clinical measures, further supporting its validity (Reiner Dahlbender, personal communication, December 1999 and June 2000). A recent study has found that mastery was significantly related to the core relationship conflict and that improvements in this relationship conflict were associated with mastery augmentation (Dahlbender, Erena, Reichenauer, & Kächele, 2000). The scale is also being successfully applied to studies of hospitalized psychiatric patients at the Istituto di Clinica Psichiatrica, Università degli Studi di Milano, Ospedale Maggiore Policlinico, Milan, Italy (Professor Gherardo Amadei, personal communication, October 1999 and June 2000).

DIRECTIONS FOR FUTURE RESEARCH

Further Development of the Theoretical Roots of Mastery

Although mastery appears to be a part of the theoretical account of most schools of psychotherapy, additional work needs to be done to integrate the models of mastery underlying the different schools of clinical theory. One example developed in this book (chapter 2) is a biopsychosocial theory, which proved to be useful because of its comprehensive psychodynamic account of mind and motivation. Other schools of clinical theory have developed similar notions of change, using different terminology and models. The way in which these theories enrich our understanding of mastery requires further examination.

Studies of Other Types of Psychotherapy

Although all of the transcripts analyzed in this study were derived from dynamic psychotherapy, psychotherapies based on other persuasions, such as cognitive therapy, experiential therapy, personal construct, and client-centered therapy, can be expected to achieve similar changes. Further studies of these other types of therapies are needed to advance the "assimilative integration" of mastery within each of these explanatory models (Messer, 1992).

Relationship Between Mastery and Other Variables

Further comparisons could be made between changes in mastery and other measures. For example, studies could examine the relationship between mastery and specific defense mechanisms (as articulated in Appendix B of the *DSM–IV*; American Psychiatric Association, 1994). The Ulm psychotherapy group in Germany has begun this work and has found predictive relationships between defensive functioning and mastery (Reiner Dahlbender, personal communication, December 1999). Studies could also examine relationships with related constructs, such as emotional intelligence and alexithymia. Advances in the understanding of narratives and narrative analysis may also enrich our understanding of mastery. Further studies on transference, insight, and the therapeutic alliance would also contribute to the understanding of mastery development.

Mastery Fluctuations Throughout Psychotherapy

The studies reported in this book include narratives from early in therapy and late in therapy. What is now required are studies that examine changes throughout the course of psychotherapy, including samples derived from the middle stage of psychotherapy. This requires sampling a greater number of sessions from throughout therapy. For example, K. I. Howard and colleagues (1993) charted the sequence of changes in process and outcome variables at different points in therapy. Sampling from across therapy would increase our understanding of the sequence of changes in different stages of mastery and how these relate to other clinical changes.

Links Between Mastery and Outcome

Some of the results reported in this book rest on finding correlations between process and outcome variables. However, a correlation between two variables does not necessarily mean that the two are causally related. It may be, for instance, that the correlation between mastery and health–sickness is in part attributable to a third variable (such as the therapeutic alliance). Further research is required on the relationship of different clinical variables to mastery. In this kind of research, it is difficult to avoid this correlation–causation dilemma, because establishing causal links requires the kind of tight control of variables that would in most cases destroy the natural phenomenon— psychotherapy—that is the object of interest. (For further discussion of such process–outcome dilemmas, see, e.g., Stiles, 1988, and Wallerstein, 1993.)

Technical Aspects of Scale Administration

The methodological implications of various decisions involved in constructing the Mastery Scale should also be investigated. For example, it was generally recommended that judges score narratives from psychotherapy without knowing when in therapy the narrative was told. In addition, narratives were usually extracted and presented to judges without a context. Studies could examine the implications of these decisions and whether different results would ensue by allowing judges more contextual knowledge of when and why a particular narrative was told. In addition, further work on the statistical aggregation of mastery scores could yield greater insights into the subtlety of the change process, such as assessing the sequences of individual mastery scores within narratives.

Therapists' Contributions to Patient Mastery

The primary focus of the Mastery Scale is on patient functioning. It would be interesting to look at the influence of therapist behaviors on the development of mastery, and especially to ascertain the impact of the therapist's degree of intensity of supportiveness versus expressiveness toward patients at different levels of mastery.

Different Diagnostic Groups and Larger Samples

The sample sizes in the studies reported in this book were modest, and further research is necessary on other populations, preferably using larger samples. It should be noted that gathering larger samples and applying such methods are not easy tasks: It is extremely time intensive and costly to design psychotherapy trials and then record, transcribe, and apply these types of content analysis methods. Although studies are reported here on patients with depression, substance dependence, and mixed diagnosis, studies with other patient populations (e.g., those diagnosed with psychosomatic disorders, anxiety, and perhaps schizophrenia) would be a welcome addition to knowledge on how mastery operates within different patient groups.

Other Complementary Ways of Assessing Mastery

Content analysis is time consuming, which discourages researchers from adopting it routinely in clinical trials. Therefore, it may be beneficial to develop other, less time-consuming ways of assessing mastery, such as a questionnaire method. It would be important to assess whether simpler tools are able to measure the same concepts or capture the same subtle therapeutic factors. In addition, refinements and changes may be made to the current scale, not only in the content categories but also (and more specifically) in the methods of scoring and compiling results.

HOW PSYCHOTHERAPY WORKS: THE DEVELOPMENT OF MASTERY

The following summary arises out of a consideration of the outcome of this mastery study. The basic efficacy of therapy rests on the establishment of a strong supportive therapeutic alliance between patients and therapists. The safety of this relationship gives patients the opportunity to explore their problems through the telling of narratives. The exploration of how long-standing patterns of problems and conflicts are currently active in patients' lives is central to the work of therapy. A principal mechanism of change in therapy is through the development of mastery, which involves the acquisition of self-control and self-understanding. Patients need not only to understand their problems and conflicts but also to feel in control of their responses to difficulties in having needs met and wishes fulfilled. Pervasive problems do not appear to be solved or cured in psychotherapy; rather, they are better mastered.

Vaillant (1993) summarized some of these ideas, although not within a causal account of mind, by stressing the importance of the therapist–patient dyad in fostering mastery:

> Another person can offer the individual in conflict a sense of shared competence and unconditional positive regard. Such support can help us achieve mastery, and once that mastery is internalized, it becomes our own. Such learned mastery wards off helplessness and becomes a potent antidote to depression. (p. 109)

Through successful therapy, the major sources of emotional conflict are mastered. In other words, patients develop an awareness and understanding of the conflict, as well as a sense of control over it, which, in turn, protect them against the re-emergence of symptoms of psychological distress.

Like the future of all sciences, the future of the science of psychotherapy will always rest on close observation. This mastery research represents one attempt to examine psychotherapy at close quarters, to discover how it works. The richest source of knowledge about psychotherapy is through studying and experiencing first-hand the actual process between therapist and patient. Psychotherapy can be a powerful emotional experience that may change both the patient and the therapist, with each learning from the other (Symington, 1986, 1996). As a pioneer of psychotherapy theory, research, and practice, Freud (1933/1964b) stated more than 65 years ago that "psychoanalysis . . . is still linked to its contact with patients for increasing its depth and for its further development" (p. 151).

REFERENCES

Alexander, L. B., & Luborsky, L. (1986). The Penn Helping Alliance Scales. In L. S. Greenberg & W. M. Pinsof (Eds.), *The psychotherapeutic process: A research handbook* (pp. 325–366). New York: Guilford Press.

Alloy, L. B., Abramson, L. Y., Metalsky, G. I., & Hartlage, S. (1988). The hopelessness theory of depression: Attributional aspects. *British Journal of Clinical Psychology, 27,* 5–21.

American Psychiatric Association. (1968). *Diagnostic and statistical manual of mental disorders* (2nd ed.). Washington, DC: Author.

American Psychiatric Association. (1980). *Diagnostic and statistical manual of mental disorders* (3rd ed.). Washington, DC: Author.

American Psychiatric Association. (1987). *Diagnostic and statistical manual of mental disorders* (3rd ed., rev.). Washington, DC: Author.

American Psychiatric Association. (1994). *Diagnostic and statistical manual of mental disorders* (4th ed.). Washington, DC: Author.

Anderson, E. M., & Lambert, M. J. (1995). Short-term dynamically oriented psychotherapy: A review and meta-analysis. *Clinical Psychology Review, 15,* 503–514.

Andrews, G., & Harvey, R. (1981). Does psychotherapy benefit neurotic patients? *Archives of General Psychiatry, 38,* 1203–1208.

Armstrong, D. M. (1968). *A materialist theory of the mind.* London: Routledge & Kegan Paul.

Aron, L. (1990). One-person and two-person psychologies and the method of psychoanalysis. *Psychoanalytic Psychology, 7,* 475–495.

Auerbach, A. H., Luborsky, L., & Johnson, M. (1972). Clinicians' predictions of psychotherapy outcome: A trial of a prognostic index. *American Journal of Psychiatry, 128,* 830–835.

Auld, F., & White, A. M. (1956). Rules for dividing interviews into sentences. *Journal of Psychology, 42,* 273–281.

Australian Bureau of Statistics. (1994). *Australian social trends 1994: Health–causes of death–youth suicide.* Canberra: Australian Government Publishing Service.

Bargh, J. A., Chaiken, S., Govender, R., & Felicia, P. (1992). The generality of the automatic attitude activation effect. *Journal of Personality and Social Psychology, 62,* 893–912.

Barlow, K., Grenyer, B., & Ilkiw-Lavalle, O. (2000). Prevalence and precipitants of aggression in psychiatric inpatient units. *Australian and New Zealand Journal of Psychiatry, 34,* 967–974.

Barron, F. (1953). An ego-strength scale which predicts response to psychotherapy. *Journal of Consulting Psychology, 17,* 327–333.

Battle, C., Imber, S., Hoehn-Saric, R., Stone, A., Nash, E., & Frank, J. (1966). Target complaints as criteria of improvement. *American Journal of Psychotherapy, 20,* 184–192.

Beck, A. T. (1976). *Cognitive therapy and the emotional disorders.* New York: International Universities Press.

Beck, A. T., & Steer, R. A. (1987). *BDI: Beck Depression Inventory manual.* San Antonio, TX: Psychological Corporation.

Beck, A. T., Ward, C. H., Mendelson, M., Mock, J., & Erbaugh, J. (1961). An inventory for measuring depression. *Archives of General Psychiatry, 4,* 561–571.

Bellack, A. S., & Hersen, M. (1998). *Comprehensive clinical psychology* (Vols. 1–11). New York: Pergamon.

Benjamin, L. S. (1993). *Interpersonal diagnosis and treatment of personality disorders.* New York: Guilford Press.

Bergin, A. E., & Garfield, S. L. (Eds.). (1994). *Handbook of psychotherapy and behaviour change* (4th ed.). New York: Wiley.

Beutler, L. E. (1991). Have all won and must all have prizes? Revisiting Luborsky et al.'s verdict. *Journal of Consulting and Clinical Psychology, 59,* 226–232.

Beutler, L. E., & Crago, M. (Eds.). (1991). *Psychotherapy research: An international review of programmatic studies.* Washington, DC: American Psychological Association.

Blacker, K. H. (1975). Tracing a memory. *Journal of the American Psychoanalytic Association, 23,* 51–68.

Blatt, S. J. (1995). The destructiveness of perfection. Implications for the treatment of depression. *American Psychologist, 50,* 1003–1020.

Blatt, S. J., Quinlan, D. M., Chevron, E. S., McDonald, C., & Zuroff, D. (1982). Dependancy and self criticism: Psychological dimensions of depression. *Journal of Consulting and Clinical Psychology, 50,* 113–124.

Blatt, S. J., Quinlan, D. M., Pilkonis, P. A., & Shea, T. M. (1995). Impact of perfectionism and need for approval on the brief treatment of depression: The National Institute of Mental Health Treatment of Depression Collaborative Research Program revisited. *Journal of Consulting and Clinical Psychology, 63*, 125–132.

Blatt, S. J., Sanislow, C. A., Zuroff, D. C., & Pilkonis, P. A. (1996). Characteristics of effective therapists: Further analyses of data from the National Institute of Mental Health Treatment of Depression Collaborative Research Program. *Journal of Consulting and Clinical Psychology, 64*, 1276–1284.

Blatt, S. J., Zuroff, D. C., Bondi, C. M., Sanislow, C. A., & Pilkonis, P. A. (1998). When and how perfectionism impedes on brief treatment of depression: Further analyses of the National Institute of Mental Health Treatment of Depression Collaborative Research Program. *Journal of Consulting and Clinical Psychology, 66*, 423–428.

Blatt, S. J., Zuroff, D. C., Quinlan, D. M., & Pilkonis, P. A. (1996). Interpersonal factors in brief treatment of depression: Further analyses of the National Institute of Mental Health Treatment of Depression Collaborative Research Program. *Journal of Consulting and Clinical Psychology, 64*, 162–171.

Book, H. E. (1998). *How to practice brief psychodynamic psychotherapy: The core conflictual relationship theme method.* Washington, DC: American Psychological Association.

Bordin, E. S. (1979). The generalizability of the psychoanalytic concept of the working alliance. *Psychotherapy: Theory, Research and Practice, 16*, 252–260.

Bordin, E. S. (1994). Theory and research on the therapeutic working alliance: New directions. In A. O. Horvath & L. S. Greenberg (Eds.), *The working alliance: Theory, research and practice* (pp. 13–37). New York: Wiley.

Bordin, E. S., Cutler, R. L., Ditmann, A. T., Harway, N. I., Rausch, H. L., & Rigler, D. (1954). Measurement problems in process research on psychotherapy. *Journal of Consulting Psychology, 18*, 79–82.

Bowlby, J. (1988). *A secure base: Clinical applications of attachment theory.* London: Routledge.

Breuer, J., & Freud, S. (1955). Studies on hysteria. In J. Strachey (Ed.), *Standard edition of the complete psychological works of Sigmund Freud* (Vol. 2, pp. 1–400). London: Hogarth Press. (Original work published 1895)

Brewin, C. R. (1985). Depression and causal attributions: What is their relation? *Psychological Bulletin, 98*, 297–309.

Brown, G. W., & Harris, T. (1978). *Social origins of depression: A study of psychiatric disorder in women.* London: Tavistock.

Buchsbaum, H., & Emde, R. (1990). Play narratives in 36-month-old children: The portrayal of early moral development and family relationships. In A. J. Solnit, P. Newbauer, S. Abrams, & A. S. Dowling (Eds.), *The psychoanalytic study of the child* (Vol. 45, pp. 129–155). New Haven, CT: Yale University Press.

Carlson, R. (1981). Studies of script theory: Adult analogs of a childhood nuclear scene. *Journal of Personality and Social Psychology, 40*, 501–510.

Chance, E. (1952). The study of transference in group therapy. *International Journal of Group Therapy, 2*, 40–53.

Chen, D., & Kandel, D. B. (1998). Predictors of cessation of marijuana use: An event history analysis. *Drug and Alcohol Dependence, 50,* 109–121.

Ciarrochi, J., Chan, A., & Caputi, P. (2000). A critical evaluation of the emotional intelligence construct. *Personality and Individual Differences, 28,* 539–561.

Cierpka, M., Zander, B., Krannich, S., Reich, G., Ratzke, K., Hombburg, H., Staats, H., & Seide, L. (1992, June). *Differences in conflictual relationship themes of male and female students.* Paper presented at the annual meeting of the Society for Psychotherapy Research, Berkeley, CA.

Clyman, R. B. (1991). The procedural organization of emotions: A contribution from cognitive science to the psychoanalytic theory of therapeutic action. *Journal of the American Psychoanalytical Association, 39*(Suppl.), 349–382.

Cohler, B. J. (1991). The life story and the study of resilience and response to adversity. *Journal of Narrative and Life History, 1,* 169–200.

Cohler, B. J., & Galatzer-Levy, R. M. (1990). Self, meaning, and morale across the second half of life. In R. A. Nemiroff & C. A. Colarusso (Eds.), *New dimensions in adult development* (pp. 214–263). New York: Basic Books.

Connolly, M. B. K., Hollon, S., & Shelton, R. (1993, June). *The development of a measure of self-understanding of interpersonal patterns.* Paper presented at the annual meeting of the Society for Psychotherapy Research, Pittsburgh, PA.

Connors, G. J., DiClemente, C. C., Carroll, K. M., Longabaugh, R., & Donovan, D. M. (1997). The therapeutic alliance and its relationship to alcoholism treatment participation and outcome. *Journal of Consulting and Clinical Psychology, 65,* 588–598.

Coyne, J. C., & Gotlib, I. H. (1983). The role of cognition in depression: A critical appraisal. *Psychological Bulletin, 94,* 472–505.

Coyne, J. C., & Gotlib, I. (1986). Studying the role of cognition in depression: Well-trodden paths and cul-de-sacs. *Cognitive Therapy and Research, 10,* 695–705.

Crisp, A. (1966). Transference, symptom emergence and social repercussion in behaviour therapy: A study of 54 treated patients. *British Journal of Medical Psychology, 39,* 179–196.

Crits-Christoph, P. (1992). The efficacy of brief dynamic psychotherapy: A meta-analysis. *American Journal of Psychiatry, 149,* 151–158.

Crits-Christoph, P., Barber, J. P., Miller, N. E., & Beebe, K. (1993). Evaluating insight. In N. E. Miller, L. Luborsky, J. P. Barber, & J. P. Docherty (Eds.), *Psychodynamic treatment research: A handbook for clinical practice* (pp. 407–422). New York: Basic Books.

Crits-Christoph, P., Cooper, A., & Luborsky, L. (1988). The accuracy of therapist's interpretations and the outcome of dynamic psychotherapy. *Journal of Consulting and Clinical Psychology, 56,* 490–495.

Crits-Christoph, P., & Luborsky, L. (1998a). Changes in CCRT pervasiveness during psychotherapy. In L. Luborsky & P. Crits-Christoph (Eds.), *Understanding transference: The core conflictual relationship theme method* (2nd ed., pp. 151–164). Washington, DC: American Psychological Association.

Crits-Christoph, P., & Luborsky, L. (1998b). Self-understanding of the CCRT. In L. Luborsky & P. Crits-Christoph (Eds.), *Understanding transference: The core con-*

flictual relationship theme method (2nd ed., pp. 213–220). Washington DC: American Psychological Association.

Crits-Christoph, P., & Mintz, J. (1991). Implications of therapist effects for the design and analysis of comparative studies of psychotherapies. *Journal of Consulting and Clinical Psychology, 59,* 20–26.

Cunningham, J. A., Sobell, L. C., & Sobell, M. B. (1998). Awareness of self-change as a pathway to recovery for alcohol abusers: Results from five different groups. *Addictive Behaviours, 23,* 399–404.

Curtis, H. C. (1979). The concept of the therapeutic alliance: Implications for the "widening scope." *Journal of the American Psychoanalytic Association, 27,* 159–192.

Dahlbender, R. W., Erena, C., Reichenauer, G., & Kächele, H. (2000). Mastery of conflictual relationship patterns in the course of psychodynamic focal therapy. *Psychotherapy, Psychosomatic Medicine and Psychology, 50,* 1–10.

Dahlbender, R. W., Volkert, M., Torres, L., Pokorny, D., Frevert, G., Reichert, S., & Kächele, H. (1992, June). *Intra- and inter-subjectivity in relationship anecdotes paradigm (RAP) interviews.* Paper presented at the annual meeting of the Society for Psychotherapy Research, Berkeley, CA.

Davanloo, H. (1980). *Short-term dynamic psychotherapy.* New York: Jason Aronson.

Deane, F. P., & Spicer, J. (1998). Validity of a simplified target complaints measure. *Assessment, 4,* 119–130.

Derogatis, L., Lipman, R. S., Covi, L., Rickels, K., & Uhlenhuth, E. H. (1970). Dimensions of outpatient neurotic pathology: Comparison of a clinical vs. an empirical assessment. *Journal of Consulting and Clinical Psychology, 34,* 164–171.

Derogatis, L. R., Rickels, K., & Rock, A. F. (1976). The SCL-90 and the MMPI: A step in the validation of a new self-report scale. *British Journal of Psychiatry, 128,* 208–289.

DeRubeis, R. J., Hollon, S. E., Evans, M. D., & Bemis, K. M. (1982). Can psychotherapies for depression be discriminated? A systematic investigation of cognitive therapy and interpersonal therapy. *Journal of Consulting and Clinical Psychology, 50,* 744–756.

Diguer, L., Barber, J., & Luborsky, L. (1993). Three concomitants: Personality disorders, psychiatric severity, and outcome of dynamic psychotherapy of major depression. *American Journal of Psychiatry, 150,* 1246-1248.

Division 12 Task Force. (1996). An update on empirically validated therapies. *Clinical Psychologist, 49,* 5–18.

Docherty, J. P., Fiester, S. J., & Shea, T. (1986). Syndrome diagnosis and personality disorder. In A. J. Frances & R. E. Hales (Eds.), *Psychiatry update: The American Psychiatric Association annual review* (Vol. 5, pp. 86–95). Washington, DC: American Psychiatric Association.

Dyck, M. (1991, July). *The empirical status of Beck's cognitive theory of depression.* Paper presented at the National Australian Behaviour Modification Association Conference, University of New South Wales, New South Wales, Australia.

Eagle, M. N. (1984). *Recent developments in psychoanalysis: A critical evaluation.* Cambridge, MA: Harvard University Press.

Eckert, R., Luborsky, L., Barber, J. P., & Crits-Christoph, P. (1990). The CCRT in patients with major depression. In L. Luborsky & P. Crits-Christoph (Eds.), *Understanding transference: The CCRT method* (pp. 222–234). New York: Basic Books.

Ekstein, R. (1956). Psychoanalytic techniques. In D. Brower & L. E. Abt (Eds.), *Progress in clinical psychology* (Vol. 2, pp. 56–71). New York: Grune & Stratton.

Elkin, I., Shea, T., Watkins, J. T., Imber, S. D., Sotsky, S. M., Collins, J. F., Glass, D. R., Pilkonis, P. A., Leber, W. R., Docherty, J. P., Fiester, S. J., & Parloff, M. B. (1989). National Institute of Mental Health Treatment of Depression Collaborative Research Programme: General effectiveness of treatments. *Archives of General Psychiatry, 46,* 971–982.

Endicott, J., Spitzer, R. L., Fleiss, J. L., & Cohen, J. (1976). The Global Assessment Scale. *Archives of General Psychiatry, 33,* 766–771.

Erickson, E. H. (1963). *Childhood and society.* New York: Norton.

Eysenck, H. J. (1952). The effects of psychotherapy: An evaluation. *Journal of Consulting Psychology, 16,* 319–324.

Fairbairn, W. R. D. (1952). A revised psychopathology of the psychoses and psychoneuroses. *Psychoanalytic studies of the personality.* London: Tavistock. (Original work published 1941)

Feffer, M. (1982). *The structure of Freudian thought.* New York: International Universities Press.

Fenichel, O. (1920–1930). *Ten years of the Berlin Psychoanalysis Institute* [Berlin]. Mimeograph.

Field, S., Barkham, M., Shapiro, D. A., & Stiles, W. B. (1994). Assessment of assimilation in psychotherapy: A quantitative case study of problematic experiences with a significant other. *Journal of Counseling Psychology, 41,* 397–406.

Fiske, D. W. (1971). The shaky evidence is slowly put together. *Journal of Consulting and Clinical Psychology, 37,* 314–315.

Fonagy, P. (1999). Memory and therapeutic action. *International Journal of Psychoanalysis, 80,* 215–223.

Frank, J. (1968). The role of hope in psychotherapy. *International Journal of Psychiatry, 5,* 383–395.

Frank, J. D. (1971). Therapeutic factors in psychotherapy. *American Journal of Psychotherapy, 25,* 350–361.

Frank, J. D. (1974). Psychotherapy: The restoration of morale. *American Journal of Psychiatry, 131,* 271–274.

French, T. M. (1958). *The reintegrative process in a psychoanalytic treatment: Vol. 3. The integration of behaviour.* Chicago: University of Chicago Press.

Freud, S. (1953). Fragment of an analysis of a case of hysteria ("Dora"). In J. Strachey (Ed.), *The standard edition of the complete psychological works of Sigmund Freud* (Vol. 7, pp. 1–122). London: Hogarth Press. (Original work published 1905)

Freud, S. (1955a). Beyond the pleasure principle. In J. Strachey (Ed.), *The standard edition of the complete psychological works of Sigmund Freud* (Vol. 18, pp. 1–64). London: Hogarth Press. (Original work published 1920)

Freud, S. (1955b). Case history: Fräulein Elisabeth von R. In J. Strachey (Ed.), *Standard edition of the complete psychological works of Sigmund Freud* (Vol. 2, pp. 135–181). London: Hogarth Press. (Original work published 1895)

Freud, S. (1955c). From the history of an infantile neurosis (the "wolf man"). In J. Strachey (Ed.), *The standard edition of the complete psychological works of Sigmund Freud* (Vol. 17, pp. 1–122). London: Hogarth Press. (Original work published 1918)

Freud, S. (1957a). Instincts and their vicissitudes. In J. Strachey (Ed.), *The standard edition of the complete psychological works of Sigmund Freud* (Vol. 14, pp. 109–140). London: Hogarth Press. (Original work published 1915)

Freud, S. (1957b). Mourning and melancholia. In J. Strachey (Ed.), *The standard edition of the complete psychological works of Sigmund Freud* (Vol. 14, pp. 237–258). London: Hogarth Press. (Original work published 1917)

Freud, S. (1957c). The unconscious. In J. Strachey (Ed.), *The standard edition of the complete psychological works of Sigmund Freud* (Vol. 14, pp. 141–158). London: Hogarth Press. (Original work published 1915)

Freud, S. (1958a). The dynamics of transference. In J. Strachey (Ed.), *The standard edition of the complete psychological works of Sigmund Freud* (Vol. 12, pp. 97–108). London: Hogarth Press. (Original work published 1912)

Freud, S. (1958b). Observations of transference-love (Further recommendations on the technique of psycho-analysis III). In J. Strachey (Ed.), *The standard edition of the complete psychological works of Sigmund Freud* (Vol. 12, pp. 157–173). London: Hogarth Press. (Original work published 1915)

Freud, S. (1958c). On the beginning of treatment (Further recommendations on the technique of psycho-analysis I). In J. Strachey (Ed.), *The standard edition of the complete psychological works of Sigmund Freud* (Vol. 12, pp. 121–144). London: Hogarth Press. (Original work published 1913)

Freud, S. (1958d). Recommendations to physicians practising psycho-analysis. In J. Strachey (Ed.), *The standard edition of the complete psychological works of Sigmund Freud* (Vol. 12, pp. 111–120). London: Hogarth Press. (Original work published 1912)

Freud, S. (1958e). Remembering, repeating and working-through (Further recommendations on the technique of psycho-analysis II). In J. Strachey (Ed.), *The standard edition of the complete psychological works of Sigmund Freud* (Vol. 12, pp. 145–156). London: Hogarth Press. (Original work published 1914)

Freud, S. (1959). Inhibitions, symptoms and anxiety. In J. Strachey (Ed.), *The standard edition of the complete psychological works of Sigmund Freud* (Vol. 20, pp. 75–172). London: Hogarth Press. (Original work published 1926)

Freud, S. (1961). The ego and the id. In J. Strachey (Ed.), *The standard edition of the complete psychological works of Sigmund Freud* (Vol. 19, pp. 3–63). London: Hogarth Press. (Original work published 1923)

Freud, S. (1963). General theory of the neuroses: Psychoanalysis and psychiatry. Part 3 of the introductory lectures on psychoanalysis. In J. Strachey (Ed.), *The standard edition of the complete psychological works of Sigmund Freud* (Vol. 16). London: Hogarth Press. (Original work published 1917)

Freud, S. (1964a). Analysis terminable and interminable. In J. Strachey (Ed.), *The standard edition of the complete psychological works of Sigmund Freud* (Vol. 23, pp. 209–253). London: Hogarth Press. (Original work published 1937)

Freud, S. (1964b). New introductory lectures on psycho-analysis. In J. Strachey (Ed.), *The standard edition of the complete psychological works of Sigmund Freud* (Vol. 22, pp. 1–182). London: Hogarth Press. (Original work published 1933)

Freud, S. (1966). Project for a scientific psychology. In J. Strachey (Ed.), *The standard edition of the complete psychological works of Sigmund Freud* (Vol. 1, pp. 279–293). London: Hogarth Press. (Original work published 1895)

Fried, D., Crits-Christoph, P., & Luborsky, L. (1998). The parallel of the CCRT for the therapist with the CCRT for other people. In L. Luborsky & P. Crits-Christoph (Eds.), *Understanding transference: The core conflictual relationship theme method* (2nd ed., pp. 165–174). Washington, DC: American Psychological Association.

Gabbard, G. O. (1990). *Psychodynamic psychiatry in clinical practice*. Washington, DC: American Psychiatric Association.

Galatzer-Levy, R. M., & Cohler, B. J. (1993). *The essential other: A developmental psychology of the self*. New York: Basic Books.

Gaston, L. (1990). The concept of the alliance and its role in psychotherapy: Theoretical and empirical considerations. *Psychotherapy, 27*, 143–153.

Gedo, J. E. (1978). *Beyond interpretation: Toward a revised theory for psychoanalysis*. New York: International Universities Press.

Gelso, C. J., & Carter, J. (1985). The relationship in counseling and psychotherapy: Components, consequences, and theoretical antecedents. *Counseling Psychologist, 13*, 155–243.

Gelso, C. J., & Carter, J. A. (1994). Components of the psychotherapy relationship: Their interaction and unfolding during treatment. *Journal of Counseling Psychology, 41*, 296–306.

Gelso, C. J., Hill, C. E., Mohr, J. J., Rochlen, A. B., & Zack, J. (1999). Describing the face of transference: Psychodynamic therapists' recollections about transference in cases of successful long-term therapy. *Journal of Counseling Psychology, 46*, 257–267.

Gelso, C. J., Kivlighan, D. M., Wine, B., Jones, A., & Friedman, S. C. (1997). Transference, insight, and the course of time-limited therapy. *Journal of Counseling Psychology, 44*, 209–217.

Gift, T., Cole, R., & Wynne, L. (1986). An interpersonal measure of hostility based on speech context. In L. A. Gottschalk, F. Lolas, & L. L. Viney (Eds.), *Content analysis of verbal behaviour: Significance in clinical medicine and psychiatry* (pp. 87–93). Berlin: Springer-Verlag.

Gill, M., & Hoffman, I. Z. (1982). A method for studying the analysis of aspects of the patient's experience of the relationship in psychoanalysis and psychotherapy. *Journal of the American Psycho-Analytic Association, 30*, 137–167.

Gottschalk, L. A. (1974). A hope scale applicable to verbal samples. *Archives of General Psychiatry, 30*, 779–785.

Gottschalk, L. A., Winget, C. N., & Gleser, G. C. (1969). *Manual of instructions for using the Gottschalk-Gleser content analysis scales: Anxiety, hostility, and social alienation—Personal disorganization.* Berkeley: University of California Press.

Greenberg, J., & Mitchell, S. A. (1983). *Object relations in psychoanalytic theory.* Cambridge, MA: Harvard University Press.

Greenson, R. R. (1967). *Technique and practice of psychoanalysis.* New York: International Universities Press.

Grenyer, B. F. S. (1994a). *Mastery Scale I: Manuale di ricerca e di attribuzione di punteggio (Italian translation).* Wollongong, New South Wales, Australia: University of Wollongong Press.

Grenyer, B. F. S. (1994b). *Mastery Scale I: A research and scoring manual.* Wollongong, New South Wales, Australia: University of Wollongong Press.

Grenyer, B. F. S., Dahlbender, R. W., & Reichenauer, G. (1998). *Mastery Scale 1: Meisterung interpersoneller Konflikte, Deutsche Manual Bearbeitung.* Ulm, Germany: Ulmer Textbank.

Grenyer, B. F. S., & Luborsky, L. (1996). Dynamic change in psychotherapy: Mastery of interpersonal conflicts. *Journal of Consulting and Clinical Psychology, 64,* 411–416.

Grenyer, B. F. S., & Luborsky, L. (1998a). The measurement of mastery of relationship conflicts. In L. Luborsky & P. Crits-Christoph (Eds.), *Understanding transference: The core conflictual relationship theme method* (2nd ed., pp. 261–272). Washington, DC: American Psychological Association.

Grenyer, B. F. S., & Luborsky, L. (1998b). Positive versus negative CCRT patterns. In L. Luborsky & P. Crits-Christoph (Eds.), *Understanding transference: The core conflictual relationship theme method* (2nd ed., pp. 55–64). Washington, DC: American Psychological Association.

Grenyer, B. F. S., Luborsky, L., & Solowij, N. (1995). *Treatment manual for supportive–expressive dynamic psychotherapy: Special adaptation for treatment of cannabis (marijuana) dependence.* Sydney, Australia: National Drug and Alcohol Research Centre.

Grenyer, B. F. S., & Solowij, N. (in press). Dynamic psychotherapy for cannabis dependence. In R. Roffman & R. Stephens (Eds.), *Cannabis dependence: Its nature, consequences and treatment.* Cambridge, England: Cambridge University Press.

Grenyer, B. F. S., Solowij, N., & Peters, R. (1996). *Marijuana: A guide to quitting.* Sydney, Australia: National Drug and Alcohol Research Centre.

Grinspoon, L., & Bakalar, J. B. (1998). The use of cannabis as a mood stabilizer in bipolar disorder: Anecdotal evidence and the need for clinical research. *Journal of Psychoactive Drugs, 30,* 171–177.

Gruber, A. J., Pope, H. G., & Brown, M. E. (1996). Do patients use marijuana as an antidepressant? *Depression, 4,* 77–80.

Gruber, A. J., Pope, H. G., & Oliva, P. (1997). Very long users of marijuana in the United States: A pilot study. *Substance Use and Misuse, 32,* 249–264.

Grünbaum, A. (1986). Précis of *The Foundations of Psychoanalysis:* A philosophical critique. *Behavioural and Brain Sciences, 9,* 217–284.

Gunderson, J. G., & Elliott, G. R. (1985). The interface between borderline personality disorder and affective disorder. *American Journal of Psychiatry, 142,* 277–288.

Hall, W., & Solowij, N. (1997). Long term cannabis use and mental health. *British Journal of Psychiatry, 171,* 107–108.

Hall, W., Solowij, N., & Lemon, J. (1994). *The health and psychological consequences of cannabis use.* Canberra: Australian Government Publishing Service.

Hamilton, M. (1960). A rating scale for depression. *Journal of Neurology, Neurosurgery and Psychiatry, 23,* 56–62.

Hamilton, M. (1967). Development of a rating scale for primary depressive illness. *British Journal of Social and Clinical Psychology, 6,* 278–296.

Harlow, H. F., & Zimmermann, R. R. (1959). Affectional responses in the infant monkey. *Science, 130,* 421–432.

Hartley, D. E., & Strupp, H. H. (1983). The therapeutic alliance: Its relationship to outcome in brief psychotherapy. In J. Masling (Ed.), *Empirical studies in analytic theories* (pp. 1–37). Hillsdale, NJ: Erlbaum.

Hartmann, H. (1958). *Ego psychology and the problem of adaptation.* New York: International Universities Press. (Original work published 1938)

Hartmann, H., Kris, E., & Loewenstein, R. M. (1964). *Papers on psychoanalytic psychology* (Psychological Issues Monograph No. 14). New York: International Universities Press.

Hendrick, I. (1943a). The discussion of the "instinct to master." *Psychoanalytic Quarterly, 12,* 561–565.

Hendrick, I. (1943b). Work and the pleasure principle. *Psychoanalytic Quarterly, 12,* 311–329.

Henry, W. P., Strupp, H. H., Schacht, T. E., & Gaston, L. (1994). Psychodynamic approaches. In A. E. Bergin & S. L. Garfield (Eds.), *Handbook of psychotherapy and behaviour change* (4th ed., pp. 467–508). New York: Wiley.

Hewitt, P. L., Flett, G. L., & Ediger, E. (1996). Perfectionism and depression: Longitudinal assessment of a specific vulnerability hypothesis. *Journal of Abnormal Psychology, 105,* 276–280.

Hiatt, D., & Hargrave, G. E. (1995). The characteristics of highly effective therapists in managed behavioral provider networks. *Behavioral Healthcare Tomorrow, 4,* 19–22.

Høglend, P., Engelstad, V., Sorbye, O., Heyerdahl, O., & Amlo, S. (1994). The role of insight in exploratory psychodynamic psychotherapy. *British Journal of Medical Psychology, 67,* 305–317.

Horowitz, L., Weckler, D., & Doren, R. (1983). Interpersonal problems and symptoms: A cognitive approach. In P. C. Kendall (Ed.), *Advances in cognitive–behavioural research and therapy* (Vol. 2, pp. 56–71). New York: Academic Press.

Horowitz, M. J. (1979). *States of mind.* New York: Plenum Press.

Horvath, A., Gaston, L., & Luborsky, L. (1993). The therapeutic alliance and its measures. In N. E. Miller, L. Luborsky, J. P. Barber, & J. P. Docherty (Eds.),

Psychodynamic treatment research: A handbook for clinical practice (pp. 247–273). New York: Basic Books.

Horvath, A. O. (1994). Research on the alliance. In A. O. Horvath & L. S. Greenberg (Eds.), *The working alliance: Theory, research and practice* (pp. 259–286). New York: Wiley.

Horvath, A. O., & Symonds, B. D. (1991). Relation between working alliance and outcome in psychotherapy: A meta-analysis. *Journal of Counseling Psychology, 38,* 139–149.

Howard, G. S. (1991). Culture tales: A narrative approach to thinking, cross-cultural psychology, and psychotherapy. *American Psychologist, 46,* 187–197.

Howard, K. I. (1993, June). *The benefits of long-term psychotherapy.* Paper presented at the 25th Society for Psychotherapy Research Annual Meeting, Pittsburgh, PA.

Howard, K. I., Kopta, S. M., Krause, M. S., & Orlinsky, D. E. (1986). The dose-effect relationship in psychotherapy. *American Psychologist, 41,* 159–164.

Howard, K. I., Krause, M. S., Saunders, S. M., & Kopta, S. M. (1997). Trials and tribulations in the meta-analysis of treatment differences: Comment on Wampold et al. (1997). *Psychological Bulletin, 122,* 221–225.

Howard, K. I., Leuger, R. J., Maling, M. S., & Martinovich, Z. (1993). A phase model of psychotherapy outcome: Causal mediation of change. *Journal of Consulting and Clinical Psychology, 61,* 678–685.

Jacobs, M. A., Muller, J. J., Eisman, H. D., Knitzer, J., & Spilken, A. (1968). The assessment of change in distress level and styles of adaptation as a function of psychotherapy. *Journal of Nervous and Mental Disease, 145,* 392–404.

Jacobson, N. S., & Truax, P. (1991). Clinical significance: A statistical approach to defining meaningful change in psychotherapy research. *Journal of Consulting and Clinical Psychology, 59,* 12–19.

Jaspers, K. (1951). *The way to wisdom.* New Haven, CT: Yale University Press.

Jones, A., Henry, R., & Grenyer, B. (2001). *Transmission of attachment patterns across generations: The role of the family environment.* Manuscript submitted for publication.

Jones, E. (1926–1936). *Decennial report of the London Clinic of Psychoanalysis.* London: Mimeograph.

Joseph, B. (1988). Transference: The total situation. In E. B. Spillius (Ed.), *Melanie Klein today: Developments in theory and practice* (Vol. 2, pp. 61–72). London: Tavistock/Routledge. (Original work published 1985)

Kächele, H., Thomä, H., Ruberg, W., & Grünzig, H.-J. (1988). Audio-recordings of the psychoanalytic dialogue: Scientific, clinical and ethical problems. In H. Dahl, H. Kächele, & H. Thomä (Eds.), *Psychoanalytic process research strategies* (pp. 179–193). Berlin: Springer-Verlag.

Kaplan, H. I., & Sadock, B. J. (1998). *Synopsis of psychiatry: Behavioral sciences/clinical psychiatry* (8th ed.). Baltimore: Williams & Wilkins.

Kazdin, A. E. (1994). Methodology, design, and evaluation in psychotherapy research. In A. E. Bergin & S. L. Garfield (Eds.), *Handbook of psychotherapy and behavior change* (4th ed., pp. 19–71). New York: Wiley.

Kelly, A. E. (2000). A self-presentational view of psychotherapy: Reply to Hill, Gelso, and Mohr (2000) and to Arkin and Hermann (2000). *Psychological Bulletin, 126,* 505–511.

Kernberg, O. F. (1972). Psychotherapy and psychoanalysis: Final report of the Menninger Foundation's psychotherapy research project. *Bulletin of the Menninger Clinic, 36,* 1–277.

Kernberg, O. F. (1984). *Severe personality disorders: Psychotherapeutic strategies.* New Haven & London: Yale University Press.

Kiloh, L. G., Andrews, G., & Neilson, M. (1988). The long-term outcome of depressive illness. *British Journal of Psychiatry, 153,* 752–759.

Klein, M. (1986). The origins of transference. In J. Mitchell (Ed.), *The selected Melanie Klein* (pp. 201–210). London: Penguin Books. (Original work published 1952)

Klein, M. H., Kupfer, D. J., & Shea, M. T. (Eds.). (1993). *Personality and depression: A current view.* New York: Guilford Press.

Klein, M. H., Mathieu-Coughlan, P., & Kiesler, D. J. (1986). The experiencing scales. In L. S. Greenberg & W. M. Pinsof (Eds.), *The psychotherapeutic process: A research handbook.* New York: Guilford.

Klerman, G. L. (1989). Depressive disorders: Further evidence for increased medical morbidity and impairment of social functioning. *Archives of General Psychiatry, 46,* 856–858.

Klerman, G. L., Weissman, M. M., Rounsaville, B. J., & Chevron, E. S. (1984). *Interpersonal psychotherapy of depression.* New York: Basic Books.

Kohut, H. (1971). *Analysis of the self: A systematic approach to the psychoanalytic treatment of narcissistic personality disorders.* New York: International Universities Press.

Kohut, H. (1977). *The restoration of the self.* New York: International Universities Press.

Kohut, H. (1978). *The search for the self.* New York: International Universities Press.

Kouri, E., Pope, H. G., Yurgelun-Todd, D., & Gruber, S. (1995). Attributes of heavy vs. occasional marijuana smokers in a college population. *Biological Psychiatry, 38,* 475–481.

Krupnick, J. L., Elkin, I., Collins, J., Simmens, S., Sotsky, S. M., Pilkonis, P. A., & Watkins, J. T. (1994). Therapeutic alliance and clinical outcome in the NIMH treatment of depression collaborative research program: Preliminary findings. *Psychotherapy, 31,* 28–35.

Krupnick, J. L., Sotsky, S. M., Simmens, S., Moyer, J., Elkin, I., Watkins, J., & Pilkonis, P. A. (1996). The role of the therapeutic alliance in psychotherapy and pharmacotherapy outcome: Findings in the National Institute of Mental Health Treatment of Depression Collaborative Research Program. *Journal of Consulting and Clinical Psychology, 64,* 532–539.

Kuhn, T. S. (1970). *The structure of scientific revolutions.* Chicago: University of Chicago Press.

Laikin, M., Winston, A., & McCullough, L. (1991). Intensive short-term dynamic psychotherapy. In P. Crits-Christoph & J. P. Barber (Eds.), *Handbook of short-term dynamic psychotherapy* (pp. 80–109). New York: Basic Books.

Lambert, M. J., & Bergin, A. E. (1994). The effectiveness of psychotherapy. In A. E. Bergin & S. L. Garfield (Eds.), *Handbook of psychotherapy and behavior change* (4th ed., pp. 143–189). New York: Wiley.

LeDoux, J. E. (1995). Emotion: Clues from the brain. *Annual Review of Psychology, 46,* 209–235.

Lee, A. S., & Murray, R. M. (1988). The long-term outcome of Maudsley depressives. *British Journal of Psychiatry, 153,* 741–751.

Liberman, B. L. (1978). The role of mastery in psychotherapy: Maintenance or improvement and prescriptive change. In J. Frank, R. Hoehn-Saric, S. Imber, B. Leberman, & A. Stone (Eds.), *Effective ingredients of successful psychotherapy* (35–72). New York: Brunner-Mazel.

Linehan, M. M. (1993). *Cognitive–behavioral treatment of borderline personality disorder.* New York: Guilford Press.

Linehan, M. M., Armstrong, H. E., Suarez, A., Allmon, D., & Heard, H. L. (1991). Cognitive–behavioural treatment of chronically parasuicidal borderline patients. *Archives of General Psychiatry, 48,* 1060–1064.

Loftus, E. F., & Ketcham, K. (1991). *Witness for the defense.* New York: St. Martin's Press.

Luborsky, L. (1954). A note on Eysenck's article "The effects of psychotherapy: An evaluation." *British Journal of Psychology, 45,* 129–131.

Luborsky, L. (1962). Clinicians' judgments of mental health: A proposed scale. *Archives of General Psychiatry, 7,* 407–417.

Luborsky, L. (1972). Another reply to Eysenck. *Psychological Bulletin, 78,* 406–408.

Luborsky, L. (1975). Clinicians' judgements of mental health: Specimen case descriptions and forms for the Health–Sickness Rating Scale. *Bulletin of the Menninger Clinic, 35,* 448–480.

Luborsky, L. (1976). Helping alliances in psychotherapy. In J. Claghorn (Ed.), *Successful psychotherapy* (pp. 92–111). New York: Brunner/Mazel.

Luborsky, L. (1977). Measuring a pervasive psychic structure in psychotherapy: The core conflictual relationship theme. In N. Freedman & S. Grand (Eds.), *Communicative structures and psychic structures* (pp. 367–395). New York: Plenum Press.

Luborsky, L. (1984). *Principles of psychoanalytic psychotherapy: A manual for supportive–expressive treatment.* New York: Basic Books.

Luborsky, L. (1994). Therapeutic alliances as predictors of psychotherapy outcomes: Factors explaining the predictive success. In A. Horvath & L. Greenberg (Eds.), *The working alliance: Theory, research, and practice* (pp. 38–50). New York: Wiley.

Luborsky, L. (1998a). A guide to the CCRT method. In L. Luborsky & P. Crits-Christoph (Eds.), *Understanding transference: The core conflictual relationship theme method* (2nd ed., pp. 15–42). Washington, DC: American Psychological Association.

Luborsky, L. (1998b). The relationship anecdotes paradigm (RAP) interview as a versatile source of narratives. In L. Luborsky & P. Crits-Christoph (Eds.),

Understanding transference: The core conflictual relationship theme method (2nd ed., pp. 109–120). Washington, DC: American Psychological Association.

Luborsky, L., & Bachrach, H. (1974). Factors influencing clinicians' judgements of mental health: Eighteen experiences with the Health–Sickness Rating Scale. *Archives of General Psychiatry, 31,* 292–299.

Luborsky, L., & Barber, J. (1994). Perspectives on seven transference-related measures applied to the interview with Ms. Smithfield. *Psychotherapy Research, 4,* 152–155.

Luborsky, L., Barber, J. P., & Crits-Christoph, P. (1990). Theory-based research for understanding the process of dynamic psychotherapy. *Journal of Consulting and Clinical Psychology, 58,* 281–287.

Luborsky, L., Barber, J. P., & Diguer, L. (1992). The meanings of narratives told during psychotherapy: The fruits of a new observational unit. *Psychotherapy Research, 2,* 277–290.

Luborsky, L., Barber, J., Schaffler, P., & Cacciola, J. (1998). The narratives told during psychotherapy and the types of CCRTs within them. In L. Luborsky & P. Crits-Christoph (Eds.), *Understanding transference: The core conflictual relationship theme method* (2nd ed., pp. 135–150). Washington, DC: American Psychological Association.

Luborsky, L., Chandler, M., Auerbach, A. H., Cohen, J., & Bachrach, H. (1971). Factors influencing the outcome of psychotherapy: A review of quantitative research. *Psychological Bulletin, 75,* 145–185.

Luborsky, L., & Crits-Christoph, P. (1989). A relationship pattern measure: The core conflictual relationship theme. *Psychiatry, 52,* 250–259.

Luborsky, L., & Crits-Christoph, P. (1990). *Understanding transference: The core conflictual relationship theme method.* New York: Basic Books.

Luborsky, L., & Crits-Christoph, P. (1998). *Understanding transference: The core conflictual relationship theme method* (2nd ed.). Washington, DC: American Psychological Association.

Luborsky, L., Crits-Christoph, P., Alexander, L., Margolis, M., & Cohen, M. (1983). Two helping alliance methods for predicting outcomes of psychotherapy: A counting signs vs. a global rating method. *Journal of Nervous and Mental Disease, 171,* 480–491.

Luborsky, L., Crits-Christoph, P., Friedman, S. H., Mark, D., & Schaffler, P. (1991). Freud's transference template compared with the core conflictual relationship theme (CCRT): Illustrations by the two specimen cases. In M. J. Horowitz (Ed.), *Person schemas and maladaptive interpersonal patterns* (pp. 167–195). Chicago: University of Chicago Press.

Luborsky, L., Crits-Christoph, P., Mintz, J., & Auerbach, A. (1988). *Who will benefit from psychotherapy? Predicting therapeutic outcomes.* New York: Basic Books.

Luborsky, L., Diguer, L., Kächele, H., Dahlbender, R., Waldinger, R., Freni, S., Krause, R., Frevert, G., Bucci, W., Drouin, M., Fischmann, T., Seganti, A., Wischmann, T., Hori, S., Azzone, P., Pokorny, D., Staats, H., Zobel, H., Grenyer, B., Soldz, S., Anstadt, T., Schauenburg, H., Benninghoven, D., Stigler, M., & I., T. (1999). *A guide to the CCRT's methods, discoveries and future.* Ulm, Germany:

University of Ulm. (On-line http://sip.medizin.uni-ulm.de/Psychotherapie/ccrt-frame.html)

Luborsky, L., Diguer, L., Luborsky, E., McLellan, T., Woody, G., & Alexander, L. (1993). Psychological health–sickness (PHS) as a predictor of outcomes in dynamic and other psychotherapies. *Journal of Consulting and Clinical Psychology, 61*, 542–548.

Luborsky, L., Diguer, L., Luborsky, E., Singer, B., Dickter, D., & Schmidt, K. A. (1993). The efficacy of dynamic psychotherapies: Is it true that "Everyone has won and all must have prizes"? In N. E. Miller, L. Luborsky, J. P. Barber, & J. P. Docherty (Eds.), *Psychodynamic treatment research: A handbook for clinical practice* (pp. 497–518). New York: Basic Books.

Luborsky, L., Diguer, L., Seligman, D. A., Rosenthal, R., Krause, E. D., Johnson, S., Halperin, G., Bishop, M., Berman, J. S., & Schweizer, E. (1999). The researcher's own therapy allegiances: A "wild card" in comparisons of treatment efficacy. *Clinical Psychology: Science and Practice, 6*, 95–106.

Luborsky, L., Mark, D., Hole, A. V., Popp, C., Goldsmith, B., & Cacciola, J. (1995). Supportive–expressive dynamic psychotherapy for depression: A time-limited version. In J. P. Barber & P. Crits-Christoph (Eds.), *Dynamic therapies for psychiatric disorders (Axis 1)* (pp. 13–42). New York: Basic Books.

Luborsky, L., McLellan, T., Woody, G. E., O'Brien, C. P., & Auerbach, A. (1985). Therapist success and its determinants. *Archives of General Psychiatry, 42*, 602–611.

Luborsky, L., Popp, C., Barber, J. P., & Shapiro, D. A. (1994). Common and special factors in different transference-related measures. Special Issue of *Psychotherapy Research, 4*(3–4), 277–286.

Luborsky, L., Singer, B., & Luborsky, L. (1975). Comparative studies of psychotherapies: Is it true that "everyone has won and all must have prizes"? *Archives of General Psychiatry, 32*, 995–1008.

Luborsky, L., & Spence, D. P. (1978). Quantitative research on psychoanalytic therapy. In S. L. Garfield & A. E. Bergin (Eds.), *Handbook of psychotherapy and behavior change: An empirical analysis* (2nd ed.). New York: Wiley.

Luborsky, L., Woody, G. E., McLellan, T., O'Brien, C. P., & Rosenzweig, J. (1982). Can independent judges recognize different psychotherapies? An experience with manual guided therapies. *Journal of Consulting and Clinical Psychology, 50*, 49–62.

Lundqvist, T. (1995). *Cognitive dysfunctions in chronic cannabis users observed during treatment*. Stockholm: Almqvist & Wiksell International.

Mackay, N. (1981). Melanie Klein's metapsychology: Phenomenological and mechanistic perspective. *International Journal of Psychoanalysis, 62*, 187–198.

Mackay, N. (1989). *Motivation and explanation: An essay on Freud's philosophy of science*. New York: International Universities Press.

Mackay, N. (1994). Cognitive therapy, constructivist metatheory, and rational explanation. *Australian Journal of Psychology, 46*, 7–12.

Mahl, G. F., Dollard, J., & Redlich, F. C. (1954). Facilities for the sound recording and observation of interviews. *Science, 120*, 235–239.

Malan, D. H. (1963). *A study of brief psychotherapy*. New York: Plenum.

Malan, D. H. (1976). *Toward the validation of dynamic psychotherapy*. New York: Plenum.

Malan, D. H., Bacal, H., Heath, E., & Balfour, F. L. (1968). A study of psychodynamic changes in untreated neurotic patients. *British Journal of Psychiatry, 114,* 525–551.

Manning, W., & DuBois, P. (1962). Correlational methods in research on human learning. *Perceptual and Motor Skills, 15,* 288–321.

Marcel, G. (1960). *The mystery of being*. Chicago: Regnery.

Martin, D. J., Garske, J. P., & Davis, M. K. (2000). Relation of the therapeutic alliance with outcome and other variables: A meta-analytic review. *Journal of Consulting and Clinical Psychology, 68,* 438–450.

Marziali, E. A. (1984). Prediction of outcome of brief psychotherapy from therapist interpretive interventions. *Archives of General Psychiatry, 41,* 301–304.

Marziali, E. A., & Sullivan, J. M. (1980). Methodological issues in the content analysis of brief psychotherapy. *British Journal of Medical Psychology, 53,* 19–27.

Maslow, A. H. (1970). *Motivation and personality* (2nd ed.). New York: Harper & Row.

Maze, J. R. (1983). *The meaning of behaviour*. London: George Allen & Unwin.

Maze, J. R. (1987). The composition of the ego in a determinist psychology. In W. J. Baker, M. E. Hyland, H. Van Rappard, & A. W. Staats (Eds.), *Current issues in theoretical psychology*. Amsterdam: North-Holland.

Maze, J. R. (1991). Representationism, realism and the redundancy of "Mentalese." *Theory and Psychology, 1,* 163–185.

Maze, J. R. (1993). The complementarity of object-relations and instinct theory. *International Journal of Psychoanalysis, 74,* 459–470.

McCullough, L. (1993). Standard and individualized psychotherapy outcome measures: A core battery. In N. E. Miller, L. Luborsky, J. P. Barber, & J. P. Docherty (Eds.), *Psychodynamic treatment research: A handbook for clinical practice* (pp. 469–496). New York: Basic Books.

Meares, R., & Coombes, T. (1994). A drive to play: Evolution and psychotherapeutic theory. *Australian and New Zealand Journal of Psychiatry, 28,* 58–67.

Meares, R., Stevenson, J., & Comerford, A. (1999). Psychotherapy with borderline patients: I. A comparison between treated and untreated cohorts. *Australian & New Zealand Journal of Psychiatry, 33,* 467–472.

Meissner, W. W. (1981). *Internalization in psychoanalysis* (Psychological Issues Monograph 50). New York: International Universities Press.

Mergenthaler, E., & Stinson, C. H. (1992). Psychotherapy transcription standards. *Psychotherapy Research, 2,* 125–142.

Messer, S. B. (1992). A critical examination of belief structures in integrative and eclectic psychotherapy. In J. C. Norcross & M. R. Goldfried (Eds.), *Handbook of psychotherapy integration* (pp. 130–165). New York: Basic Books.

Messer, S. B., & Warren, C. S. (1995). *Models of brief psychodynamic therapy: A comparative approach*. New York: Guilford Press.

Miller, N. E., Luborsky, L., Barber, J. P., & Docherty, J. P. (1993). *Psychodynamic treatment research: A handbook for clinical practice.* New York: Basic Books.

Mintz, J., & Kiesler, D. J. (1982). Individualized measures of psychotherapy outcome. In P. C. Kendall & J. N. Butcher (Eds.), *Handbook of research methods in clinical psychology* (pp. 491–534). New York: Wiley.

Mitchell, S. A. (1988). *Relational concepts in psychoanalysis: An integration.* Cambridge, MA: Harvard University Press.

Morey, L. C. (1988). Personality disorders in DSM-III, and DSM-III-R: Convergence, coverage and internal consistency. *American Journal of Psychiatry, 145,* 573–577.

Morgan, C. D., & Murray, H. A. (1935). A method for investigating fantasies: The thematic apperception test. *Archives of Neurology and Psychiatry, 34,* 289–306.

Murray, C. J. L., & Lopez, A. D. E. (1996). *Global burden of disease: A comprehensive assessment of mortality and disability from diseases, injuries and risk factors in 1990 and projected to 2020.* Boston, MA: Harvard University Press.

Najavits, L. M., & Weiss, R. D. (1994). Variations in therapist effectiveness in the treatment of patients with substance use disorders: An empirical review. *Addictions, 89,* 679–688.

Nathan, P. E. (2000). Practice guidelines: Not yet ideal. *American Psychologist, 53,* 290–299.

O'Connor, L. E., Edelstein, S., Berry, J. W., & Weiss, J. (1994). Changes in the patient's level of insight in brief psychotherapy: Two pilot studies. *Psychotherapy, 31,* 533–544.

Orange, D., Atwood, G., & Stolorow, R. (1997). *Working intersubjectively: Contextualism in psychoanalytic practice.* Hillsdale, NJ: Analytic Press.

Orlinsky, D. E., Grawe, K., & Parks, B. K. (1994). Process and outcome in psychotherapy-Noch Einmal. In A. E. Bergin & S. L. Garfield (Eds.), *Handbook of psychotherapy and behaviour change* (4th ed., pp. 270–378). New York: Wiley.

Perry, J. C., Augusto, F., & Cooper, S. H. (1989). Assessing psychodynamic conflicts: I. Reliability of the idiographic conflict formulation method. *Psychiatry, 52,* 289–301.

Pfeffer, A. Z. (1963). The meaning of the analyst after analysis: A contribution to the theory of therapeutic results. *Journal of the American Psychoanalytic Association, 11,* 229–244.

Piper, W. E., Azim, F. A., Joyce, S. A., & McCallum, M. (1991). Transference interpretations, therapeutic alliance and outcome in short-term individual psychotherapy. *Archives of General Psychiatry, 48,* 946–953.

Piper, W. E., Debbane, E. G., Bienvenu, J.-P., Carufel, F., & Garant, J. (1986). Relationships between object focus of therapist interpretations and outcome in short-term individual psychotherapy. *British Journal of Medical Psychology, 59,* 1–11.

Piper, W. E., Joyce, A. S., McCallum, M., & Azim, H. F. (1998). Interpretive and supportive forms of psychotherapy and patient personality variables. *Journal of Consulting and Clinical Psychology, 66,* 558–567.

Piper, W. E., McCallum, M., Joyce, A. S., Azim, H. F., & Ogrodniczuk, J. S. (1999). Follow-up findings for interpretive and supportive forms of psychotherapy and patient personality variables. *Journal of Consulting and Clinical Psychology, 67,* 267–273.

Popp, C. A., Diguer, L., Luborsky, L., Faude, J., Johnson, S., Morris, M., Schaffer, N., Schaffler, P., & Schmidt, K. (1996). Repetitive relationship themes in waking narratives and dreams. *Journal of Consulting and Clinical Psychology, 64*, 1073–1078.

Popp, C., Diguer, L., Luborsky, L., Faude, J., Johnson, S., Morris, M., Schaffer, N., Schaffler, P., & Schmidt, K. (1998). The parallel of the CCRT from waking narratives with the CCRT from dreams: A further validation. In L. Luborsky & P. Crits-Christoph (Eds.), *Understanding transference: The core conflictual relationship theme method* (2nd ed., pp. 187–196). Washington, DC: American Psychological Association.

Popper, K. (1959). *The logic of scientific discovery.* London: Dent. (Original work published 1934)

Price, P. B., & Jones, E. E. (1998). Examining the alliance using the psychotherapy process Q-set. *Psychotherapy, 35*, 392–399.

Quality Assurance Project. (1990, 1991). Ideal treatment outlines in psychiatry [Collected reprint series]. *Australian and New Zealand Journal of Psychiatry, 25*, 392–411.

Rabkin, J. G., & Klein, D. F. (1987). The clinical measurement of depressive disorders. In A. J. Marsella, R. M. A. Hirschfeld, & M. M. Katz (Eds.), *The measurement of depression* (pp. 30–86). New York: Guilford Press.

Rapaport, D. (1967). *The collected papers of David Rapaport.* New York: Basic Books.

Reilly, D., Didcott, P., Swift, W., & Hall, W. (1998). Long-term cannabis use: Characteristics of users in an Australian rural area. *Addiction, 93*, 837–846.

Reis, S., & Grenyer, B. F. S. (2001). Precursors to anaclitic and introjective depression subtypes. Manuscript submitted for publication.

Robins, H., & Kulbok, P. A. (1988). Epidemiologic studies in suicide. In A. J. Frances & R. E. Hales (Eds.), *Review of psychiatry* (Vol. 7, pp. 56–71). Washington, DC: American Psychiatric Press.

Rogers, C. R. (1942). The use of electrically recorded interviews in improving psychotherapeutic techniques. *American Journal of Orthopsychiatry, 12*, 429–434.

Rogers, C. R. (1957). The necessary and sufficient conditions of therapeutic personality change. *Journal of Consulting Psychology, 21*, 95–103.

Rogers, C. R., & Dymond, R. F. (Eds.). (1954). *Psychotherapy and personality change.* Chicago: University of Chicago Press.

Rosenzweig, S. (1936). Some implicit common factors in diverse methods of psychotherapy. *American Journal of Orthopsychiatry, 6*, 412–415.

Rosenzweig, S. (1954). A transvaluation of psychotherapy: A reply to Eysenck. *Journal of Abnormal and Social Psychology, 49*, 298–304.

Rotter, J. B. (1966). Generalized expectancies for internal versus external control of reinforcement. *Psychological Monographs: General and Applied, 80*(1), 1–28.

Russell, R. L., & Van Den Broek, P. (1992). Changing narrative schemas in psychotherapy. *Psychotherapy, 29*, 344–354.

Sacks, H., Schegloff, E. A., & Jefferson, G. A. (1974). A simplest systematics for the organization of turn-taking in dyadic conversation. *Language, 50*, 697–735.

Sartorius, N. (1979). Research on affective psychoses within the framework of the WHO Programme. In M. Schon & E. Stromgren (Eds.), *Origin, prevention and treatment of affective disorders* (pp. 51–72). London: Academic Press.

Schacht, T., Binder, J., & Strupp, H. (1984). *Psychotherapy in a new key: A guide to time-limited dynamic psychotherapy*. New York: Basic Books.

Schachter, J., & Luborsky, L. (1998). Who's afraid of psychoanalytic research? Analysts' attitudes towards reading clinical versus empirical research papers. *International Journal of Psychoanalysis, 79*, 965–969.

Schafer, R. (1976). *A new language for psychoanalysis*. New Haven, CT: Yale University Press.

Schafer, R. (1999). Recentering psychoanalysis: From Heinz Hartmann to the contemporary British Kleinians. *Psychoanalytic Psychology, 16*, 339–354.

Schlesinger, N., & Robbins, F. P. (1975). The psychoanalytic process: Recurrent patterns of conflict and changes in ego functions. *Journal of the American Psychoanalytic Association, 23*, 761–782.

Seligman, M. E. P. (1995). The effectiveness of psychotherapy: The *Consumer Reports* study. *American Psychologist, 50*, 965–974.

Seligman, M. E. P., & Csikszentmihalyi, M. (2000). Positive psychology: An introduction. *American Psychologist, 55*, 5–14.

Seligman, M. E. P., & Elder, G. (1985). Learned helplessness and life-span development. In A. Sorenson, F. Weinert, & L. Sherrod (Eds.), *Human development and the life course: Multidisciplinary perspectives* (pp. 377–427). Hillsdale, NJ: Erlbaum.

Shapiro, D. A., Firth-Cozens, J., & Stiles, W. B. (1989). The question of therapists' differential effectiveness: A Sheffield psychotherapy project addendum. *British Journal of Psychiatry, 154*, 383–385.

Shapiro, D. H., & Bates, D. E. (1990). The measurement of control and self-control: Background, rationale, and description of a control content analysis scale. *Psychologia, 33*, 147–162.

Shea, M. T., Pilkonis, P. A., Beckham, E., Collins, J. F., Elkin, I., Sotsky, S. M., & Docherty, J. P. (1990). Personality disorders and treatment outcome in the NIMH Treatment of Depression Collaborative Research Program. *American Journal of Psychiatry, 147*, 711–718.

Silberschatz, G., Curtis, J. T., & Nathans, S. (1989). Using the patient's plan to assess progress in psychotherapy. *Psychotherapy, 26*, 40–46.

Silberschatz, G., Curtis, J. T., Sampson, H., & Weiss, J. (1991). Mount Zion Hospital and Medical Center: Research on the process of change in psychotherapy. In L. E. Beutler & M. Crago (Eds.), *Psychotherapy research: An international review of programmatic studies* (pp. 56–64). Washington, DC: American Psychological Association.

Simons, J., Correia, C. J., Carey, K. B., & Borsari, B. E. (1998). Validating a five-factor marijuana motives measure: Relations with use, problems, and alcohol motives. *Journal of Counseling Psychology, 45*, 265–273.

Simpson, J. A., & Rholes, W. S. (1998). Attachment in adulthood. In J. A. Simpson & W. S. Rholes (Eds.), *Attachment theory and close relationships* (pp. 3–24). New York: Guilford Press.

Smith, M. L., & Glass, G. V. (1977). Meta-analysis of psychotherapy outcome studies. *American Psychologist, 32*, 752–760.

Smith, M. L., Glass, G. V., & Miller, T. I. (1980). *The benefits of psychotherapy.* Baltimore, MD: Johns Hopkins University Press.

Solowij, N. (1998). *Cannabis and cognitive functioning.* Cambridge, England: Cambridge University Press.

Solowij, N., & Grenyer, B. F. S. (2001). The long term effects of cannabis on psyche and cognition. In F. Grotenhermen (Ed.), *Cannabis and cannabinoids: Pharmacology, toxicology and therapeutic potential.* London: Haworth Press.

Solowij, N., Grenyer, B. F. S., Chesher, G., & Lewis, J. (1995). Biopsychosocial changes associated with cessation of cannabis use: A single case study of acute and chronic cognitive effects, withdrawal and treatment. *Life Sciences, 56*, 2127–2134.

SPSS-X. (1988). *SPSS-X user's guide* (3rd ed.). Chicago: SPSS, Inc.

Stephens, R. S., Roffman, R. A., & Simpson, E. E. (1993). Adult marijuana users seeking treatment. *Journal of Consulting and Clinical Psychology, 61*, 1100–1104.

Stephens, R. S., Roffman, R. A., & Simpson, E. E. (1994). Treating adult marijuana dependence: A test of the relapse prevention model. *Journal of Consulting and Clinical Psychology, 62*, 92–99.

Stern, D. (1985). *The interpersonal world of the infant: A view from psychoanalysis and developmental psychology.* New York: Basic Books.

Stevenson, J., & Meares, R. (1992). An outcome study of psychotherapy for patients with borderline personality disorder. *American Journal of Psychiatry, 149*, 358–362.

Stevenson, J., & Meares, R. (1999). Psychotherapy with borderline patients: II. A preliminary cost benefit study. *Australian and New Zealand Journal of Psychiatry, 33*, 473–477.

Stiles, W. B. (1988). Psychotherapy process-outcome correlations may be misleading. *Psychotherapy, 25*, 27–35.

Stiles, W. B. (1994). Drugs, recipes, babies, bathwater and psychotherapy process-outcome relations. *Journal of Consulting and Clinical Psychology, 62*, 955–959.

Stiles, W. B., Elliott, R., Llewelyn, S. P., Firth-Cozens, J. A., Margison, F. R., Shapiro, D. A., & Hardy, G. (1990). Assimilation of problematic experiences by clients in psychotherapy. *Psychotherapy, 27*, 411–420.

Stiles, W. B., Meshot, C. M., Anderson, T. M., & Sloan, W. W. (1992). Assimilation of problematic experiences: The case of John Jones. *Psychotherapy Research, 2*, 81–101.

Stiles, W. B., Morrison, L. A., Haw, S. K., Harper, H., Firth-Cozens, J., & Shapiro, D. A. (1991). Longitudinal study of assimilation in exploratory psychotherapy. *Psychotherapy, 28*, 195–206.

Stiles, W. B., & Shapiro, D. A. (1994). Disabuse of the drug metaphor: Psychotherapy process-outcome correlations. *Journal of Consulting and Clinical Psychology, 62*, 942–948.

Stiles, W. B., Shapiro, D. A., & Elliott, R. (1986). "Are all psychotherapies equivalent?" *American Psychologist, 41*, 165–180.

Stone, M. H., Stone, D. K., & Hurt, S. W. (1987). Natural history of borderline patients treated by intensive hospitalization. *Psychiatric Clinics of North America, 10*, 185–206.

Strachey, J. (1934). The nature of the therapeutic action of psycho-analysis. *International Journal of Psycho-Analysis, 15*, 127–159.

Strunk, W., & White, E. B. (2000). *Elements of style* (4th ed.). Boston: Allyn & Bacon.

Strupp, H. H. (1960). Nature of psychotherapist's contribution to treatment process: Some research results and speculations. *Archives of General Psychiatry, 3*, 219–231.

Strupp, H. H. (1970). Specific vs nonspecific factors in psychotherapy and the problem of control. *Archives of General Psychiatry, 23*, 393–401.

Strupp, H. H. (1992). The future of psychodynamic psychotherapy. *Psychotherapy, 29*, 21–27.

Strupp, H. H., & Binder, J. L. (1984). *Psychotherapy in a new key*. New York: Basic Books.

Sullivan, H. S. (1953). *The interpersonal theory of psychiatry*. New York: Norton.

Symington, N. (1986). *The analytic experience: Lectures from the Tavistock*. London: Free Association Books.

Symington, N. (1996). *The making of a psychotherapist*. New York: International Universities Press.

Teasdale, J. D. (1983). Negative thinking in depression: Cause, effect, or reciprocal relationship? *Advances in Behaviour Research and Therapy, 5*, 3–25.

Teller, V., & Dahl, H. (1981, August). *The framework for a model of psychoanalytic inference*. Paper presented at the Seventh International Joint Conference on Artificial Intelligence, Vancouver, Canada.

Tichenor, V., & Hill, C. E. (1989). A comparison of six measures of working alliance. *Psychotherapy, 26*, 195–199.

Toukmanian, S. G., & Rennie, D. L. (Eds.). (1992). *Psychotherapy process research: Paradigmatic and narrative approaches*. Newbury Park, CA: Sage.

Vaillant, G. E. (1993). *The wisdom of the ego*. Cambridge, MA: Harvard University Press.

Viney, L. L. (1983). The assessment of psychological states through content analysis of verbal communications. *Psychological Bulletin, 94*, 542–563.

Viney, L. L., & Bousfield, L. (1990). Narrative analysis: A method of psychosocial research for AIDS-affected people. *Social Science and Medicine, 32*, 757–765.

Wallerstein, R. S. (1986). *Forty-two lives in treatment: A study of psychoanalysis and psychotherapy*. New York: Guilford Press.

Wallerstein, R. S. (1993). Psychoanalysis as science: Challenges to the data of psychoanalytic research. In N. E. Miller, L. Luborsky, J. P. Barber, & J. P. Docherty (Eds.), *Psychodynamic treatment research: A handbook for clinical practice* (pp. 96–108). New York: Basic Books.

Wampold, B. E., Mondin, G. W., Moody, M., Stich, F., Benson, K., & Ahn, H. (1997). A meta-analysis of outcome studies comparing bona fide psychotherapies: Empirically, "all must have prizes." *Psychological Bulletin, 122,* 203–215.

Waskow, I., & Parloff, M. (Eds.). (1975). *Psychotherapy change measures.* Washington, DC: U.S. Government Printing Office.

Weiner, B. (1988). Attribution theory and attributional therapy: Some theoretical observations and suggestions. *British Journal of Clinical Psychology, 27,* 99–104.

Weiss, J. (1986). A broad look at the theory. In J. Weiss, H. Sampson, & Mount Zion Psychotherapy Research Group (Eds.), *The psychoanalytic process: Theory, clinical observations, and empirical research* (pp. 323–336). New York: Guilford Press.

Weiss, J. (1990a). The nature of the patient's problems and how in psychoanalysis the individual works to solve them. *Psychoanalytic Psychology, 7,* 105–113.

Weiss, J. (1990b). Unconscious mental functioning. *Scientific American, 262,* 103–109.

Weiss, J. (1993). *How psychotherapy works: Process and technique.* New York: Guilford Press.

Weiss, J., Sampson, H., & Mount Zion Psychotherapy Research Group. (1986). *The psychoanalytic process: Theory, clinical observations, and empirical research.* New York: Guilford Press.

Weissman, M. M. (1995). *Mastering depression through interpersonal psychotherapy: Patient workbook.* New York: Psychological Corporation.

Weissman, M. M., Klerman, G. L., Paykel, E. S., Prusoff, B., & Hanson, B. (1974). Treatment effects on the social adjustment of depressed patients. *Archives of General Psychiatry, 30,* 771–778.

White, R. W. (1959). Motivation reconsidered: The concept of competence. *Psychological Review, 66,* 297–333.

White, R. W. (1960). Competence and the psychosexual stages of development. In M. R. Jones (Ed.), *Nebraska symposium on motivation* (pp. 97–141). Lincoln: University of Nebraska Press.

White, R. W. (1963). Ego and reality in psychoanalytic theory: A proposal regarding independent ego energies (Monograph No. 11). *Psychological Issues, 3*(3).

Winnicott, D. W. (1956). On transference. *International Journal of Psycho-Analysis, 37,* 386–388.

Winnicott, D. W. (1965). *The maturational process and the facilitating environment: Studies in the theory of emotional development.* London: Hogarth Press.

Zuardi, A. W., Morais, S. L., Guimarães, F. S., & Mechoulam, R. (1995). Antipsychotic effect of cannabidiol. *Journal of Clinical Psychiatry, 56,* 485–486.

INDEX

Battle, C., 99, 103
BDI. *See* Beck Depression Inventory
Beck, A. T., x, 4, 171, 188, 190
Beck Depression Inventory (BDI), 171,
    174, 190
Beebe, K., 3
Behaviorism, 17
Bellack, A. S., 10
Bemis, K. M., 6
Benjamin, L. S., 179
Bergin, A. E., 5, 10, 40, 108
Berry, J. W., 50
Beutler, L. E., 7, 10
Bibring, Edward, 19
Bienvenu, J.-P., 158
Binder, J. L., 43, 124
Biopsychosocial drive theory, 16–18, 20,
    24–25, 33, 186, 199
Bipolar disorder, 170
Blacker, K. H., 49
Blatt, S. J., 7, 170, 171, 176
Blocking defenses, 70–71
Bondi, C. M., 171
Book, H. E., 130
Bordin, E. S., 8, 62, 142
Borsari, B. E., 185
Bousfield, L., 41
Bowlby, J., 36, 165
Breuer, J., 25
Brewin, C. R., 170
Brown, G. W., 170
Brown, M. E., 186
Buchsbaum, H., 147

Cacciola, J., 149
Cannabis use, 185–193
Caputi, P., 51
Carey, K. B., 185
Carlson, R., 43
Carroll, K. M., 142
Carter, J. A., 142
Carufel, F., 158
Case studies, single, 5
CCRTs. *See* Core conflictual relationship
    themes
Chaiken, S., 152
Chan, A., 51
Chance, E., 42
Chandler, M., 5
Chen, D., 186
Chesher, G., 185
Chevron, E. S., 4, 171

Children, 19, 29, 147, 148
Ciarrochi, J., 51
Cierpka, M., 148
Clyman, R. B., 27
Cognitive ambivalence, expressions of,
    77–78
Cognitive confusion, references to, 77
Cognitive depression, 170
Cognitive psychology, 26
Cognitive theory, 17
Cognitive therapy, 4
Cohen, J., x, 5, 102
Cohen, M., 91
Cohler, B. J., 41, 165, 179
Cole, R., 61
Comerford, A., 178
Competence, 3, 19, 21
Connolly, M. B. K., 50
Connors, G. J., 142
Control—mastery theory, 18, 20
Coombes, T., 35
Cooper, A., 42
Core conflictual relationship themes
        (CCRTs), 43–48, 50, 52, 100,
        146–157
    elements of, 43–44
    mastery of four-category positive and
        negative, 152–156
    and mastery of positive and negative
        transference patterns, 150–152
    and Mastery Scale, 101
    and measurement of repetition com-
        pulsion, 146–147
    and narratives, 44, 147–150
    and self-understanding, 48
    usefulness of, 43, 46–47, 130
Core relationships, mastery of, 157–166
Correia, C. J., 185
Covi, L., x, 47, 104
Coyne, J. C., 17, 170
Crago, M., 7, 10
Crisp, A., 42
Crits-Cristoph, P., x, 4, 6, 7, 17, 40, 42–44,
    46–48, 50, 90, 99, 100, 113,
    146–148, 157, 159
Csikszentmihalyi, M., viii, 3
Cunningham, J. A., 185
Curtis, H. C., 8
Curtis, J. T., 10, 42

Dahl, H., 43
Dahlbender, R. W., 148, 201

Level 1 in (lack of impulse control), 69–73
Level 2 in (introjection/projection of negative affects), 73–77
Level 3 in (difficulties in understanding and control), 77–79
Level 4 in (interpersonal awareness), 79–82
Level 5 in (self-understanding), 82–86
Level 6 in (self-control), 86–89
outcome measures with, 102–104
Phase 1 of (collection/preparation of samples for analysis), 58–66
Phase 2 of (application of scale to samples), 66–89
Phase 3 of (compilation of sample scores), 89–91
reliability/validity of, 97–114
research method, 99–106
research results, 106–114
scorable clauses in, 66
scoring procedure for, 100–101
transcription of verbal samples, 61–65
Mathieu-Coughlan, P., x
Maze, J. R., 17, 21, 34, 35
McCallum, M., 9, 124
McCullough, L., 51, 98
McDonald, C., 171
McLellan, T., 6, 7, 188
Meares, R., 35, 178
Mechoulam, R., 186
Meissner, W. W., 52
Mendelson, M., x, 171
Menninger, Karl, 19
Menninger Foundation, 102
Mergenthaler, E., 62
Meshot, C. M., 49
Messer, S. B., 33, 202
Metalsky, G. I., 3
Miller, N. E., 3, 40
Miller, T. I., 6
Mintz, J., 4, 7, 103, 159
Mitchell, S. A., 33
Mock, J., x, 171
Mohr, J. J., 50
Morais, S. L., 186
Morale, 3
Morey, L. C., 179
Morgan, C. D., 43, 58
Motivation, 17, 22, 25–26

Mt. Zion Psychotherapy Research Group, 10, 18, 24
Muller, J. J., 3
Murray, C. J. L., 169
Murray, H. A., 43, 58
Murray, R. M., 170

Najavits, L. M., 7
Narratives
interpretation of, 147–150
in psychotherapy, 40, 41, 43–44
quantification of, 147–148
Nathan, P. E., 6
Nathans, S., 42
National Institute of Mental Health Treatment of Depression Collaborative Research Program study, 170
Naturalistic psychotherapy, 59
Negative affects, 73–77
helplessness, expressions of, 76–77
introjection of, 73–74
projection of, from others, 74–75
projection of, onto others, 74
withdrawal, references to interpersonal, 76
Neilson, M., 170
Neuroticism, 4

Object relations theory, 34–35
O'Brien, L. P., 6, 7
Occam's razor, 23
O'Connor, L. E., 50
Ogrodniczuk, J. S., 9
Oliva, P., 186
Optimism, 3
Orange, D., 33
Orlinsky, D. E., 6, 7, 8, 40
Others
considering point of view of, 80–81
projection of negative affects from, 74–75
projection of negative affects onto, 74
questioning reactions of, 79–80
Overwhelmed, being emotionally, 69

Parks, B. K., 7
Parloff, M., 103
Paykel, E. S., 170
Penn depression study, 147
Penn Helping Alliance Counting Signs Method, 144, 145

234   INDEX

ABOUT THE AUTHOR

Brin F. S. Grenyer, PhD, is a senior lecturer in the Department of Psychology at the University of Wollongong in Sydney, Australia, where he is engaged in practice, research, and supervision. He is deputy director of clinical psychology training, a research coordinator in the Illawarra Institute for Mental Health, and holds a conjoint clinical appointment in the Illawarra Area Mental Health Service. In addition to publishing widely, he has collaborated for many years on research at the National Drug and Alcohol Research Center in Sydney and has established links with psychotherapy researchers and practitioners in the United States, Italy, Germany, and Sweden. Dr. Grenyer is married to a psychologist; they have two children and live among the rainforest palms and groves at Austinmer Beach, New South Wales, Australia.